T0091751

Early praise for *Build Talking Apps*

This book will take you on a journey into the exciting world of voice applications and Alexa. Craig has found a way to make a very technical subject accessible to anyone that is interested in learning about this new (and natural) way to communicate with computers. After reading it, I hope you are as excited about the future of voice and ambient computing as I am!

➤ **Jeff Blankenburg**
Chief Technical Evangelist, Amazon Alexa

Craig has done it again. He's written the first comprehensive guide to programming a technology that will be mainstream in a few years—Alexa Skill development. He's beautifully organized all the key elements, giving developers the foundation they need to both deliver customer value through skills today and to carry them into the future as the Alexa Skill ecosystem evolves.

➤ **Cornelia Davis**
Alexa Product Management, Amazon

While we haven't reached science fiction level computing just yet, conversational UIs are quickly becoming a must-have in our application arsenal. Whether you're new to the space or you've been building skills for years, Craig can help. It's all here, from getting started to polishing your app to getting it published.

➤ **Nate Schutta**
Architect, VMware

Certainly the best introduction I've seen yet to actually building an Alexa Skill, covering real challenges and solutions you will encounter building your own applications. Craig has a knack for entertainingly explaining the core concepts well, with useful analogies throughout.

➤ **Miles Woodroffe**
CTO

Craig Walls brings his wealth of experience to the Alexa arena and does the comprehensive job you would expect from him. Alexa is a hard topic to cover as there are so many aspects to it, but Craig explains them all. Though I've been writing skills for four years I learned new things from this book.

➤ **Brian Tarbox**
 AWS Community Hero, Wabi Sabi Software

Lays a solid foundation for skill development and introduced valuable intermediate-level topics one would apply to give an app extra polish to set it apart from so many others. Importantly, it was a fun read with many easily understood code examples. I highly recommend this book for anyone doing Alexa skill development.

➤ **Jack Frosch**
 Software Architect and Developer, Objistics, Inc.

A guide to creating your own Alexa apps from conception to publication including a continuous integration approach and without losing your yellow brick road.

➤ **Jesús Chamizo**
 Software Engineer, Professional Coded Solutions

Written in a meticulous manner, this is one of the most complete Alexa books I've seen by far. Well done!

➤ **Dzulkiflee Taib "Goldzulu"**
 Founder, VoiceTechGuy

Build Talking Apps

Develop Voice-First Applications for Alexa

Craig Walls

The Pragmatic Bookshelf

Raleigh, North Carolina

Many of the designations used by manufacturers and sellers to distinguish their products are claimed as trademarks. Where those designations appear in this book, and The Pragmatic Programmers, LLC was aware of a trademark claim, the designations have been printed in initial capital letters or in all capitals. The Pragmatic Starter Kit, The Pragmatic Programmer, Pragmatic Programming, Pragmatic Bookshelf, PragProg and the linking *g* device are trademarks of The Pragmatic Programmers, LLC.

Every precaution was taken in the preparation of this book. However, the publisher assumes no responsibility for errors or omissions, or for damages that may result from the use of information (including program listings) contained herein.

For our complete catalog of hands-on, practical, and Pragmatic content for software developers, please visit *https://pragprog.com*.

The team that produced this book includes:

CEO: Dave Rankin
COO: Janet Furlow
Managing Editor: Tammy Coron
Development Editor: Jacquelyn Carter
Copy Editor: Karen Galle
Indexing: Potomac Indexing, LLC
Layout: Gilson Graphics
Founders: Andy Hunt and Dave Thomas

For sales, volume licensing, and support, please contact *support@pragprog.com*.

For international rights, please contact *rights@pragprog.com*.

ISBN-13: 978-1-68050-725-6
Book version: P1.0—April 2022

Contents

Acknowledgments

As a virtual assistant, Alexa can do some amazing things and can be a great help in many tasks. However, Alexa isn't much help when I say, "Alexa, help me write a book." That's why I'm super grateful to everyone who helped me make this book a reality.

First, I'd like to thank my editor, Jackie Carter. She guided me through the writing process and made sure I stayed on track. It's been great working with her again and I look forward to our next writing project.

Many thanks to all of the reviewers who provided feedback on the work in progress along the way to make this book the best it can be: Alessandro Bahgat, Jeff Blankenburg, Jesús Chamizo, Cornelia Davis, Jack Frosch, Srey Sang, Nate Schutta, Ken Sipe, Lalit Surampudi, Dzulkiflee Taib, Brian Tarbox, Erik Weibust, and Miles Woodroffe.

A shout out to my fellow speakers on the No Fluff Just Stuff conference tour as well as everyone who attended my sessions over the years. I have learned so much from all of you and knowing that I'll be standing at the front of the room sharing what I know pushes me to stay sharp and learn new things, including the material that went into this book.

As always, I'd like to thank the Phoenicians. Without their contribution, this book would not have been possible.

Finally, all of my love and thanks to my beautiful wife, Raymie, and to my amazing daughters, Maisy and Madi, for encouragement, inspiration, and your enduring love through yet another writing project.

Introduction

If you're reading this, then it's a safe bet that you're a software developer. If so, then what drew you to this craft?

Speaking for myself, I was drawn to working with computers early on by the way that computers were portrayed in the science fiction shows that I watched as a kid. In shows like *Star Trek*, the crew of the Enterprise could talk to the ship's computer, and the computer would answer with a spoken response. Will Robinson would talk to the robot on *Lost in Space*, and the robot would talk back, often warning him of danger. Fast-forward to modern-day science fiction, who wouldn't want a computer like Iron Man's Jarvis to assist with your work?

When I finally got to use a real computer, I was a bit disappointed that I couldn't talk to my Commodore VIC-20. And even if I tried, it wouldn't do anything or talk back in response. Where was my talking computer? Oh well, that's why it's called science *fiction*.

Nevertheless, I continued to pursue a career in software development as I observed that science fiction often eventually becomes science fact. The computers we have today are far more powerful than the writers of science fiction would have imagined. The tablet that Captain Picard used in his ready room on *Star Trek: The Next Generation* is now commonplace in tablet devices such as the iPad. Smart watches worn by many these days rival anything James Bond ever had on his wrist. And recently, voice assistants such as Alexa have given us a talking computer that's not entirely unlike Jarvis.

As a software developer, there are very few things more exciting than writing code that implements what was once science-fiction. That's exactly what we'll do in this book—write code that implements science fiction with Alexa and voice-first applications.

Who Should Read This Book?

This book is for software developers who are interested in creating voice-first user interfaces or adding voice to their existing applications. We'll be developing in JavaScript using Node.js, so some experience with the JavaScript language and tooling will be helpful, but even those new to or unfamiliar with JavaScript should be able to follow along (and maybe learn JavaScript in a fun way).

About This Book

This book will introduce you to the exciting topic of voice user interfaces, building applications known as "skills" for the Alexa platform.

We'll start where all good learning projects start, with a simple "Hello World" skill that we'll deploy to Alexa and talk to. Then, before diving in deep, you'll learn techniques for testing Alexa skills, with both semi-automated and completely automated tests.

Next, you'll learn how to parameterize our conversations with Alexa using *slots*. When the user leaves out important information or says something that doesn't make sense, you'll learn how to create dialogs where Alexa can elicit missing details and validate that the information given is acceptable.

Often, voice interfaces must collaborate with other applications. We'll explore options for integrating Alexa skills with external applications and APIs.

Next, we'll look at how to change how Alexa speaks and sounds, and even include special sound effects and music in her responses using the Speech Synthesis Markup Language (SSML). That will lead right into a discussion of how to add localization to our skills so that Alexa can speak in the user's own language (and even change her voice to include the language's accent).

Then we'll see how voice-first applications aren't necessarily voice-only applications, by creating visual experiences that complement Alexa's vocal responses when our skill is launched on screen-enabled devices such as Echo Show and Fire TV.

Following our exploration of visual interfaces, we'll see how skills can act in response to out-of-band events when the user isn't actively using the skill. This includes handling events that are triggered when the user modifies the skill's settings as well as notifying the user of events.

Next, you'll learn how to monetize skills by offering in-skill purchases, allowing the user to purchase goods, both tangible and virtual.

We'll then unleash our skill to the world by publishing it. You'll learn what the requirements for publication are as well as perform some last-minute fine tuning to ensure that our skill is ready for real-world use.

Finally, we'll have a look at a relatively new way to create rich conversational interactions using Alexa Conversations. Like Dialogs we learned about earlier in the book, Conversations involve a question and answer session between Alexa and the user to achieve some outcome. But where Conversations shine is in how they allow the user to change their answers and take tangents in the conversational flow.

Online Resources

The examples and source code shown in this book can be found under the source code link on the Pragmatic Bookshelf website.[1]

Please report any errors or suggestions using the errata link that is available on the Pragmatic Bookshelf website.[2]

If you like this book and it serves you well, I hope that you will let others know about it—your reviews really do help. Tweets and posts are a great way to help spread the word. You can find me on Twitter at @habuma, or you can tweet @pragprog directly.

Craig Walls
April 2022

---

1. https://pragprog.com/book/cwalexa/build-talking-apps
2. https://pragprog.com/book/cwalexa/build-talking-apps

CHAPTER 1

Alexa, Hello

Voice is powerful. The words you say can make someone smile and laugh, with equal capacity for bringing tears or stirring anger. The spoken word can inspire, educate, and command. New parents are overjoyed when their baby says their first word, while veteran parents are often exasperated by the words said by their teenager. The ability to speak and be heard is one of the most versatile and potent abilities given to humans.

Until recently, however, computers and the applications we use haven't been able to share that power with us. We have been forced to communicate with computers by typing, clicking, tapping, and reading a screen—an interface that is natural to computers, even if unnatural to humans.

Voice platforms such as Amazon Alexa are changing the human-to-computer interface. Applications can now listen to what we say and respond with spoken words that we can hear. We can now talk to our applications in a conversational style that is very much the same as how we communicate with each other.

Having an Alexa device in the room changes how you do everyday things. Here are just a few examples:

- If you want to know what the weather forecast is, you can ask "Alexa, what's the weather?" instead of navigating to a weather website on your computer.

- Rather than fumble with the buttons on an alarm clock, you can say, "Alexa, set an alarm for 6:00 a.m."

- To find out when a movie is playing, you can ask, "Alexa, when is *Doctor Sleep* playing nearby?" which is much more convenient than looking it up on your phone or in a newspaper.

And this is just a sampling of what Alexa can do. Once you start talking with Alexa, you may start to think that there's nothing she doesn't know or can't do. But in reality, her abilities are only limited by what *skills* have been developed for her. While Alexa may be able to tell you what time the local Taco Bell closes or if your flight is on time, there'll always be things she doesn't know or know how to do.

Skills are voice-enabled applications that are written for Alexa to expand her capabilities. This is analogous to how mobile applications expand the capabilities of smartphones and tablets, or web applications expand the functionality of the internet. By developing Alexa skills you will be able to reach Alexa users with your ideas, content, and/or business in much the same way that websites and mobile applications do for the internet and mobile devices.

Creating custom skills is what this book is all about. In this chapter, we'll start by quickly getting to know what goes into building a skill. Then we'll install some essential tools for working with skills and write some code that implements a custom skill that we can actually talk to. First, let's establish a foundation by understanding how Alexa itself works.

How Alexa Works

It's easy to think of Alexa as an omniscient voice that lives inside of some speaker device in your house or car, and that always-present access to Alexa is what makes her such a useful assistant. In reality, however, all of Alexa's know-how lives in the cloud.

When you ask Alexa a question, the device you are speaking to sends a sound capture of what was heard to the Alexa Voice Service (AVS), a cloud-based service that applies Natural Language Processing (NLP) to interpret what Alexa hears and translates it into a speech request that is then forwarded to application code—a skill—that handles the request.

The skill itself typically executes as a function in AWS Lambda. It is also possible to develop the skill as a conventional REST API that is hosted outside of AWS Lambda, anywhere that can be reached by Alexa. That approach, however, is less common. We won't be covering this style of skill in this book.

After a skill has finished processing the request, it returns a response which goes back to AVS. AVS translates the skill's response into a voice response that it sends back to the Alexa device for her to speak out loud.

A Tale of Two Kinds of Functions

As with many terms used in software development, the word "function" has overloaded meanings. With regard to Alexa skills, there are two ways that the term "function" may be used. When talking about where a skill's fulfillment implementation is deployed, the word "function" refers to an application that is deployed to AWS Lambda. On the other hand, when we're mucking about with some JavaScript code, "function" means a block of code that performs a particular task.

The following diagram illustrates how an Alexa request and response flow from the user's spoken query through AVS, the skill running in AWS Lambda, and then back to the user's device.

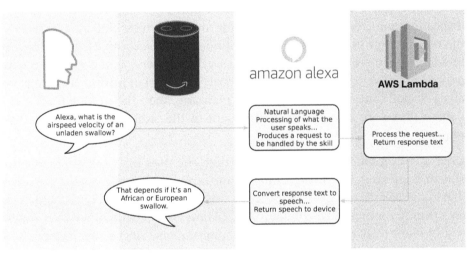

For the purposes of developing Alexa skills, it's not important to understand how the Alexa device works or the inner-workings of Alexa's NLP service. It is important, however, to understand how Alexa takes what she hears and directs the request to the relevant function running in AWS Lambda. So let's take a deeper dive into the rightmost portion of the diagram to see what makes a skill tick.

Dissecting Skills

Skills are composed of two essential elements: the fulfillment implementation, which is code that provides the skill's behavior, and the interaction model that describes how a human may interact with the skill.

The interaction model's main purpose is to assist Alexa's NLP in understanding what is said and where requests should be sent. It defines three things:

- An *invocation name*: The name by which a skill may be launched

- *Utterances*: Sample questions, commands, or phrases that a user might say to the skill

- *Intents*: Unique and precise commands that the user intends for Alexa to perform, mapped to one or more utterances

The invocation name acts as the trigger that launches a skill so that a user may talk to it. It's roughly the voice equivalent of clicking an icon to launch a desktop application. Although Alexa has many built-in capabilities that do not require an invocation name, custom skills usually require a unique invocation name so that Alexa can know for sure which skill should receive the request. For example, suppose that a space travel planning skill has an invocation name of "star port seventy five," the user might say, "open star port seventy five," or "ask star port seventy five to plan a trip." If there were another skill that also provided travel planning, then the unique invocation name will ensure that the request is sent to the skill that the user had in mind.

Once a conversation with a skill is started, the user may ask a question or state a command. The funny thing about humans, though, is that we often find many diverse ways to say the same thing. In a space travel planning skill, for example, someone might say, "let's plan a trip," but another user might say, "I want to plan a vacation." Still someone else might say, "schedule a tour." These are all examples of utterances, each capturing a different way of saying what might mean the same thing.

Regardless of how the user stated their question or command, intents narrow a skill's utterances into one or more discrete operations. Although simple skills may only do one thing or answer one type of question, many skills are capable of performing many related tasks. For the space travel planning skill, you might plan a trip, ask for information about a destination, or ask when your trip starts. There may be several utterances for each of these, but ultimately these are three distinct tasks. For each task, there will be a unique intent to capture what the skill is expected to do in response to an utterance.

To understand the relationship between utterances and intents, consider the diagram on page 5 that illustrates the interaction model for the space travel skill.

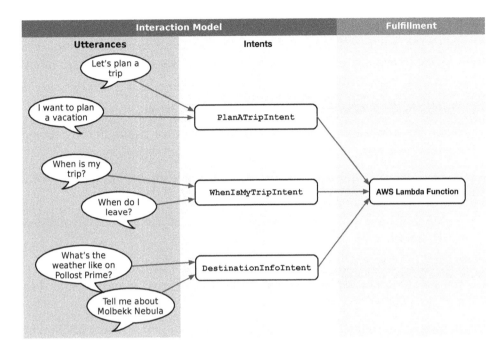

As shown here, the space travel skill can do three things: plan a trip, answer when a trip starts, and provide information about a destination. Those three individual actions are captured as the three intents in the middle column, each mapped to a couple of utterances in the leftmost column.

Regardless of what utterance a user says or which intent is chosen, all requests are ultimately sent to the fulfillment implementation for handling. As mentioned earlier, skill fulfillment is commonly implemented as a function deployed to AWS Lambda. Functions, by definition, take input, perform a single operation, and then return the result of that operation. But if the function only performs a single operation, how can a skill's fulfillment function handle requests for several intents? The answer comes from intent routing.

Once the Lambda function accepts a request, it will internally route the request to different code branches based on the request's content, including the request's intent. This is the same as the Front Controller Pattern[1] employed in many web frameworks for routing requests through a single front-end handler to distinct command objects. The only difference is that instead of routing web requests to command objects, the Lambda function routes intent requests to distinct intent handlers.

---

1.   https://martinfowler.com/eaaCatalog/frontController.html

Put simply, the Lambda function that implements a skill's functionality appears to do one thing from an outside point of view: Process intent requests from Alexa. Internally, however, it may do many things, responding to many different (but related) questions or commands spoken by the user.

In a nutshell, the Alexa skill can be described as follows:

- Skills are applications that expand Alexa's native capability to provide custom behavior.

- A skill has one fulfillment implementation, typically deployed as an AWS Lambda function.

- A skill may have one or many related operations, each discretely defined by an intent.

- Users of a skill may say what they intend for the skill to do in very different ways. Utterances capture different ways a user may interact with a skill and are mapped to more precise intents.

Developing Alexa skills involves defining the interaction model and fulfillment implementation to create custom capabilities for Alexa. Making that possible, Amazon provides the Alexa Skills Kit (ASK), a set of APIs, SDKs, and tools for developing Alexa skills. We'll soon see how to use ASK's JavaScript SDK to create our first Alexa skill. But before we go heads-down in developing a skill, let's install the ASK CLI, one of the most useful tools you'll put in your Alexa toolbox.

Installing the ASK CLI

The ASK CLI is a Swiss Army knife for Alexa developers, providing dozens of handy utilities. Among other things, we're going to use the ASK CLI throughout this book to create new skill projects, deploy skills, and test skills.

Before you install the ASK CLI, you'll need to install a few prerequisite command line tools:

- Node.js and npm[2]—We'll be developing Alexa skills in JavaScript using Node.js and using npm to install library dependencies and the ASK CLI itself.

- Git CLI[3]—When initializing a new Alexa skill project, the ASK CLI acts as a Git client to clone a template project.

---

2.   https://nodejs.org/en/download
3.   https://git-scm.com/book/en/v2/Getting-Started-Installing-Git

There's a good chance that you already have all of these prerequisites installed. If not, then follow the instructions at the respective download pages before attempting to install the ASK CLI.

To install the ASK CLI, use the npm install command:

```
$ npm install --global ask-cli
```

Depending on your operating system and user permissions, you may need to perform this as sudo:

```
$ sudo npm install --global ask-cli
```

Be patient. It may take several moments for npm to install everything needed for the ASK CLI and install it. When it finishes, you can verify that it installed by using it to tell you which version is installed:

```
$ ask --version
2.26.0
```

Ultimately, the skills you create will be deployed to and will run in AWS Lambda. The ASK CLI can help you deploy them, but to do so, it will need to be authorized to access you AWS developer account. The ask configure command initializes the ASK CLI to obtain that authorization. Start by typing ask configure at the command line:

```
$ ask configure
```

Your web browser should open and prompt you to sign in with your Amazon developer credentials. From the sign-in page, provide your Amazon developer credentials and sign in. If you've not yet created an Amazon developer account, you'll need to do so by clicking the "Create your Amazon Developer account" button on the sign-in screen. If you already have an Amazon account (for shopping) then you won't need to create a new account. Instead, you can add developer capabilities your existing Amazon account. This will enable you to interact with the skills you develop using any Alexa devices associated with that account.

After signing into your Amazon developer account, you'll be presented with a page that requests several permissions for the ASK CLI to have access to your account. The page will look a little something like the screenshot on page 8.

While the list of permissions being requested may seem daunting, they are all directly relevant to developing and deploying Alexa skills and it's important to accept them before moving on.

Once you've granted the ASK CLI authority to access your Amazon developer account, you will be shown a very basic text message in the browser instructing you to close the browser and return to the command line to continue setup.

If your web browser doesn't open to the sign-in page, it may be because you're running ask init in an environment without a web browser, such as from a Docker container. In that case, you can initialize the ASK CLI specifying --no-browser to the ask init command:

```
$ ask configure --no-browser
```

In "no-browser" mode, the ASK CLI will provide you with a URL to copy and paste into a browser's address bar on some other machine. From there you will go through the same sign-in and authorization steps, but in the end you'll be given an authorization code to provide to the ASK CLI when prompted with "Please enter the Authorization Code".

Next, you'll be asked if you want to link your AWS account in order to host skills. There are several options for hosting skills, including hosting them in AWS Lambda. But for now, we're going to use a different hosting option called "Alexa-hosted skills", which we'll discuss more in the next section. Respond with "No" to skip linking your AWS account at this time.

Linking Your AWS Account

Although we're skipping the AWS Linking configuration, you can always run ask configure again later if you decide to use AWS Lambda hosting.

When asked if you want to link your AWS account, respond with "Yes." You'll be asked for your AWS Access Key ID and AWS Secret Access Key. If you've developed with AWS previously, you may already have these. If not, then you'll need to obtain your AWS credentials[a] and use them to answer the prompts from the ASK CLI.

---

a.   https://developer.amazon.com/docs/smapi/manage-credentials-with-ask-cli.html#create-aws-credentials

---

After answering all of the configuration questions, the ASK CLI will be ready for you to start developing skills. Let's give it a spin by using it to create a new project that will be the foundation for a travel planning skill.

Creating Your First Alexa Skill

Through this book, we're going to build an Alexa skill for Star Port 75 Travel, a fictional travel agency specializing in interstellar travel destinations. Using the skill we create, adventurous travelers will be able to plan an out-of-this-world vacation. As the book progresses, we'll add features to capture the user's travel plans, book travel with external systems, support multiple languages and locales, remind the user of their upcoming trips, and much more. We'll start simple in this chapter, though, creating a voice application that simply welcomes the user to Star Port 75 Travel.

To get started, we're going to use the ASK CLI to bootstrap the project. Among the many commands that the ASK CLI offers is the new command, which creates a new skill project, including the project's directory structure, the skill manifest, interaction model, and some elementary code on which to add custom behavior.

The ASK CLI vs. the Alexa Developer Console

The ASK CLI isn't the only option for developing Alexa skills. You can also create and deploy Alexa skills using the Alexa Developer Console.[a] In fact, almost everything we're going to do throughout this book using the ASK CLI can also be achieved in your web browser via the developer console.

We're going to focus on using the ASK CLI as we develop the Star Port 75 Travel skill, only occasionally using the developer console—usually for manually testing the skill. Working in the CLI affords us more opportunities to use additional tooling and version control for our skill's code. But feel free to explore the developer console and use it if you find it useful.

---

a.   https://developer.amazon.com/alexa/console/ask

Bootstrapping any Alexa skill project starts with typing ask new at the command line and answering a few questions:

```
$ ask new
Please follow the wizard to start your Alexa skill project ->
? Choose the programming language you will use to code your skill:
  (Use arrow keys)
> NodeJS
  Python
  Java
```

The first question asks which language you want to develop with. The ASK SDK is available for NodeJS, Python, and Java. You're welcome to choose any language you like for your skills, but there are so many more resources and tools available when working with NodeJS, so that's the option we'll use for the Star Port 75 skill.

After selecting the language, you'll be asked to select the deployment option for hosting your skill:

```
$ ask new
Please follow the wizard to start your Alexa skill project ->
? Choose the programming language you will use to code your skill:   NodeJS
? Choose a method to host your skill's backend resources:
> Alexa-hosted skills
  Host your skill code by Alexa (free).
  AWS with CloudFormation
  Host your skill code with AWS services and provision with AWS
  CloudFormation (requires AWS account)
  AWS Lambda
  Host your skill code on AWS Lambda (requires AWS account).
  _____
  self-hosted and manage your own hosting
```

Here you have four options: Alexa-hosted, AWS with CloudFormation, AWS Lambda, and self-hosting. We're going to choose "Alexa-hosted skills". Alexa-hosted skills is a free option that is suitable for many Alexa skills, including the one we're going to build. By choosing Alexa-hosted skills, Alexa will provision AWS Lambda endpoints in all three Alexa-service regions, an Amazon S3 bucket for media resources, an Amazon DynamoDB database that your skill can use to persist data, and an AWS CodeCommit Git repository for your Alexa project. Because all of that is set up for you, Alexa-hosted skills are by far the easiest option for getting started.

Note that if you were to select AWS Lambda or AWS with CloudFormation hosting here instead of Alexa-hosted skills, you will need to have linked your AWS account at the time you ran ask configure. You will also be asked a slightly different set of questions.

After selecting to deploy with Alexa-hosted skills, you'll be asked to specify the default region.

```
$ ask new
Please follow the wizard to start your Alexa skill project ->
? Choose the programming language you will use to code your skill: NodeJS
? Choose a method to host your skill's backend resources: Alexa-hosted skills
  Host your skill code by Alexa (free).
? Choose the default region for your skill:  (Use arrow keys)
> us-east-1
  us-west-2
  eu-west-1
```

Although Alexa-hosted skills will be deployed in all three regions supported for Alexa skills, you still must designate one as the default region. Pick the region closest to your users. Here, we'll choose "us-east-1".

After selecting the default hosting region, you'll be asked for the name of the skill:

```
$ ask new
Please follow the wizard to start your Alexa skill project ->
? Choose the programming language you will use to code your skill:  NodeJS
? Choose a method to host your skill's backend resources:  Alexa-hosted skills
  Host your skill code by Alexa (free).
? Choose the default region for your skill:  us-east-1
? Please type in your skill name:  starport-75
```

By default, the skill will be named "Hello World Skill". But we'll want to change that to "starport-75" for our skill.

Finally, you'll be asked to specify a directory name for the project to be created in. This can be different than the skill's name, but for our purposes, "starport-75" is a fine choice:

```
$ ask new
Please follow the wizard to start your Alexa skill project ->
? Choose the programming language you will use to code your skill:  NodeJS
? Choose a method to host your skill's backend resources:  Alexa-hosted skills
  Host your skill code by Alexa (free).
? Choose the default region for your skill:  us-east-1
? Please type in your skill name:  starport-75
? Please type in your folder name for the skill project (alphanumeric):
  starport-75
```

After giving the project directory name, the project will be created. You can change into that directory and have a look around.

Now that our project has been initialized, let's take a quick tour of the project structure.

Exploring the Project

At a high level the directory structure of the newly created Alexa skill project will look like the following results from running a tree command:

```
$ tree
.
├── ask-resources.json
├── lambda
│   ├── index.js
│   ├── local-debugger.js
│   ├── package.json
│   └── util.js
└── skill-package
    ├── interactionModels
    │   └── custom
    │       └── en-US.json
    └── skill.json
```

Of all of the files in the project, there are three files that are most significant:

- *skill-package/interactionModels/custom/en-US.json*: This file defines the skill's interaction model for U.S. English. Later, in Chapter 8, Localizing Responses, on page 195 we'll expand the interaction model to other languages and locales.

- *lambda/index.js*: This is the source code for the fulfillment implementation. It contains JavaScript code for handling Alexa requests.

- *skill-package/skill.json*: This is the skill's deployment manifest, which describes some essential information about the skill and is used when deploying the skill.

As we continue to develop our skill, we'll touch these three files the most. We'll definitely edit en-US.json, and index.js in this chapter; we'll tweak skill.json several times throughout this book to configure additional capabilities in our skill.

The Only Thing Constant Is Change

Because the ask new command is essentially acting as a Git client, cloning the chosen project template from an actively developed Git repository, it's quite possible that the resulting project structure and code will vary with what is shown in this book. It will likely remain similar enough for easy comparison, however.

There are also a handful of files and directories that are important and helpful in building and deploying a skill:

- *lambda/package.json*—This is a typical Node package definition specifying the modules that are required to support the skill. This includes, among other things, the ASK SDK. As you continue to evolve your skill, you might find yourself using the npm command line tool to add more modules to the project.

- *lambda/local-debugger.js*—This script enables you to test and debug your Alexa skill with locally running fulfillment code. It is deprecated in favor of a much simpler way to run skills locally (which is covered in Appendix 1, Running and Debugging Skill Code Locally, on page 343). You may delete it from the project or just ignore it.

- *lambda/util.js*—This is a utility script that simplifies resolving URLs to images, sounds, and other resources stored in Amazon's S3 service. We won't need this script initially, so we'll ignore it for now.

- *ask-resources.json*—This file describes where the skill's resources are placed in the project.

Even though these files are important, it's rare that you'll change them often or at all.

Now that we've taken the nickel tour of the "Hello World" template project, let's dive even deeper into the code, starting with a look at the interaction model defined in skill-package/interactionModels/custom/en-US.json.

Describing the Interaction Model

Each skill defines its own interaction model, essentially defining how a user is expected to interact with the skill. While the interaction model can be created from scratch, the ASK CLI will give us a simple interaction model for U.S. English in skill-package/interactionModels/custom/en-US.json to get started with. For any brand new project based on the "Hello World" template, the interaction model will look like this:

```
hello/starport-75/skill-package/interactionModels/custom/en-US.json
{
  "interactionModel": {
    "languageModel": {
      "invocationName": "change me",
      "intents": [
        {
          "name": "AMAZON.CancelIntent",
          "samples": []
        },
        {
          "name": "AMAZON.HelpIntent",
          "samples": []
        },
        {
          "name": "AMAZON.StopIntent",
          "samples": []
        },
        {
          "name": "HelloWorldIntent",
          "slots": [],
          "samples": [
            "hello",
            "how are you",
            "say hi world",
            "say hi",
            "hi",
            "say hello world",
            "say hello"
          ]
        },
        {
          "name": "AMAZON.NavigateHomeIntent",
          "samples": []
        }
      ],
      "types": []
    }
  },
  "version": "1"
}
```

As mentioned before, the interaction model describes two main things: the skill's invocation name and the mappings of utterances to the intents supported by the skill. As shown here, the invocation name is "change me". That means that if we were to deploy this skill, a user would be able to open it by saying, "open change me." But since that is a horrible invocation name, we'll definitely want to change it to give it a name more befitting its purpose. Since we're developing a skill for Star Port 75 Travel, we should change it to "star port seventy five" like this:

```
{
  "interactionModel": {
    "languageModel": {
      "invocationName": "star port seventy five",
      ...
    }
  }
}
```

With the invocation name set this way, we'll be able to launch the skill by saying, "Alexa, open star port seventy five."

Note that the invocation name is all lowercase and the words "seventy five" are spelled out rather than using a numerical representation. These are, in fact, requirements for the invocation name, enforced by the platform. There are several rules around invocation names,[4] but succinctly it must be two or more words, start with a letter and can only contain lower case letters, spaces, apostrophes, and periods. If we were to set the invocation name to "Star Port 75 Travel", it would be rejected when we get around to deploying it later because the digits "75" are not allowed.

In addition to the invocation name, the interaction model also defines intents supported by the skill along with sample utterances for each of those intents. The invocation model in skill-package/interactionModels/custom/en-US.json provided by the "Hello World" template defines five intents, four of which are Amazon built-in intents and one which is a domain-specific intent defined by the skill itself.

HelloWorldIntent is the one intent that is specific to this skill. In a little while, we'll see code that handles requests for this intent. But for now, notice that it has several sample utterances. Ultimately, we're developing a travel planning skill and not a "hello world" skill. But for now, just to get started, we'll leave this intent in place.

---

4. https://developer.amazon.com/en-US/docs/alexa/custom-skills/choose-the-invocation-name-for-a-custom-skill.html#cert-invocation-name-req

The remaining intents are Amazon built-in intents to cover situations common to most skills. These intents do not list any sample utterances in their samples property because they are already pre-associated with utterances appropriate to their purpose by the platform. For example, the intent named AMAZON.HelpIntent is pre-associated with the "help" utterance. You do not need to explicitly list "help" or any other sample utterances, but you may list additional utterances if you want the help intent to respond to a non-default utterance. For example, the following snippet from skill-package/interactionModels/custom/en-US.json will have Alexa respond with help information if the user says "huh":

```
{
  "name": "AMAZON.HelpIntent",
  "samples": [
    "huh"
  ]
},
```

The AMAZON.CancelIntent and AMAZON.StopIntent intents match when the user says "cancel" and "stop," but as with any intent, you are welcome to additional utterances to their sample list. They are often synonymous with each other. For our skill, they both are used to exit the skill if the user says "cancel" or "stop." However, in some skills, the words "cancel" and "stop" might have different meanings. For example, "cancel" may have the semantics of canceling an order in some skills, but not exiting the skill. Because of this, they are expressed as two separate intents so that you can associate different behavior with each.

It's important to realize that because this file is named en-US.json, it only describes the interaction model for English speaking users in the United States locale. To support other languages, we can create similar files in the models directory whose names are based on the language and locale we want to support. For now, we'll start with U.S. English, then internationalize our skill later in Chapter 8, Localizing Responses, on page 195.

Throughout this book, we'll modify the interaction model, adding new custom intents and seeing other kinds of built-in intents. But for now, let's see how to write fulfillment code that handles requests from Alexa.

Handling Requests

While the interaction model describes the interaction between a user and your skill, the fulfillment endpoint defines how the skill should respond to requests. As mentioned earlier, the fulfillment endpoint is typically deployed as a function on AWS Lambda that handles speech requests. For skills created with the ASK CLI for the "Hello World" template, a starting point fulfillment implementation is given in the lambda/index.js file.

If you open that file in your favorite text editor, you'll see a line at the top that looks like this:

```
hello/starport-75/lambda/index.js
const Alexa = require('ask-sdk-core');
```

This line imports the ASK SDK module and assigns it to a constant named Alexa. The Alexa constant will be referenced throughout the fulfillment implementation code to access SDK functionality.

One place you'll find the Alexa constant in use is at the end of the lambda/index.js file where it is used to create a skill builder object through which request handlers will be registered:

```
hello/starport-75/lambda/index.js
exports.handler = Alexa.SkillBuilders.custom()
    .addRequestHandlers(
        LaunchRequestHandler,
        HelloWorldIntentHandler,
        HelpIntentHandler,
        CancelAndStopIntentHandler,
        SessionEndedRequestHandler,
        IntentReflectorHandler,
        )
    .addErrorHandlers(
        ErrorHandler,
        )
    .lambda();
```

As you can see, we're currently using the skill builder to register seven request handlers in the call to addRequestHandlers(). This includes handlers for Amazon's built-in intents, handlers for the skill lifecycle (LaunchRequestHandler and SessionEndedRequestHandler), and the handler for the intent named HelloWorldIntent.

You'll notice that a special error handler is registered in a call to addErrorHandlers() to handle any errors that may occur while processing a request.

Finally, the last thing we do with the skill builder is call lambda(), which builds a Lambda function that acts as a front-controller for all requests, dispatching them to one of the registered request handlers.

The request handlers, themselves, are objects that expose two functions, canHandle() and handle(). For example, consider the following request handler that handles the intent named HelloWorldIntent:

```
hello/starport-75/lambda/index.js
const HelloWorldIntentHandler = {
  canHandle(handlerInput) {
    return Alexa.getRequestType(handlerInput.requestEnvelope)
                                           === 'IntentRequest'
      && Alexa.getIntentName(handlerInput.requestEnvelope)
                                           === 'HelloWorldIntent';
  },
  handle(handlerInput) {
    const speakOutput = 'Hello World!';
    return handlerInput.responseBuilder
      .speak(speakOutput)
      .getResponse();
  }
};
```

The canHandle() function examines the given handler input, which includes
information about the request being handled, and decides whether or not the
handler is able to handle the request. If it can, it should return true; otherwise
it returns false indicating that this particular handler isn't the one for handling
the request. In this particular example, the first thing that canHandle() checks
is that the request is an intent request, and not some other type of request
such as a launch request or session-end request. Then it checks that the
intent's name is HelloWorldIntent. If so, then this handler is the one for the job.

Assuming that canHandle() returns true, the handle() method will be called next.
Since, at this point, the skill is little more than a garden-variety Hello World
example, the handle() method is fairly basic as far as handlers go. After
assigning the legendary greeting to a constant, it references a response builder
from the given handlerInput to build a response. By calling the speak() function,
we are asking Alexa to speak the words "Hello World!" through the Alexa
device's speaker.

Even though at this point, the Star Port 75 skill is nothing more than a "hello
world" skill, let's make a few small customizations so that Alexa will give a
greeting fitting to the interstellar travel business:

```
hello/starport-75/lambda/index.js
const HelloWorldIntentHandler = {
  canHandle(handlerInput) {
    return Alexa.getRequestType(handlerInput.requestEnvelope)
                                           === 'IntentRequest'
      && Alexa.getIntentName(handlerInput.requestEnvelope)
                                           === 'HelloWorldIntent';
  },
  handle(handlerInput) {
    const speakOutput = 'Have a stellar day!';
    return handlerInput.responseBuilder
```

```
      .speak(speakOutput)
      .getResponse();
  }
};
```

With this change, Alexa will now say, "Have a stellar day!" instead of the trite "Hello world" greeting.

Taking inventory of the rest of the lambda/index.js file, you'll notice that in addition to the HelloWorldIntentHandler, there are five other request handlers. Where HelloWorldIntentHandler exists to handle the skill-specific intent named HelloWorldIntent, the other handlers are there to handle a few of Amazon's built-in intents and requests:

- LaunchRequestHandler—Handles a launch request when the skill is first launched

- HelpIntentHandler—Handles the built-in AMAZON.HelpIntent intent whenever a user asks for help

- CancelAndStopIntentHandler—Handles the built-in AMAZON.CancelIntent and AMA-ZON.StopIntent intents. These will be sent if the user says "Cancel" or "Stop" to leave the skill.

- SessionEndedRequestHandler—Handles a request to end the session

- ErrorHandler—Handles any errors that may occur. This does not necessarily mean that Alexa doesn't understand what the user said, but it might mean that some error is thrown from one of the other handlers while handling a different request.

- IntentReflectorHandler—An intent handler used for testing and debugging. It will handle requests for any intents that aren't handled by other intent handlers and echo the otherwise unhandled intent's name. You may choose to keep it around if you want, but you should probably remove it before publishing your skill.

The handler named LaunchRequestHandler, for instance, will be invoked upon a request of type LaunchRequest. This is the request that is sent to a skill when the skill first opens—in this case, when the user says, "Alexa, open star port seventy five." It looks like this:

```
hello/starport-75/lambda/index.js
const LaunchRequestHandler = {
  canHandle(handlerInput) {
    return Alexa.getRequestType(handlerInput.requestEnvelope)
                                          === 'LaunchRequest';
  },
```

```
  handle(handlerInput) {
    const speakOutput =
         'Welcome, you can say Hello or Help. Which would you like to try?';
    return handlerInput.responseBuilder
       .speak(speakOutput)
       .reprompt(speakOutput)
       .getResponse();
  }
};
```

As you can see, LaunchRequestHandler isn't much different from HelloWorldIntentHandler. It creates a response passing a welcome message to speak(). But it also passes the message to reprompt() to repeat the message after a moment if the user doesn't say anything.

The out-of-the-box welcome message is fine for a generic "hello world" skill, but it isn't good enough for Star Port 75 Travel. Let's tweak it to give a more befitting welcome message:

```
hello/starport-75/lambda/index.js
const LaunchRequestHandler = {
  canHandle(handlerInput) {
    return Alexa.getRequestType(handlerInput.requestEnvelope)
                                              === 'LaunchRequest';
  },
  handle(handlerInput) {
    const speakOutput =
         'Welcome to Star Port 75 Travel. How can I help you?';
    return handlerInput.responseBuilder
       .speak(speakOutput)
       .reprompt(speakOutput)
       .getResponse();
  }
};
```

The other request handlers and messages are fine as-is, but feel free to tweak them if you'd like.

We're just getting started with the Star Port 75 skill, but the two request handlers and messages we've touched should serve as a fine introduction to writing custom Alexa skills. There's a lot more we'll add to the skill as we progress through the book. Before we deploy what we have created and try it out, let's add a couple of helpful components to the skill, starting with a catch-all intent for utterances that don't match any other intents.

Adding a Fallback Handler

Even though the sample utterances defined for the HelloWorldIntent serve as a guide to Alexa's NLP service to match utterances to the intent, it's not necessary for the user to speak those precise phrases to trigger the intent. Other utterances that the NLP considers reasonably close to the sample utterances will also match. In fact, without any further changes, almost any utterance that doesn't match one of Alexa's built-in intents will match the HelloWorldIntent.

For example, if the user were to say "watermelon," that might be close enough to trigger the HelloWorldIntent. Actually, it's not that "watermelon" is all that close to "hello," but rather it's not any closer to any other intent.

In cases like that, it's usually better for Alexa to gracefully respond that she didn't understand what the user said than to reply with a nonsensical answer. For that, Amazon provides the built-in AMAZON.FallbackIntent. AMAZON.FallbackIntent is a catch-all intent that is triggered when the user's utterance doesn't match any other intent's sample utterances.

To take advantage of AMAZON.FallbackIntent, we must declare it in the interaction model just like any other intent by adding the following JSON to skill-package/interactionModels/custom/en-US.json:

```
{
  "name": "AMAZON.FallbackIntent",
  "samples": []
},
```

It's not necessary to specify sample utterances for AMAZON.FallbackIntent, although if you find that certain utterances are incorrectly matching to other intents, you can list them under AMAZON.FallbackIntent to ensure that they're directed there.

As with any other intent, we must also create an intent handler that will respond to the intent:

```
hello/starport-75/lambda/index.js
const FallbackIntentHandler = {
  canHandle(handlerInput) {
      return Alexa.getRequestType(handlerInput.requestEnvelope)
                                          === 'IntentRequest'
          && Alexa.getIntentName(handlerInput.requestEnvelope)
                                          === 'AMAZON.FallbackIntent';
  },
  handle(handlerInput) {
      const speakOutput =
          'Sorry, I don\'t know about that. Please try again.';
```

```
        return handlerInput.responseBuilder
            .speak(speakOutput)
            .reprompt(speakOutput)
            .getResponse();
    }
};
```

Finally, be sure to register the intent handler with the skill builder:

hello/starport-75/lambda/index.js
```
exports.handler = Alexa.SkillBuilders.custom()
    .addRequestHandlers(
        LaunchRequestHandler,
        HelloWorldIntentHandler,
        HelpIntentHandler,
        CancelAndStopIntentHandler,
        FallbackIntentHandler,
        SessionEndedRequestHandler,
        IntentReflectorHandler,
        )

    ...

    .lambda();
```

Because AMAZON.FallbackIntent is just another intent, like any other intent, FallbackIntentHandler can be registered among the other handlers in any order. It's only important that it be listed before IntentReflectorHandler, since that handler doesn't inspect the intent name and will therefore match any intent if listed higher.

Now, if a user were to say "watermelon," "kangaroo," "zip-a-dee-doo-dah," or anything else that doesn't match any other intent, it will be directed to AMAZON.FallbackIntent and handled by the FallbackIntentHandler.

If during testing, or after the skill has been published, you find that some utterances that you'd expect to be directed as AMAZON.FallbackIntent are being directed as another intent, you can adjust the fallback intent's sensitivity level in the interaction model:

```
{
  "interactionModel": {
    "languageModel": {
      "invocationName": "star port seventy five",
      "intents": [
        ...
      ],
      "types": [],
      "modelConfiguration": {
        "fallbackIntentSensitivity": {
          "level": "HIGH"
```

```
            }
          }
        }
      }
    }
  }
}
```

The fallback intent sensitivity level can be set to "LOW", "MEDIUM", or "HIGH". The default sensitivity level is "LOW". Raising it will cause more utterances to be routed to the fallback intent handler.

Up to this point, we've been hard-coding all of the text that Alexa will speak in the request handler. That will work fine, but we can do better. Let's see how to extract those strings so that they can be managed independent of the request handler.

Externalizing Strings

Right now, while our skill is rather basic, it seems natural to just hard-code the response text in the handle() functions as we have done. But as our skill evolves, it will be helpful to manage all of those strings in one place. And when we get to Chapter 8, Localizing Responses, on page 195, the responses will be different depending on the user's preferred language and hardcoded strings won't be an option.

To help with externalization of strings, we'll add the i18next module to our project:

```
$ npm install --prefix lambda i18next
```

This module enables internationalization of string values. Even though we're only supporting English output at this point, it's easier to externalize the strings now while there are only a few strings to manage than to wait until we have several strings to extract.

To use the i18next module, we'll first need to require() it in index.js:

hello/starport-75/lambda/index.js
```
const i18next = require('i18next');
const languageStrings = require('./languageStrings');
```

In addition to the i18next module, we also require() a local module named languageStrings which will contain the externalized string values. We'll define that module in a moment, but first let's use both of these modules to extend the handlerInput object with a utility function to lookup a string by name:

hello/starport-75/lambda/index.js
```
const LocalisationRequestInterceptor = {
  process(handlerInput) {
```

```
        i18next.init({
            lng: Alexa.getLocale(handlerInput.requestEnvelope),
            resources: languageStrings
        }).then((i18n) => {
            handlerInput.t = (...args) => i18n(...args);
        });
    }
};
```

LocalisationRequestInterceptor is a request interceptor that adds a t() function to handlerInput. When a request comes into our skill, this interceptor's process() function will use the user's locale and the languageStrings module to initialize the i18next module and then use the resulting i18n function to lookup a string from the externalized file.

The interceptor code is brief, but a little complex. But when you see it in action, it will make more sense.

So that the interceptor can do its job, we'll need to register it with the skill builder:

hello/starport-75/lambda/index.js
```
exports.handler = Alexa.SkillBuilders.custom()

    ...

    .addRequestInterceptors(
        LocalisationRequestInterceptor
        )
    .lambda();
```

Revisiting the intent handler for HelloWorldIntent, we can use the new t() function to lookup a the text with a key of "HELLO_MSG":

hello/starport-75/lambda/index.js
```
const HelloWorldIntentHandler = {
  canHandle(handlerInput) {
    return Alexa.getRequestType(handlerInput.requestEnvelope)
                                              === 'IntentRequest'
        && Alexa.getIntentName(handlerInput.requestEnvelope)
                                              === 'HelloWorldIntent';
  },
  handle(handlerInput) {
    const speakOutput = handlerInput.t('HELLO_MSG');
    return handlerInput.responseBuilder
        .speak(speakOutput)
        .getResponse();
  }
};
```

When handlerInput.t() is called, it will return the greeting as defined in languageStrings.js under the "HELLO_MSG" key:

```
hello/starport-75/lambda/languageStrings.js
module.exports = {
    en: {
      translation: {
        WELCOME_MSG: 'Welcome to Star Port 75 Travel. How can I help you?',
        HELLO_MSG: 'Have a stellar day!',
        HELP_MSG: 'You can say hello to me! How can I help?',
        GOODBYE_MSG: 'Goodbye!',
        REFLECTOR_MSG: 'You just triggered {{intentName}}',
        FALLBACK_MSG: 'Sorry, I don\'t know about that. Please try again.',
        ERROR_MSG: 'Sorry, I had trouble doing what you asked. ' +
                  'Please try again.'
    }
  }
}
```

Notice that the top-level key in languageStrings.js is "en", which is shorthand for "English". Later we may add additional languages to this file, but for now English is all we need. Underneath the "en" key is a set of strings for all of the intents in our skill. Specifically, the "HELLO_MSG" entry is mapped to the message we want Alexa to speak to users when the HelloWorld-Intent is handled. We can apply the other strings in the skill's other request handlers the same way, by calling handlerInput.t() instead of hard-coding the responses.

Now we're ready to deploy our skill and kick the tires.

Deploying the Skill

How you deploy a skill depends on whether the skill is Alexa-hosted or AWS Lambda-hosted. Since we chose Alexa-hosting, all we need to do to deploy our skill is to commit and push our skill using the git command line:

```
$ git add .
$ git commit -m "Initial customization for Star Port 75"
$ git push
```

Alexa-hosted skills are backed by AWS CodeCommit, which offers a private Git repository. When you push your Alexa-hosted skill code to CodeCommit, it will automatically be deployed for you within a few minutes of submitting the git push command.

If, however, you chose AWS Lambda-hosting for your skill, then you'll be responsible for providing your own source code control. To deploy the skill, you can use the ask deploy command like this:

```
$ ask deploy
```

After hitting the enter key, the ASK CLI takes care of the rest. Among other things, it deploys the interaction model to ASK and builds it to be ready to take requests. It also deploys the fulfillment code to AWS Lambda for you, freeing you from having to work with AWS Lambda directly. It takes a few moments to complete, but once it does, your skill will be deployed and ready to use.

That said, it is only available on Alexa devices connected to your Amazon account, so don't start calling your friends and family or blasting an email announcement to the world just yet. Deploying a skill with ask deploy only makes it available for testing with devices and tools connected to your account. In order to make your skill available for general consumption, you'll need to publish it. We'll see how to publish skills in Chapter 13, Publishing Your Skill, on page 289.

For now, however, it's good enough to do a few manual tests against your skill. If you own an Alexa-enabled device associated with your developer account, simply say, "Alexa, open star port seventy five." If all goes well, she should respond with "Welcome to the Star Port 75 Travel. How can I help you?" Then, if you follow up by saying "Hello" or "Say Hello," she will reply with "Have a stellar day!"

The Alexa Device in Your Pocket

If you're just getting started with Alexa skill development, it's possible that you've not yet purchased an Alexa device. That's okay. You may already have an Alexa device without knowing it.

The Alexa companion application is an application that Alexa users can install on their mobile devices or access via a web browser[a] to manage their Alexa devices and other aspects of their Amazon account as it pertains to Alexa.

Among other things, the mobile version of the Alexa companion application can function as an Alexa device itself. With the application open on your mobile device, simply start talking to it like any other Alexa device by saying "Alexa" and then asking it questions or opening your skill.

---

a. https://alexa.amazon.com

While trying out a custom skill on a real Alexa device is very satisfying, you don't need an Alexa device to try out your skill. Another option you'll find useful is to sign into the ASK developer console,[5] find your skill in the list of available skills, then click on the "Test" tab to use the Alexa Simulator. The following screenshot shows a brief test session in the simulator:

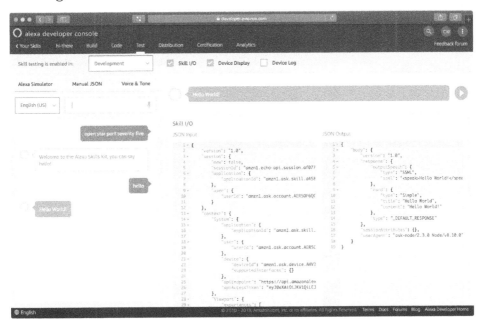

In the left-hand panel, you can either type what you want to say to Alexa, or click and hold the microphone icon and speak what you want to say. Your conversation will appear in the speech bubbles below the text box. In this screenshot, we've asked her to open the skill we've created in this chapter and then said "Hello" to her.

In the panel on the right, you'll be shown JSON for the most recent request and response. This is useful for debugging more complex skills. But for our simple skill, it's just interesting information. We'll take a deeper look at this JSON later in the book, as we need it to understand how our skills work.

Another way to try out your Alexa skill is with Visual Studio Code.[6] Aside from being a fantastic editor for developing your Alexa skills, Visual Studio Code with the Alexa Skills Toolkit extension[7] offers a great way to test your

---

5. https://developer.amazon.com/alexa/console/ask

6. https://code.visualstudio.com/

7. https://developer.amazon.com/en-US/docs/alexa/ask-toolkit/get-started-with-the-ask-toolkit-for-visual-studio-code.html

skill that's similar to the "Test" tab in the developer console. If the ASK extension is installed, you'll be able to click on the Alexa logo on the activity bar and then select "Test skill > Open simulator" in the left-hand menu to see an in-editor Alexa simulator. This screenshot shows what working with the simulator in Visual Studio code looks like:

Notice that the simulator in Visual Studio Code offers the option of exporting a session via the "Export" button (near the top). This will save the user's utterances in a JSON file. Then later you can replay it by selecting "Test skill > Replay session" from the left-hand menu.

Wrapping Up

Voice applications are an exciting next step in the evolution of human-computer interaction. Alexa, one of the leading voice platforms, enables users to use the natural interface of voice to perform tasks, ask questions, and be entertained.

Skills are applications that expand Alexa's capabilities beyond her native functions. Skills can provide information, tackle business tasks, entertain, or anything you can dream of. The Alexa Skills Kit (ASK) provides tools, APIs, SDKs, and examples to help software developers produce voice-first applications.

Skills are composed of an interaction model, which describes how a human may interact with the skill, and a fulfillment implementation, which executes the logic to process questions and commands from the user. The interaction model itself describes utterances, samples of things a user may say to the skill, mapped to intents, which precisely capture what the user intended to say.

One of the most useful tools you'll use as an Alexa skill developer is the ASK CLI, a command line tool that provides many useful functions for developing skills, including bootstrapping a new skill project and deploying the project.

Another useful tool that ASK makes available is the developer console where you can test a skill through a web interface rather than using an actual Alexa-enabled device. Even so, manually testing with the developer console is only one way to test skills.

Before we get too carried away learning new techniques and building new functionality into our Alexa skill, it will be helpful to get to know some of the options for testing Alexa skills. Therefore, in the next chapter we'll look at several ways to test Alexa skills, both manual and automated, and even including ways of testing a skill without deploying it to the Alexa platform and AWS Lambda. This will give us the tools to consistently ensure that the code we're developing does what we expect it to do.

CHAPTER 2

Testing Alexa Skills

Software testing is a very important part of any application's development cycle and provides the means for knowing that the application's functionality is correct. Alexa skills are no exception. Although the vocal nature of Alexa skills presents some unique twists in testing, it's still important to write tests that ensure that the skill does what you expect and operates correctly as you continue to build out the skill's functionality.

Knowing that we'll need to write tests as we flesh out the functionality of our skill, let's take a moment to learn some useful testing techniques and tools that meet the unique nature of voice applications.

Considering Skill Testing Styles

Fortunately, there are several useful tools in the Alexa development ecosystem for testing skills. In fact, there are enough choices that it can be difficult to know which testing tool to use. To help you understand which testing tools are the best fit for a particular circumstance, consider that there are three styles of testing for Alexa skills:

- Vocal/Manual
- Non-Vocal/Semi-automated
- Non-Vocal/Fully automated

Vocal testing is almost completely manual, requiring that you speak to an Alexa-enabled device or simulator and listen to the response to know if your skill is behaving as expected. One of the key benefits of vocal testing is that it is virtually the same as what your end-user will experience when they use your skill. Also, unlike the other non-vocal testing styles, you will be able to verify how your skill *sounds*. This is incredibly important if your skill includes sound effects, music, or uses the Speech Synthesis Markup Language (SSML) to alter Alexa's voice or tone. (We'll look at SSML in Chapter 6, Embellishing Response Speech, on page 131).

While vocal testing has its benefits, it also has a few limitations. First, it requires that the skill be deployed before you can test it. If changes are required between test runs, you must wait for the skill to be redeployed, which gets in the way of quick feedback on your changes. With vocal testing, it is also not easy to reliably repeat a vocal test and ensure that you said and heard the same things each time. Finally, vocal testing is difficult, and perhaps even rude, to conduct in a crowded place such as an office, airplane, or StarBucks.

Non-vocal testing, as its name suggests, does not require speaking or listening to a skill, thereby sparing those around you from hearing your conversation with Alexa. Instead, non-vocal testing involves submitting your questions and commands in textual form, either by manually typing them in or as part of a script. When submitted as a script, the tests can be reliably repeated and run as many times as necessary.

Semi-automated non-vocal testing still relies on you to verify the results manually, albeit by reading results instead of listening to them. It also requires that the skill be deployed before you can test it, and thus the feedback loop can still be lengthy. In spite of these limitations, semi-automated non-vocal testing can be nearly as flexible as vocal testing when it comes to trying different things, allowing you to mix repeatable tests with ad-hoc tests if you like.

While vocal testing of a skill brings us as close to the user experience as possible and semi-automated testing is useful for ad hoc testing and debugging of Alexa skills, both techniques are unfortunately dependent on human participation. And humans are notoriously unreliable when it comes to doing repeated tasks such as software testing.

Computers, on the other hand, excel at automatically performing repeated tasks. Therefore, if we are looking for a way to reliably and frequently verify that our skill is behaving as we expect it to behave, then we should consider writing fully automated tests.

Fully automated non-vocal testing is repeatable, and verification of results is scripted as part of the test itself, requiring no visual or audible verification. This makes it a perfect fit for a CI/CD pipeline to build and deploy your skill automatically when changes are made. In this style of skill testing, the skill does not need to be deployed. This means that the feedback loop is tight, enabling you to develop faster and with confidence that your changes are good.

The biggest downside of fully automated testing is that it is far removed from the actual user experience, and as such there's no way to experience the skill as your users will experience it. But being able to reliably repeat tests and verify results makes it incredibly powerful.

Because vocal testing requires no special techniques or tooling, aside from an Alexa device to talk to, you're welcome to establish your own strategy for vocal testing. In this chapter, we're going to focus on techniques for non-vocal testing. We'll start by looking at how to write semi-automated tests that let us interact with our skill by typing our queries and reading responses.

Semi-Automated Testing

Semi-automated testing of an Alexa skill involves automatically sending a request to your skill, but still manually verifying the response. This style of testing is most useful when debugging, especially if the debugging session requires repeating the same flow of intents multiple times.

We're going to look at three options for semi-automated testing of Alexa skills, using the ASK CLI and TestFlow. First up, let's see how to use the ASK CLI to test a skill.

Testing with the ASK CLI

We've already used the ASK CLI to bootstrap our Alexa skill project and to deploy it. But the ASK CLI has many more tricks up its sleeves, including the dialog subcommand which opens a shell within which you can interact with the skill by typing utterances and reading the responses.

To use the ask dialog command in interactive mode, you'll need specify the --locale parameter to provide a locale that you want to use when interacting with the skill. For example, here's how to start a session with ask dialog in the U.S. English locale:

```
$ ask dialog --locale en-US
```

Once the dialog session starts, you will be shown a User > prompt at which you can type in what you want to say to Alexa. Alexa will reply in lines that begin with Alexa >, followed by a new User > prompt for you to say something else. For instance, here's a simple dialog session interacting with the Star Port 75 skill:

```
User  > open star port seventy five
Alexa > Welcome to Star Port 75 Travel. How can I help you?
User  > hello
Alexa > Have a stellar day!
User  > .quit
```

Here, we are launching the skill by typing "open" followed by the skill's invocation name. Alexa replies with the launch request handler's greeting. Then we say "hello" and Alexa replies by saying, "Have a stellar day!" Finally, we type in the special .quit command to end the dialog session.

Even though testing with ask dialog involves typing queries and reading Alexa's responses, it's a very similar experience to speaking to an actual Alexa-enabled device. But what if, in the course of developing a skill, you find yourself needing to run through the same dialog session many times? Maybe you try something, make a few changes to your skill's fulfillment code, and then want to try the same dialog again?

As it turns out, ask dialog supports interaction record and playback. To record an ask dialog session, start it up as normal and type whatever queries you want to interact with Alexa. When you're done, use the special .record command. You'll be prompted to supply a filename for the recorded interaction. Here's the same ask dialog session as before, using the .record command to save the interaction for later replay:

```
$ ask dialog --locale en-US
User  > open star port seventy five
Alexa > Welcome to Star Port 75 Travel. How can I help you?
User  > hello
Alexa > Have a stellar day!
User  > .record test/askdialog/launch-and-hello.json
Created replay file at test/askdialog/launch-and-hello.json
User  > .quit
```

This will create a JSON file named launch-and-hello.json, which looks like this:

test/starport-75/test/askdialog/launch-and-hello.json
```
{
  "skillId": "amzn1.ask.skill.8f0c022e-65ee-4c73-a889-c10ad5bc74de",
  "locale": "en-US",
  "type": "text",
  "userInput": [
    "open star port seventy five",
    "hello"
  ]
}
```

The recorded script captures the skill's ID and locale, as well as an array containing the text provided as input by the user. With this script in hand, you can now replay it as many times as you want by running ask dialog with the --replay parameter:

```
$ ask dialog --replay test/askdialog/launch-and-hello.json
[Info]: Replaying file test/askdialog/launch-and-hello.json.
User  >  open star port seventy five
Alexa >  Welcome to Star Port 75 Travel. How can I help you?
User  >  hello
Alexa >  Have a stellar day!
User  >
```

Because the script provides the locale, there's no need to specify it when starting ask dialog. And, rather than have you type your query at the User > prompt, the --replay parameter will do that for you.

One thing that the replay script does not contain is the .quit command to exit the dialog session. Therefore, once the replay script has completed, you can either continue poking at your skill with more queries or type .quit to exit the session. Optionally, you could have created the script with --append-quit to have the .quit command included in the script:

```
User  > .record test/askdialog/launch-and-hello.json --append-quit
Created replay file at launch-and-hello.json (appended `.quit` to list of
utterances).
```

You'll find ask dialog useful for ad hoc testing sessions with your skill. And with the record/replay feature, you can have it automatically play through a pre-defined testing session. It's still up to you, however, to visually inspect the responses coming back from Alexa to ensure they are what you expect from your skill.

One of the drawbacks of all of the testing techniques shown so far is that they require you to deploy your skill before you can test it. This is limiting in that you won't be able to test your skills if you aren't connected to the internet (such as if you are on a flight). And even if you are online, at the very least the feedback cycle is longer because you'll have to wait on your skill to deploy before you can test it.

Thankfully, not all testing tools require that a skill be deployed. Let's have a look at TestFlow, a semi-automated testing tool that supports repeatedly running conversations with a skill, but without requiring that the skill be deployed.

Testing with TestFlow

TestFlow is a testing tool which simply fires intents at your skill's fulfillment code and reports the text from the response. The primary benefit of using TestFlow is that because it doesn't attempt to understand utterances and instead directly executes request handlers in fulfillment code, you do not need to deploy your skill or even be online when running tests.

To get started with TestFlow, you'll need to download it into the skill project. It can go in any directory, but in the interest of good project organization, let's put it in the test/testflow directory (relative to the project's root directory). You'll need to first create the directory like this:

```
$ mkdir -p test/testflow
```

TestFlow is fully contained in a single JavaScript file named testflow.js, which you can pull from the project's GitHub repository.[1] Using curl, you can fetch testflow.js like this:

```
$ curl https://raw.githubusercontent.com/robm26/testflow/master/testflow.js \
    -o test/testflow/testflow.js
```

After downloading the script, you'll need to edit it, changing the SourceCodeFile constant near the top to correctly reference the location of the skill's fulfillment code. Assuming that you have downloaded testflow.js into the test/testflow directory of the Star Port 75 skill project, the SourceCodeFile constant should be set like this:

```
test/starport-75/test/testflow/testflow.js
const SourceCodeFile = '../../lambda/index.js';
```

Next, you'll need a directory where your TestFlow tests will live. In TestFlow, the test cases are known as dialogs, so create a dialogs directory at the root of the skill project:

```
$ mkdir test/testflow/dialogs
```

By default, TestFlow will run a dialog definition named default.txt from the dialogs directory. So, let's create our first dialog definition by creating the default.txt file in the dialogs directory, asking TestFlow to launch the skill and say hello:

```
test/starport-75/test/testflow/dialogs/default.txt
LaunchRequest
HelloWorldIntent
```

---

1. https://github.com/robm26/testflow

The dialog definition is nothing more than a list of intent names, with one intent name on each line. In the interest of simplicity, TestFlow doesn't consider the skill's interaction model and therefore it won't execute the test based on utterances. Instead, it will invoke the canHandle() function on each of the skill's request handlers to find a handler that can handle the given intent. When it finds one, it then invokes the handle() function on the matching handler to produce results.

To see TestFlow in action, run the testflow.js file from the test/testflow directory using node:

```
$ cd test/testflow
$ node testflow.js
Running testflow on ../../lambda/index.js using dialog sequence file
./dialogs/default.txt

1 LaunchRequest
    Welcome to Star Port 75 Travel. How can I help you?
-----------------------------------------------------------------

2 HelloWorldIntent
    Have a stellar day!
=================================================================
```

If you get an error that says something like "Cannot find module ask-sdk-core", then you'll need to install the Node dependencies. Temporarily switch over to the lambda directory and install the dependencies before running TestFlow again:

```
$ cd ../../lambda
$ npm install
$ cd ../test/testflow
$ node testflow.js
```

As TestFlow runs, it steps through each of the intents listed in default.txt and displays the response text from the matching handler.

TestFlow would be of very limited use if it could only run through the intents listed in default.txt. Typically, your skill will have several potential dialog flows and you'll want to define a dialog for each of them. Thus while default.txt is just the default dialog, you can create additional dialog definitions, naming them appropriately.

For example, suppose we wanted to test what would happen if the user asked for help after launching the request. The following dialog definition launches the skill, asks for help, then triggers the intent named HelloWorldIntent:

```
test/starport-75/test/testflow/dialogs/with_help.txt
LaunchRequest
AMAZON.HelpIntent
HelloWorldIntent
```

To run this dialog, you just need to specify the dialog definition filename as a parameter when running testflow.js:

```
$ node testflow.js with_help.txt
Running testflow on ../../lambda/index.js using dialog sequence file
./dialogs/with_help.txt

1 LaunchRequest
    Welcome to Star Port 75 Travel. How can I help you?
-----------------------------------------------------------------

2 AMAZON.HelpIntent
    You can say hello to me! How can I help?
-----------------------------------------------------------------

3 HelloWorldIntent
    Have a stellar day!
=================================================================
```

As with ask dialog, you're still responsible for visually inspecting the results of the test and determining if the skill is behaving as you wish. But unlike ask dialog, you do not need to have deployed your skill before you can test it.

In either case, however, the need to visually inspect the response lends itself to human error, including accidentally overlooking bugs in the skill response. Moreover, if the skill is built and deployed through a continuous integration/continuous deployment (CI/CD) pipeline, there's no way to verify the results before deployment. Tools like ask dialog and TestFlow are semi-automatic in that they are able to automatically run through a predefined dialog flow, but are unable to automatically verify results.

Proper and complete testing of a skill requires that the skill be exercised through various dialog scenarios *and* that the responses be automatically verified. Let's have a look at a couple of fully automated options for testing Alexa skills.

Automated Testing with Alexa Skill Test Framework

The Alexa Skill Test Framework is a JavaScript framework for writing automated tests against Alexa skills. Unlike the semi-automated testing tools described in the previous section, the Alexa Skill Test Framework is able to verify the response from a skill. But like TestFlow, the Alexa Skill Test Framework is able to test a skill without requiring that the skill be deployed first. Consequently, you will get a quick turnaround on feedback from the test during development.

The Alexa Skill Test Framework is based on the Mocha testing tool, so before you start writing tests, you'll need to install the Mocha command line tool (assuming that you have not already done so for some other JavaScript project):

```
$ npm install --global mocha
```

Next, you'll need to install the Alexa Skill Test Framework as a development library in your project, along with the Mocha and Chai testing libraries. The following command line session switches into the lambda directory and installs the necessary libraries:

```
$ cd lambda
$ npm install ask-sdk-test mocha chai --save-dev
```

To enable Mocha to run when npm test is issued at the command line, you'll also need to edit the package.json file, replacing the default value for the test script with "mocha". After this tweak, the scripts section of package.json should look like this:

```
"scripts": {
    "test": "mocha"
},
```

Now we're ready to write some tests. We'll create our first test that will launch the skill and exercise the intent named HelloWorldIntent. Create a new directory named test under the lambda directory, and within the test directory, create a new file named hello-test.js and add the following test code:

```
test/starport-75/lambda/test/hello-test.js
'use strict';

const test = require('ask-sdk-test');
const skillHandler = require('../index.js').handler;

const skillSettings = {
  appId: 'amzn1.ask.skill.00000000-0000-0000-0000-000000000000',
  userId: 'amzn1.ask.account.VOID',
  deviceId: 'amzn1.ask.device.VOID',
  locale: 'en-US',
};

const alexaTest = new test.AlexaTest(skillHandler, skillSettings);

describe('Star Port 75 Travel - Hello Test', function() {
  describe('LaunchRequest', function() {
    alexaTest.test([
      {
```

```
        request: new test.LaunchRequestBuilder(skillSettings).build(),
        saysLike: 'Welcome to Star Port 75 Travel. How can I help you?',
          repromptsNothing: false,
          shouldEndSession: false,
      },
    ]);
  });
  describe('HelloWorldIntent', function() {
    alexaTest.test([
      {
        request: new test.IntentRequestBuilder(
              skillSettings, 'HelloWorldIntent').build(),
        saysLike: 'Have a stellar day!'
      },
    ]);
  });
});
```

The first few lines of hello-test.js import the ask-sdk-test library and the skill's main handler which is exported from index.js.

Then, some essential skill settings are established, including the skill's ID, a test user ID, a test device ID, and the locale. The values given for the skill ID, user ID, and device ID are merely fake test values and do not have to match an actual skill, user, or device. They are only needed when testing more advanced skills that work with data from a user's Amazon account.

The handler and skill settings are then used to create an AlexaTest object that will be used to make assertions against the skill's request handlers in the test.

What follows is the test definition itself. It is structured as a test suite that wraps nested test cases. At the test suite level, the call to describe() names the test suite as Star Port 75 Travel - Hello Test and is given a function that wraps the two tests contained by the test suite.

Within the test suite there are two test cases, named LaunchRequest and HelloWorld-Intent by the calls to describe(). Each of these is given a function that contains the test details. Specifically, each test is described as a call to alexaTest.test(), which is given an array of test descriptors.

The test descriptors specify the kind of request, either a launch request or a named intent request, as well as the expectations of making the request. For example, in the test named HelloWorldIntent, the test descriptor specifies that if the skill is sent an intent request for HelloWorldIntent, then the output speech should be "Have a stellar day!"

There are other properties we could specify in the test descriptor to make assertions against the request and response, but they don't apply to such a simple skill. As we build out our skill and write new tests, we'll see other ways to make assertions in the test descriptor.

With the test written, we are now ready to run it and see if the skill satisfies the test's expectations. You can run the test with npm like this:

```
$ npm test

> hello-world@1.1.0 test
> mocha


  Star Port 75 Travel - Hello Test
    LaunchRequest
      ✓ returns the correct responses
    HelloWorldIntent
      ✓ returns the correct responses


  2 passing (32ms)
```

As you can see, the test completed with two passing tests. But what if the skill didn't meet the test's expectations? In that case, you might see something like this when you run the test:

```
$ npm test

> hello-world@1.1.0 test
> mocha


  Star Port 75 Travel - Hello Test
    LaunchRequest
      ✓ returns the correct responses
    HelloWorldIntent
      1) returns the correct responses


  1 passing (35ms)
  1 failing

  1) Hello World Skill
       HelloWorldIntent
         returns the correct responses:

      Speech did not contain specified text. Expected Have a stellar day
      to be like Have a stellar day!
      + expected - actual

      -false
      +true
```

Here, it shows that one test passed and one test failed. For the failing test, it shows the expectation, following by the actual value. In this case, it seems that the closing exclamation mark is missing from the output speech value.

Recall that one of the benefits of testing with the Alexa Skill Test Framework is that it doesn't require that the skill be deployed before you can verify that it behaves as you expect. And, since the test cases are written in JavaScript, you have the full flexibility of the language to define the test expectations.

Even so, at this point our test only sends a request and performs basic assertions against the response, not really taking advantage of the flexibility of JavaScript. Let's take a look at another testing framework that employs YAML files to declare your test's expectations and get a test coverage as a side-effect.

Automated Testing with Bespoken's BST

Bespoken is a company with a focus on testing and monitoring voice applications. Among other things, they offer a handful of open-source tools for testing Alexa skills. Most notable among those tools is the BST CLI which enables YAML-based unit testing of Alexa skills.

BST comes in the form of a command line tool that you can use to setup an Alexa skill project for testing, run tests, and even measure test coverage to ensure that all corners of your skill's code are covered by tests. It also features a unique "Virtual Alexa" under the covers that does a pretty good job of understanding your skill's interaction model so that you can test your skill without even deploying it.

Before you can use BST, you will need to install its command line tool, the BST CLI.

Setting Up BST

Much like the ASK CLI, the BST CLI is installed using npm. Here's how to install it:

```
$ npm install bespoken-tools --global
```

Since it is a command line tool and not a library, the --global flag will tell npm to install it as a global package, rather than as a dependency in the local project's package.json. This also makes it handy for testing any skill you may write, not just the current skill.

The BST CLI is based on the Jest[2] JavaScript testing framework. As such, you get many of the same benefits as you would get using Jest on a non-skill project. In particular, we'll see in a moment that the BST CLI offers test coverage so that we can know what parts of your code aren't covered by a test.

Before we can write and run tests with the BST CLI, we need to initialize BST for our project. The quickest way of initializing BST is with the bst init command. Type bst init at the command line and from the root of the skill project:

```
$ bst init
BST: v2.6.0  Node: v17.6.0
Remember, you can always contact us at https://gitter.im/bespoken/bst.

Welcome to the Bespoken CLI.
We'll set up all you need for you to start testing your voice apps.
Please tell us:
? What type of tests are you creating - unit, end-to-end: (Use arrow keys)
> unit
  end-to-end
```

The bst init command will then ask you a series of questions about your project and the type of tests you want to create. The questions you will need to answer are:

- The type of tests—This can be either "unit" or "end-to-end". BST supports both locally run unit tests as well as end-to-end testing of a deployed skill. For now, we're going to focus on writing unit tests, so select "unit".

- The name of the project—Our project is named "starport-75", so that's a good answer for this question. Even so, the only place that this name is used by BST is in a sample test that it creates. We'll likely change that test later anyway, so the name you provide here doesn't matter much.

- The voice platform—BST supports writing tests for both Alexa and Google Assistant. Since we're developing an Alexa skill, choose "Alexa".

- Handler name—This is the relative path from the testing.json file to the handler implementation. Enter "lambda/index.js" and press enter.

- The locale—For now, we're focusing on U.S. English, so the default answer will do fine. We'll add support for multiple languages in Chapter 8, Localizing Responses, on page 195.

The full bst init session, including the answers for our project, is shown here:

---

2.   https://jestjs.io

```
$ bst init
```

```
BST: v2.6.0  Node: v17.6.0
Use bst speak to interact directly with Alexa.

Welcome to the Bespoken CLI.
We'll set up all you need for you to start testing your voice experiences.
Please tell us:
? What type of tests are you creating - unit, end-to-end: unit
? Enter the name of your voice experience: starport-75
? Select the platform you are developing for Alexa
? Please provide the name of your handler file (or leave blank for index.js):
  lambda/index.js
? Enter the locale for your tests.
If you are targeting multiple locales, please separate them by a comma: en-US

That's it! We've created your voice app test files and you can find them under
the "test" folder. To run them, simply type:
bst test
Learn more about testing for voice at https://read.bespoken.io
```

Great! Now our project has been configured for BST unit tests and there's even a sample unit test already written for us. The BST configuration will be found in a file named testing.json at the root of the project and the tests will be in test/unit relative to the project root. But before we can run the test or write new tests, we'll need to tweak the configuration a little to specify the location of the interaction model.

By default, the bst command assumes that the interaction model is located at models/en-US.json (relative to the project root). But that default path refers to the location of the interaction model in projects created by an older version of the ASK CLI. In projects created by the current ASK CLI, the interaction model is in skill-package/interactionModels/custom/en-US.json. Therefore, open the testing.json file and change it to look like this:

test/starport-75/testing.json
```
{
  "handler": "lambda/index.js",
  "interactionModel": "skill-package/interactionModels/custom/en-US.json",
  "locales": "en-US"
}
```

As you can see, the handler property is set to the relative path of the fulfillment code's main Javascript file. The locales property is set to "en-US" so that all tests will execute as if the device were U.S. English by default.

If you'd like, you may also relocate testing.json so that it's in the test/unit directory alongside the BST tests. If you do that, you'll need to change the paths in testing.json to be relative to the new location:

test/starport-75/test/unit/testing.json

```
{
  "handler": "../../lambda/index.js",
  "interactionModel":
     "../../skill-package/interactionModels/custom/en-US.json",
  "locales": "en-US"
}
```

Now that BST is set up, let's see what it can do. Although we haven't written any tests yet, bst init gave us a simple test to start with. Let's run it and see how it fares.

Running BST Tests

To run BST tests, type bst test at the command line (from the project root):

$ bst test --jest.collectCoverage=false

```
BST: v2.6.0  Node: v17.6.0
Did you know? You can use the same YAML syntax for both your end-to-end
and unit tests. Find out more at https://read.bespoken.io.

 FAIL  test/unit/index.test.yml
  My first unit test suite (en-US)
    Launch and ask for help
      ✕ LaunchRequest (508ms)
      ✕ AMAZON.HelpIntent (1ms)

  ● My first unit test suite (en-US) › Launch and ask for help ›
    LaunchRequest

    Expected value at [prompt] to ==

        Welcome to starport-75
      Received:
        <speak>Welcome to Star Port 75 Travel. How can I help you?</speak>
      Timestamp:
        2020-01-03T08:29:44.444

  ● My first unit test suite (en-US) › Launch and ask for help ›
    AMAZON.HelpIntent

    Expected value at [prompt] to ==
        What can I help you with?
      Received:
        <speak>You can say hello to me! How can I help?</speak>

      11 | - LaunchRequest : "Welcome to starport-75"
      12 | - AMAZON.HelpIntent :
    > 13 |    - prompt : "What can I help you with?"
      14 |

      at test/unit/index.test.yml:13:0
      Timestamp:
        2020-01-03T08:29:44.446
```

```
Test Suites: 1 failed, 1 total
Tests:       1 failed, 1 total
Snapshots:   0 total
Time:        1.867s
Ran all test suites.
```

As shown here, bst test was run with --jest.collectCoverage=false as a parameter. BST collects test coverage metrics, which can be useful in determining how much and what parts of your skill's fulfillment code is not covered by tests. At this point, however, we're just getting started and the test coverage report will just be extra noise. Setting --jest.collectCoverage=false disables test coverage reporting. Once we've written a few more tests, we'll leave that parameter off to check how much of our code is covered by tests.

What's most notable in the results from bst init is that the test in test/unit/index.test.yml has failed. More specifically, it failed on two assertions:

- When launching the skill, it was expecting the response to be "Welcome to starport-75", but instead it received "Welcome to Star Port 75 Travel. How can I help you?"

- When asking for help, it expected to receive "What can I help you with?" but instead it got "You can say hello to me! How can I help?"

If you take a look at test/unit/index.test.yml, it's easy to see how those expectations are set:

```
---
configuration:
  description: My first unit test suite
---
- test : Launch and ask for help
- LaunchRequest : "Welcome to starport-75"
- AMAZON.HelpIntent :
  - prompt : "What can I help you with?"
```

This test specification has two parts, the configuration and a test case, separated by a triple dash (---). The configuration is rather simple and only specifies a description of the test. The test case, however, deserves a bit more explanation.

The first line specifies the name of the test case. In this case, the name is "Launch and ask for help". This is what will be displayed in the test results.

The next line instructs BST to send a launch request to the skill and to expect "Welcome to starport-75" as the response. Obviously, this is not how our skill responds to a launch request, so we should change it to expect "Welcome to Star Port 75 Travel. How can I help you?"

The next few lines instruct BST to send an intent request for the built-in AMAZON.HelpIntent. The line that starts with prompt asserts that the response speech from the intent should be "What can I help you with?" We should change this to "You can say hello to me! How can I help?" so that it matches what the skill's implementation actually returns.

After making those tweaks to the test specification, here's what it should look like:

```
test/starport-75/test/unit/index.test.yml
---
configuration:
  description: My first unit test suite
---
- test : Launch and ask for help
- LaunchRequest : "Welcome to Star Port 75 Travel. How can I help you?"
- AMAZON.HelpIntent :
  - prompt : "You can say hello to me! How can I help?"
```

Let's try running the test again to see if it fares better after these changes:

```
$ bst test --jest.collectCoverage=false

BST: v2.6.0  Node: v17.6.0
Use bst launch to mimic someone opening your skill.

 PASS  test/unit/index.test.yml
  My first unit test suite (en-US)
    Launch and ask for help
      ✓ LaunchRequest (401ms)
      ✓ AMAZON.HelpIntent (1ms)

Test Suites: 1 passed, 1 total
Tests:       1 passed, 1 total
Snapshots:   0 total
Time:        1.799s
Ran all test suites.
```

Fantastic! The test now passes! With that initial test settled, let's write a few more tests to cover some of the other request handlers in our skill.

Writing Tests for BST

At this point the main request handler is HelloWorldIntentHandler, so we should write a test for it next. Following the example set in index.test.yml, we'll create a new test specification in a file named hello.test.yml:

```
test/starport-75/test/unit/hello.test.yml
---
configuration:
  description: Hello world intent tests

---
- test: Hello World intent
- HelloWorldIntent:
  - prompt: Have a stellar day!
```

Just like index.test.yml, the test specification in hello.test.yml is divided into two sections. The first section specifies some test-specific configuration for this particular test. In this case, it only specifies a description of the test specification. The other section is an actual test case. The test submits an intent request for the HelloWorldIntent, asserting that the response's output speech is "Have a stellar day!"

The test specifies the intent to invoke by the intent name (for example, HelloWorldIntent). But we can also build a test around an utterance. For example, instead of submitting a request directly to the intent named HelloWorldIntent, you can build the test around what would happen if the user were to say "Hello":

```
test/starport-75/test/unit/hello.test.yml
---
- test: Hello World Utterance
- "Hello":
  - prompt: Have a stellar day!
```

To see our new test specification in action, run the bst test command:

```
$ bst test --jest.collectCoverage=false
```

```
BST: v2.6.0  Node: v17.6.0
bst test lets you have a complete set of unit tests using a simple YAML
format. Find out more at https://read.bespoken.io.

 PASS  test/unit/index.test.yml
  My first unit test suite (en-US)
    Launch and ask for help
      ✓ LaunchRequest (76ms)
      ✓ AMAZON.HelpIntent (1ms)

 PASS  test/unit/hello.test.yml
  Hello world intent tests (en-US)
    Hello World intent
      ✓ HelloWorldIntent (4ms)
    Hello World Utterance
      ✓ Hello (8ms)

Test Suites: 2 passed, 2 total
Tests:       3 passed, 3 total
```

```
Snapshots:   0 total
Time:        0.879s, estimated 2s
Ran all test suites.
```

As you can see, bst test ran both test specifications, including both test cases in hello.test.yml. But sometimes you might want to focus attention on a single test specification. You can do this by passing the test specification filename as a parameter to bst test. For example, to only run the tests in hello.test.yml:

$ bst test hello.test.yml

In addition to HelloWorldIntent, our fulfillment includes several handlers for Amazon's built-in intents—AMAZON.StopIntent, AMAZON.CancelIntent, and AMAZON.FallbackIntent—as well as a request handler for SessionEndedRequest. Even though all of these handlers are fairly simple, we should still write some tests for them. The following test specification in standard-handlers.test.yml should do fine:

```
test/starport-75/test/unit/standard-handlers.test.yml
---
configuration:
  description: Tests for standard request handlers

---
- test: Cancel request
- AMAZON.CancelIntent:
  - prompt: Goodbye!

---
- test: Stop request
- AMAZON.StopIntent:
  - prompt: Goodbye!

---
- test: Fallback Intent
- AMAZON.FallbackIntent:
  - prompt: Sorry, I don't know about that. Please try again.

---
- test: Session ended request
- SessionEndedRequest:
```

This test specification, unlike the others we've seen so far, has four test cases, each separated by a triple dash. The three intent handler tests simply assert the response's output speech. As for the test for SessionEndedRequest, it doesn't assert anything. That's because the request handler for SessionEndedRequest doesn't do much. But having this test will at least ensure that the handler is executed with no errors.

Now that we have tests covering both our HelloWorldIntent as well as tests to cover Amazon's built-in intents and requests, let's run them all and see how they fare:

```
$ bst test --jest.collectCoverage=false
```

```
BST: v2.6.0  Node: v17.6.0
Use bst utter to interact with your skill, and we will handle your
intents for you.
 PASS  test/unit/standard-handlers.test.yml
  Tests for standard request handlers (en-US)
    Cancel request
      ✓ AMAZON.CancelIntent (291ms)
    Stop request
      ✓ AMAZON.StopIntent (4ms)
    Fallback Intent
      ✓ AMAZON.FallbackIntent (1ms)
    Session ended request
      ✓ SessionEndedRequest (1ms)

 PASS  test/unit/hello.test.yml
  Hello world intent tests (en-US)
    Hello World intent
      ✓ HelloWorldIntent (5ms)
    Hello World Utterance
      ✓ Hello (2ms)

 PASS  test/unit/index.test.yml
  My first unit test suite (en-US)
    Launch and ask for help
      ✓ LaunchRequest (6ms)
      ✓ AMAZON.HelpIntent (2ms)

Test Suites: 3 passed, 3 total
Tests:       7 passed, 7 total
Snapshots:   0 total
Time:        1.203s
Ran all test suites.
```

Awesome! All tests are passing! It would seem that there's nothing left to test. But how can know for sure that we're testing everything?

Measuring Test Coverage

If we run the tests again without the --jest.collectCoverage=false parameter, we'll get a test coverage report that will give us an idea of how much of our skill's code remains untested:

```
$ bst test
```

```
BST: v2.6.0  Node: v17.6.0
```

```
...
---------------|---------|----------|---------|---------|--------------------|
File           | % Stmts | % Branch | % Funcs | % Lines | Uncovered Line #s  |
---------------|---------|----------|---------|---------|--------------------|
All files      |    7.66 |     7.14 |   31.25 |    7.78 |                    |
 lambda        |      84 |      100 |   83.33 |      84 |                    |
  index.js     |      84 |      100 |   83.33 |      84 |        14,16,44,46 |
 test/astf     |       0 |      100 |       0 |       0 |                    |
  hello-test.js|       0 |      100 |       0 |       0 |... 12,21,22,32,33  |
 test/testflow |       0 |        0 |       0 |       0 |                    |
  testflow.js  |       0 |        0 |       0 |       0 |... 97,601,607,615  |
---------------|---------|----------|---------|---------|--------------------|
Test Suites: 2 passed, 2 total
Tests:       6 passed, 6 total
Snapshots:   0 total
Time:        2.004s
Ran all test suites.
```

Oh my! According to this test coverage report, only about 7% of our skill's code is covered by tests. Even with the tests we've written, we've still got a long way to go.

But wait a minute. Several of the Javascript files listed in the test coverage report are for things that shouldn't be tested, such as tests we wrote earlier in this chapter with TestFlow and Alexa Skill Testing Framework. And all of those have 0% coverage, which is definitely bringing down our overall coverage. We should exclude those files from test coverage.

To exclude files from test coverage, we need to set the jest.coveragePathIgnorePatterns property in our BST configuration. Edit the testing.json file in test/unit so that it looks like this:

test/starport-75/test/unit/testing.json

```
{
  "handler": "../../lambda/index.js",
  "interactionModel":
      "../../skill-package/interactionModels/custom/en-US.json",
  "locales": "en-US",
  "jest": {
    "coveragePathIgnorePatterns": [
      "<rootDir>/lambda/util.js",
      "<rootDir>/lambda/local-debugger.js",
      "<rootDir>/lambda/test.*",
      "<rootDir>/test/.*"
    ]
  }
}
```

Here, we're setting the jest.coveragePathIgnorePatterns property so that it ignores any Javascript files under the test and lambda/test directories, which should take care of the TestFlow and Alexa Skills Testing Framework files. It also ignores the util.js and local-debugger.js files. Since we're not even using these right now, there's no reason to include them in the test coverage report.

Now, if we run it again, the test coverage table should be much less daunting:

```
$ bst test
BST: v2.6.0  Node: v17.6.0

...

----------|----------|----------|----------|----------|-------------------|
File      | % Stmts  | % Branch | % Funcs  | % Lines  | Uncovered Line #s |
----------|----------|----------|----------|----------|-------------------|
All files |   77.14  |    100   |    75    |   77.14  |                   |
 index.js |   77.14  |    100   |    75    |   77.14  |... 36,139,140,142 |
----------|----------|----------|----------|----------|-------------------|
Test Suites: 3 passed, 3 total
Tests:       7 passed, 7 total
Snapshots:   0 total
Time:        1.874s, estimated 2s
Ran all test suites.
```

That's a lot better, but we're still not quite at 100%. There seems to be some untested code remaining in index.js. If you take a quick look at index.js you'll find that we still have two handlers that we've not written tests for: ErrorHandler and IntentReflectorHandler.

Unfortunately, ErrorHandler is difficult to test properly. In order for the error handler to be triggered, we'd need to simulate an error condition in one of the other request handlers. All of our other request handlers are too simple to cause an error, so the only way to test ErrorHandler at this point would be to fabricate a failure condition.

As for IntentReflectorHandler, it only exists for purposes of debugging the interaction model and we'll eventually remove it before publishing our skill. So it doesn't make much sense to write a test for it.

Fortunately, we can exclude those two handlers from the test by adding a simple comment just before each of them:

test/starport-75/lambda/index.js
```
/* istanbul ignore next */
const IntentReflectorHandler = {
    ...
};
/* istanbul ignore next */
const ErrorHandler = {
    ...
};
```

Where BST is based on Jest, Jest uses another library named istanbul under the covers to track code coverage. By placing a comment with the phrase istanbul ignore next just before a code block in Javascript, that code block will be excluded from test coverage. In this case, the comment is placed just before the IntentReflectorHandler, so that entire handler will be excluded from test coverage.

Now that those two handlers are excluded from test coverage, let's try running the tests one more time to see how our coverage has improved:

```
$ bst test

BST: v2.6.0  Node: v17.6.0

...

----------|----------|----------|----------|----------|-------------------|
File      | % Stmts  | % Branch | % Funcs  | % Lines  | Uncovered Line #s |
----------|----------|----------|----------|----------|-------------------|
All files |     100  |     100  |     100  |     100  |                   |
 index.js |     100  |     100  |     100  |     100  |                   |
----------|----------|----------|----------|----------|-------------------|
Test Suites: 3 passed, 3 total
Tests:       7 passed, 7 total
Snapshots:   0 total
Time:        1.877s, estimated 2s
Ran all test suites.
```

Achievement unlocked! We now have 100% test coverage. As we continue to develop our skill, we can know that it is meeting our expectations if we maintain a high level of test coverage.

The text-based test results and coverage metrics are useful feedback as we run our tests. But you may want a more polished test report produced that can be published on a project dashboard or sent in a status email. Don't worry, BST has you covered. Let's take a look at BST's HTML-based test reports.

Viewing Test Results in a Web Browser

As a side-effect of running tests through bst test, you also get a few nice HTML-based test reports. One of those test reports, in test_output/report/index.inline.html, shows the test results in the following screenshot:

At the top of the test results report, you'll see a link named "Coverage". Clicking this link will open the report in test_output/coverage/lcov-report/index.html, a test coverage report, shown in this screenshot:

This page shows a summary of test coverage for each JavaScript file in the project, but if you click on the filename, you'll be shown the source for that file, with uncovered code highlighted in red:

Detailed test results and test coverage reports are one of the best features of using the BST CLI for testing. And, just like the Alexa Skill Testing Framework, you do not need to deploy your skill before you test it with bst test.

Automated testing, with either the Alexa Skill Test Framework or BST CLI, is a great way to test a skill frequently, getting quick feedback that lets you know if you've made any changes that break how your skill is expected to work. And, as we'll see next, with a little bit of scripting, you can even leverage those automated tests to prevent a broken skill from being deployed.

Wrapping Up

Testing is one of the most important practices of any software project, including Alexa skill projects. Establishing a suite of tests will help ensure that the code you create does what you expect it to do, and continues to fulfill your expectations as development progresses. Although the voice-first aspect makes testing Alexa skills somewhat unique, there are several tools and libraries that make it easy to ensure that the skills you develop do what you expect them to do.

Testing skills with semi-automated tools, such as with the ASK CLI's simulate and dialog commands, makes it possible to script a conversation with Alexa. You will still need to manually verify the responses, but scripts can provide a repeatable performance (although at the expense of losing the ability to hear a response).

Tools like the Alexa Skill Test Framework and Bespoken's BST provide a fully automated testing experience, enabling repeatability and automated verification of responses. BST even provides test coverage support to help identify bits of your skill's code that aren't covered by a test.

Having set a foundation for testing Alexa skills, we're now ready to proceed with building out the Star Port 75 Travel skill. In the next chapter, we'll add some essential conversational capabilities to our skill, enabling the user to specify parameters as input. As we build out the skill functionality, we'll apply some of the testing techniques learned in this chapter to ensure that the skill behaves correctly.

CHAPTER 3

Parameterizing Intents with Slots

Much of human communication is made up of sentences that have parameters. Someone might say, "The weather is cold today." But on a different day, they may say, "The weather is warm today." The only difference between these two sentences is the words "cold" and "warm." They change the meaning of the sentence, but the purpose is the same with both: to describe the weather.

The same holds true when talking to Alexa. You might ask her to play Mozart. Or you might ask her to play Van Halen. Either way, the objective is the same (to play some music) although the specifics are different (Mozart vs. Van Halen).

The main thing that Star Port 75 Travel wants to offer to their clientele through their Alexa skill is the ability to schedule a trip to one of their several planetary destinations. For example, one potential space traveler might say something like "Schedule a trip to Mercury leaving Friday and returning next Thursday." Another user may have a different trip in mind and say, "Plan a trip between June 9th and June 17th to visit Mars."

Although these two requests are worded differently, their purpose is the same: to schedule a trip. The specifics—the destination, departure date, and return date—are parameters that define the trip that is to be scheduled. When handling such requests in an Alexa skill, these parameters are known as *slots*. We're going to use slots in this chapter to handle parameters in the utterances spoken by the skill's users.

Adding Slots to an Intent

The Star Port 75 Travel skill needs to be able to book trips for spacefaring adventurers based on three parameters: the destination, the departure date, and the return date. To enable this, we'll add a new intent to the skill that accepts those parameters in slots. But first, let's start by writing a BST test specification that captures and asserts what we want the intent to do:

slots/starport-75/test/unit/schedule-trip.test.yml
```yaml
---
configuration:
  locales: en-US

---
- test: Schedule a trip
- "Schedule a trip to Mercury leaving Friday and returning next Thursday":
  - prompt: I've got you down for a trip to Mercury,
            leaving on Friday and returning next Thursday.

---
- test: Plan a trip
- "Plan a trip between June 9th and June 17th to visit Mars":
  - prompt: I've got you down for a trip to Mars,
            leaving on June 9th and returning June 17th.
```

These tests cover two possible ways of wording a request to schedule a trip. But even more interesting, they each cover different values for the three parameters and assert that those values are reflected in the intent's response.

The first step toward making these tests pass is to define the new intent in the interaction model. As with the HelloWorldIntent, we'll add a new entry to skill-package/interactionModels/custom/en-US.json within the intents property. And, just like HelloWorldIntent, we'll give it a name and a list of sample utterances. But as you can see from this interaction model excerpt, ScheduleTripIntent has a few new tricks:

slots/starport-75/skill-package/interactionModels/custom/en-US.json
```json
"intents": [

...

  {
    "name": "ScheduleTripIntent",
    "samples": [
      "schedule a trip to {destination} leaving {departureDate} and
        returning {returnDate}",
      "plan a trip between {departureDate} and {returnDate}
        to visit {destination}"
    ],
    "slots": [
      {
        "name": "destination",
        "type": "AMAZON.City"
      },
```

```
      {
        "name": "departureDate",
        "type": "AMAZON.DATE"
      },
      {
        "name": "returnDate",
        "type": "AMAZON.DATE"
      }
    ]
  }
]
```

The first thing you'll notice is that the sample utterances don't have any explicitly stated destination or date values. Instead, they have placeholders in the form of variable names wrapped in curly-braces. These represent the places in the utterance where the slots will be provided.

The slots themselves are defined in the slots property. Each has a name and a type. The name must match exactly with the placeholder in the utterances. As for type, Amazon provides several built-in types,[1] including types for dates, numbers, and phone numbers. Amazon also provides nearly 100 slot types that identify a list of potential values such movie names, sports, book titles, and cities.

The slots defined in ScheduleTripIntent take advantage of two of Amazon's built-in types: AMAZON.City and AMAZON.DATE. It makes sense that the "departureDate" and "returnDate" slots are typed as AMAZON.DATE. But you might be wondering why "destination" is defined as AMAZON.City. Put simply, it's because Amazon doesn't define a built-in type for "planets" or any other astronomical locations. We'll create a custom type for planets in the next section. But until we get around to that, AMAZON.City will be a fine temporary stand-in.

Slot types are used as hints to help Alexa's natural language processing match what a user says to an intent. For example, suppose that the user asks to plan a trip to Seattle, but pronounces the city as "see cattle." The natural language processor may hear "see cattle," but since that sounds a lot like "Seattle," it can infer that the user meant "Seattle" based on the slot type AMAZON.City.

On the other hand, suppose that the user asks to plan a trip to "Jupiter," which is not a city included in the AMAZON.City type. Alexa's natural language processor will hear "Jupiter" and since no entry in the AMAZON.City type sounds

---

1. https://developer.amazon.com/docs/custom-skills/slot-type-reference.html

anything like that, it will give the user benefit of the doubt and give "Jupiter" as the slot's value.

Now that we've defined the intent, sample utterances, and slots in the inter-action model, we need to write the intent handler. Rather than pile it on along with the other intent handlers in index.js, let's split it out into its own JavaScript module. This will help keep the skill's project code more organized and prevent index.js from growing unwieldy. The intent handler's code, defined in lambda/Sched-uleTripIntentHandler.js, looks like this:

```
slots/starport-75/lambda/ScheduleTripIntentHandler.js
const Alexa = require('ask-sdk-core');

const ScheduleTripIntentHandler = {
  canHandle(handlerInput) {
    return Alexa.getRequestType(
            handlerInput.requestEnvelope) === 'IntentRequest'
      && Alexa.getIntentName(
            handlerInput.requestEnvelope) === 'ScheduleTripIntent';
  },
  handle(handlerInput) {
    const destination =
        Alexa.getSlotValue(handlerInput.requestEnvelope, 'destination');
    const departureDate =
        Alexa.getSlotValue(handlerInput.requestEnvelope, 'departureDate');
    const returnDate =
        Alexa.getSlotValue(handlerInput.requestEnvelope, 'returnDate');

    const speakOutput = handlerInput.t('SCHEDULED_MSG',
        {
          destination: destination,
          departureDate: departureDate,
          returnDate: returnDate
        });

    return handlerInput.responseBuilder
      .speak(speakOutput)
      .withShouldEndSession(true)
      .getResponse();
  },
};

module.exports=ScheduleTripIntentHandler;
```

You'll want to be sure to register this new intent handler with the skill builder, just like we did with HelloWorldIntentHandler. The intent handler can be imported into index.js using require() and then added to the list of handlers like this:

```
slots/starport-75/lambda/index.js
const HelloWorldIntentHandler = require('./HelloWorldIntentHandler');
const ScheduleTripIntentHandler = require('./ScheduleTripIntentHandler');
const StandardHandlers = require('./StandardHandlers');

  ...

exports.handler = Alexa.SkillBuilders.custom()
    .addRequestHandlers(
        HelloWorldIntentHandler,
        ScheduleTripIntentHandler,
        StandardHandlers.LaunchRequestHandler,
        StandardHandlers.HelpIntentHandler,
        StandardHandlers.CancelAndStopIntentHandler,
        StandardHandlers.FallbackIntentHandler,
        StandardHandlers.SessionEndedRequestHandler,
        StandardHandlers.IntentReflectorHandler)
    .addErrorHandlers(
        StandardHandlers.ErrorHandler)
    .addRequestInterceptors(
        LocalisationRequestInterceptor)
    .lambda();
```

As with the HelloWorldIntentHandler, ScheduleTripIntentHandler is defined by two functions: canHandle() to determine if the intent handler is capable of handling the request's intent, and handle() to handle the request if so.

The most significant and relevant difference in ScheduleTripIntentHandler, however, is in the first few lines of the handle() function. They use the Alexa.getSlotValue() function to extract the values of the "destination", "departureDate", and "returnDate" slots and assign them to constants of their own. Those constants are referenced in an object passed to the t() function when looking up the "SCHEDULED_MSG" message assigned to speakOutput.

For that to work, we'll need to define "SCHEDULED_MSG" to languageStrings.js.

```
slots/starport-75/lambda/languageStrings.js
module.exports = {
  en: {
    translation: {
      ...
      SCHEDULED_MSG: "I've got you down for a trip to {{destination}}, " +
          "leaving on {{departureDate}} and returning {{returnDate}}",
      ...
    }
  }
}
```

As you can see, embedded within the "SCHEDULED_MSG" string are place-holders, denoted by double-curly-braces, that will be replaced with the properties from the object we passed to the t() function.

With the new intent defined in the interaction model and its corresponding intent handler and language string written, we've just added basic trip scheduling support to the skill. Let's run the tests and see if it works:

```
% bst test --jest.collectCoverage=false schedule-trip.test.yml

BST: v2.6.0  Node: v17.6.0
Did you know? You can use the same YAML syntax for both your end-to-end
and unit tests. Find out more at https://read.bespoken.io.

 PASS  test/unit/schedule-trip.test.yml
   en-US
     Schedule a trip
       ✓ Schedule a trip to Mercury leaving Friday and returning next Thursday
     Plan a trip
       ✓ Plan a trip between June 9th and June 17th to visit Mars

Test Suites: 1 passed, 1 total
Tests:       2 passed, 2 total
Snapshots:   0 total
Time:        1.128s, estimated 2s
Ran all test suites.
```

As you can see, both tests passed! We've successfully used slots to handle variable input from the user when booking a trip! For brevity's sake, we can run bst test with --jest.collectCoverage=false so that the test coverage report is not in the output. And, the test specification's name is passed as a parameter in order to focus on the tests relevant to our new intent.

Although it works, there's still room for improvement. Ultimately our skill is for planning interplanetary travel. Therefore, AMAZON.City isn't really the best slot type for our needs. But before we swap it out for a custom planets slot type, let's take a quick look at how some entities may offer more information than just the entity's name.

Fetching Entity Information

While testing the previous example, if you inspected the intent request closely enough, you may have spotted something very interesting about the resolved slot value. Specifically, not only did the value have a name, it also had an id property whose value is a URL.

For example, if the city spoken in place of the city slot were Paris, the request might look a little like this:

```
"city": {
  "name": "city",
  "value": "Paris",
  "resolutions": {
    "resolutionsPerAuthority": [
      {
        "authority": "AlexaEntities",
        "status": {
          "code": "ER_SUCCESS_MATCH"
        },
        "values": [
          {
            "value": {
              "name": "Paris",
              "id": "https://ld.amazonalexa.com/entities/v1/1z1ky..."
            }
          }
        ]
      }
    ]
  },
  "confirmationStatus": "NONE",
  "source": "USER",
  "slotValue": {
    "type": "Simple",
    "value": "Paris",
    "resolutions": {
      "resolutionsPerAuthority": [
        {
          "authority": "AlexaEntities",
          "status": {
            "code": "ER_SUCCESS_MATCH"
          },
          "values": [
            {
              "value": {
                "name": "Paris",
                "id": "https://ld.amazonalexa.com/entities/v1/1z1ky..."
              }
            }
          ]
        }
      ]
    }
  }
}
```

As it turns out, the URL in the id property can be fetched with an HTTP GET request to lookup additional information about the resolved entity. This is a relatively new feature called *Alexa Entities* and at this time is currently in Beta for skills deployed in the following locales:

- English (AU)
- English (CA)
- English (IN)
- English (UK)
- English (US)
- French (FR)
- German (DE)
- Italian (IT)
- Spanish (ES)

(We'll talk more about locales in Chapter 8, Localizing Responses, on page 195.)

In the case of a slot whose type is AMAZON.City, that includes details such as the average elevation, which larger government boundaries the city is contained within (for example, metroplex, state, country), and the human population of the city. While not all skills will need this extra information, it can come in very handy for skills that do.

For example, suppose that we were building a skill with an intent that provided population information for a city. Such an intent might be defined like this:

```
slots/city-population/skill-package/interactionModels/custom/en-US.json
{
  "name": "CityPopulationIntent",
  "slots": [
    {
      "name": "city",
      "type": "AMAZON.City"
    }
  ],
  "samples": [
    "what is the population of {city}",
    "tell me about {city}",
    "how many people live in {city}",
    "how big is {city}"
  ]
},
```

The expectation is that if the user were to ask, "What is the population of Paris?" then Alexa would respond with the number of people living in Paris.

Without Alexa Entities, you'd have to maintain a database of city population data or perhaps delegate out to some API that provides such information. But with Alexa Entities, the information is readily available to your skill, just for the asking.

The way to ask for entity data is to make an HTTP GET request to the URL in the id property, providing an API access token in the Authorization header of the request. The API access token is made available in the intent's request envelope and can be easily be obtained with Alexa.getApiAccessToken() like this:

```
const apiAccessToken =
    Alexa.getApiAccessToken(handlerInput.requestEnvelope);
```

You'll also need the request's locale, which is just as readily available from the request envelope:

```
const locale = Alexa.getLocale(handlerInput.requestEnvelope);
```

With the entity URL, locale, and an access token in hand, making the request for entity information can be done using any JavaScript client library that you like. For our project, we'll use the Axios client library. You can install it by issuing the following command from the project's root directory:

```
$ npm install --prefix=lambda axios
```

With Axios installed, the following snippet shows how to request entity information:

```
slots/city-population/lambda/index.js
const resolvedEntity = resolutions.values[0].value.id;
const headers = {
  'Authorization': `Bearer ${apiAccessToken}`,
  'Accept-Language':locale
};

const response =
    await axios.get(resolvedEntity, { headers: headers });
```

Here, the first resolution is chosen and its ID is assigned to a constant named resolvedEntity. The value of resolvedEntity is not just a simple ID, but also the URL of the entity to be fetched. Therefore, it is passed in as the URL parameter to axios.get() to retrieve entity details.

Assuming that the request is successful, the response will include a JSON document with several properties that further define the resolved entity.

As an example, here's a sample of what you'll get if the entity is the city of Paris:

```
{
    "@context": {
    ...
```

```
    },
    "@id": "https://ld.amazonalexa.com/entities/v1/1z1kyo7XwxYGAKcx5F3TCf",
    "@type": [ "City" ],
    "averageElevation": [{ "@type": "unit:Meter", "@value": "28" }],
    "capitalOf": [
        {
            "@id": "https://ld.amazonalexa.com/entities/v1/LGYtKPDONTW...",
            "@type": [ "Country" ],
            "name": [{ "@language": "en", "@value": "France" }]
        }
    ],
    "countryOfOrigin": {
        "@id": "https://ld.amazonalexa.com/entities/v1/LGYtKPDONTWCtt6...",
        "@type": [ "Country" ],
        "name": [{ "@language": "en", "@value": "France" }]
    },
    "humanPopulation": [{ "@type": "xsd:integer", "@value": "2140000" }],
    "locatedWithin": [
        {
            "@id": "https://ld.amazonalexa.com/entities/v1/DAy2cvRGvSB...",
            "@type": [ "Place" ],
            "name": [{ "@language": "en", "@value": "Paris" }]
        },
        {
            "@id": "https://ld.amazonalexa.com/entities/v1/1NlBgtwDmHb...",
            "@type": [ "Place" ],
            "name": [{ "@language": "en", "@value": "Île-de-France" }]
        },
        {
            "@id": "https://ld.amazonalexa.com/entities/v1/LGYtKPDONTW....",
            "@type": [ "Country" ],
            "name": [{ "@language": "en", "@value": "France" }]
        }
    ],
    "name": [{ "@language": "en", "@value": "Paris" }]
}
```

Without looking any further, your skill can use any of this information as it sees fit, including reporting the population of the city. But also notice that some of the properties include their own URLs in @id properties. So, for example, if you wanted your skill to dig even deeper into the country that Paris is the capital of, you could make another request, following the URL in the @id property from the countryOfOrigin property.

All we need for a simple city population skill, however, is the value from the humanPopulation property. The following fetchPopulation() function shows how we might fetch the population for a given set of resolutions and API access token:

slots/city-population/lambda/index.js

```
const fetchPopulation = async (resolutions, locale, apiAccessToken) => {
  const resolvedEntity = resolutions.values[0].value.id;
  const headers = {
    'Authorization': `Bearer ${apiAccessToken}`,
    'Accept-Language':locale
  };

  const response =
      await axios.get(resolvedEntity, { headers: headers });
  if (response.status === 200) {
    const entity = response.data;
    if ('name' in entity && 'humanPopulation' in entity) {
      const cityName = entity.name[0]['@value'];
      const population = entity.humanPopulation[0]['@value'];
      const popInfo = {
        cityName: cityName,
        population: population
      };
      return popInfo;
    }
  } else {
    return null;
  }
};
```

After sending the GET request for the entity, if the response is an HTTP 200
(OK) response, then it extracts the value of the humanPopulation property from
the response. We'll also need to know the fully resolved entity name for our
intent's response, so while fetching the population, we also fetch the value
of the name property. Both are packed up in an object and returned to the
caller.

As for how fetchPopulation() is used, here's the intent handler which asks for the
population and uses the city name and population from the returned object
to produce a response to the user:

slots/city-population/lambda/index.js

```
const CityPopulationIntentHandler = {
  canHandle(handlerInput) {
    return Alexa.getRequestType(
            handlerInput.requestEnvelope) === 'IntentRequest'
        && Alexa.getIntentName(
            handlerInput.requestEnvelope) === 'CityPopulationIntent';
  },
  async handle(handlerInput) {
    const apiAccessToken =
          Alexa.getApiAccessToken(handlerInput.requestEnvelope);
    const slot =
          Alexa.getSlot(handlerInput.requestEnvelope, 'city');
```

```
    const resolutions = getSlotResolutions(slot);
    const locale = Alexa.getLocale(handlerInput.requestEnvelope);

  if (resolutions) {
      const popInfo =
          await fetchPopulation(resolutions, locale, apiAccessToken);

      if (popInfo !== null) {
        const speechResponse =
            `${popInfo.cityName}'s population is ${popInfo.population}.`
        return handlerInput.responseBuilder
            .speak(speechResponse)
            .getResponse();
      }
  }

  const reprompt = 'What city do you want to know about?';
  const speakOutput =
      "I don't know what city you're talking about. Try again. "
      + reprompt;
  return handlerInput.responseBuilder
    .speak(speakOutput)
    .reprompt(reprompt)
    .getResponse();
  }
};
```

This handler leans on a couple of helper functions to extract the slot resolutions from the given slot:

slots/city-population/lambda/index.js
```
const getSlotResolutions = (slot) => {
    return slot.resolutions
        && slot.resolutions.resolutionsPerAuthority
        && slot.resolutions.resolutionsPerAuthority.find(resolutionMatch);
};

const resolutionMatch = (resolution) => {
    return resolution.authority === 'AlexaEntities'
        && resolution.status.code === 'ER_SUCCESS_MATCH';
};
```

With all of this in place, if the user were to ask for the population of Paris, Alexa will respond by saying, "Paris's population is 2,140,000."

Not all built-in slot types support Alexa entities. Several slot types do, however, including:

- AMAZON.Person
- AMAZON.Movie
- AMAZON.Animal
- AMAZON.City

- AMAZON.Country
- AMAZON.Book
- AMAZON.Author
- AMAZON.TVSeries
- AMAZON.Actor
- AMAZON.Director
- AMAZON.Food
- AMAZON.MusicGroup
- AMAZON.Musician
- AMAZON.MusicRecording
- AMAZON.MusicAlbum

Of course, each slot type will have information relevant to that type. AMA-ZON.Movie, for example, won't have a humanPopulation property, but it will have a property named entertainment:castMember that is an array of actors who were in the movie. Each entry in the entertainment:castMember array is itself a reference to a person with an @id that you can use to look up additional information about the actor, such as their birthday.

Now let's take our skill beyond the confines of Earth and create a custom type that represents planetary destinations instead of relying on the built-in AMAZON.City type.

Creating Custom Types

If Star Port 75 Travel were a travel company specializing in international travel, then AMAZON.City would be the perfect type for the destination slot. But Star Port 75 has its sights set higher, so to speak, so a type that represents planetary destinations seems more fitting.

Although Amazon provides an impressive number of types to cover many cases, they do not offer a type that represents planets. But they do make it possible to define custom types in the interaction model as entries in the types property, a child of the languageModel property and a sibling of the intents property. For the purposes of our planet type, we're going to define a new type called PLANETS, which will include all nine planets in Earth's solar system (and yes, we'll count Pluto as a planet). Here's an excerpt from the interaction model showing the new PLANETS type, and where it fits in the interaction model:

slots/starport-75/skill-package/interactionModels/custom/en-US.json
```
{
  "interactionModel": {
    "languageModel": {
```

```
      "invocationName": "star port seventy five",
      "intents": [
...
      ],
      "types": [
        {
          "name": "PLANETS",
          "values": [
            {
              "id": "MERCURY",
              "name": {
                "value": "Mercury"
              }
            },
            {
              "id": "VENUS",
              "name": {
                "value": "Venus"
              }
            },
            {
              "id": "EARTH",
              "name": {
                "value": "Earth"
              }
            },
            {
              "id": "MARS",
              "name": {
                "value": "Mars"
              }
            },
...
          ]
        }
      ]
    }
  }
}
```

The types property is an array where each entry represents a type. Each type
has a name and an array of possible values. In this case, our custom type is
named PLANETS and includes nine values in the array of values, one for each
planet in our solar system. (For brevity's sake, only the first four planets are
shown here, but the entries for the remaining five follow a similar pattern.)

Each entry in the values property is known as an *entity*. In its simplest form,
each entity has an ID and a name. The name is the word or phrase that the
user might speak when saying that value in an utterance. The ID must

uniquely identify the value and can be almost anything, not necessarily an actual word. For the list of planets, however, it is easy enough to just set the ID to the planet's name in all uppercase lettering.

Now that we have defined our custom PLANETS type, we can use it instead of AMAZON.City in the ScheduleTripIntent's destination slot:

```
"slots": [
  {
    "name": "destination",
    "type": "PLANETS"
  }
]
```

At this point the tests should still pass and our skill should still behave as it did before creating the custom type. The only difference it makes is more internal—in how Alexa's natural language processing will interpret the values given when selecting the intent. While it makes little difference at the moment, it helps Alexa to know more definitively that "Jupiter" is a planet and not just the name of a city. If there were some ambiguity in selecting an intent, the one with a planet slot would win over one with cities.

The custom PLANETS type is perfect for space travel destinations. But you won't always need to create a completely new type. Sometimes, it's sufficient to extend one of Amazon's built-in types with custom values.

Extending Built-In Types

Suppose that instead of space travel, you were building a more conventional travel application for scheduling travel to international cities. In that case, you'd probably be fine with the built-in AMAZON.City type for most cases.

But what if you offered travel to cities that aren't covered by the AMAZON.City type? For example, suppose that you'd like to include travel to some of the smaller towns in southeastern New Mexico, including Jal, Eunice, and Hobbs. These towns aren't covered by Amazon's built-in AMAZON.City type. But we can change that by extending AMAZON.City with a few custom values.

To extend a built-in type, simply declare it in the interaction model as if it were a completely custom type. For example, the following excerpt shows how to extend AMAZON.City to include a few of New Mexico's smaller towns:

```
"types": [
  {
    "name": "AMAZON.City",
    "values": [
      {
```

```
        "id": "JAL",
        "name": {
          "value": "Jal"
        }
      },
      {
        "id": "EUNICE",
        "name": {
          "value": "Eunice"
        }
      },
      {
        "id": "HOBBS",
        "name": {
          "value": "Hobbs"
        }
      }
    ]
  }
]
```

Here, the type's name is the same as the built-in type, and includes three
custom values. But, unlike a completely custom type, which will only include
the values declared in the interaction model, this type will include all of the
values that already come with AMAZON.City as well as the new values.

The Star Port 75 Travel skill doesn't have a need for a type that's an extension
to a built-in type, so there's no need to work it into the interaction model.

But we will use the custom PLANETS type for scheduling trips. Let's see how to
make it even more flexible by handling alternative names for the type's values.

Enabling Flexibility with Synonyms

If you were to ask anyone who is even vaguely familiar with astronomy to list
the planets in our solar system, they would probably give you the names of
the nine planets that we've provided as the values in our custom type. But
some of those planets have nicknames. Mars, for example, is colloquially
known as "the red planet." Some might refer to Saturn as "the ringed planet."
Even Earth has a few nicknames, including "the third rock from the sun."

In order to make conversations with Alexa feel more natural, it helps if she
can understand these nicknames and interpret them to mean the more formal
name. This can be done by adding synonyms to the values in the custom
type. For example, have a look at the following snippet from skill-package/interac-
tionModels/custom/en-US.json, showing the first four entries from the PLANETS type,
each with a new synonyms property:

slots/starport-75/skill-package/interactionModels/custom/en-US.json

```
"types": [
  {
    "name": "PLANETS",
    "values": [
      {
        "id": "MERCURY",
        "name": {
          "value": "Mercury",
          "synonyms": [
            "the one closest to the sun",
            "the swift planet"
          ]
        }
      },
      {
        "id": "VENUS",
        "name": {
          "value": "Venus",
          "synonyms": [
            "the morning star",
            "the evening star"
          ]
        }
      },
      {
        "id": "EARTH",
        "name": {
          "value": "Earth",
          "synonyms": [
            "the blue planet",
            "the big blue marble",
            "the third rock from the sun"
          ]
        }
      },
      {
        "id": "MARS",
        "name": {
          "value": "Mars",
          "synonyms": [
            "the red planet"
          ]
        }
      },
...
    ]
  }
]
```

As you can see, each of the entries is given an array of alternate names in the synonyms property. Mercury, for instance may be referred to as "the one closest to the sun" or "the swift planet," in addition to its official name, "Mercury." This makes it possible for a user to plan a trip to Mercury by saying something like "Schedule a trip to the swift planet leaving June 9th and returning June 17th." To prove that it works, the following test can be added to the schedule-trip.test.yml file:

```
- test: Plan a trip (synonym)
- "Schedule a trip to the swift planet leaving June 9th and
                          returning June 17th":
  - prompt: I've got you down for a trip to
          Mercury, leaving on June 9th and returning June 17th.
```

Let's see what happens when we run the test:

```
$ bst test --jest.collectCoverage=false schedule-trip.test.yml
BST: v2.6.0  Node: v17.6.0
Pro tip! Each of our tools have elements you can customize, like user ID
or the locale. Learn more by using your favorite Bespoken tool and the
--help option.
 FAIL  test/schedule-trip.test.yml
  en-US
    Schedule a trip
      ✓ Schedule a trip to Mercury leaving Friday and returning
        next Thursday
    Plan a trip
      ✓ Plan a trip between June 9th and June 17th to visit Mars
    Plan a trip (synonym)
      ✗ Schedule a trip to the swift planet leaving June 9th and
        returning June 17th

  ● en-US › Plan a trip (synonym) › Schedule a trip to the swift planet
    leaving June 9th and returning June 17th

    Expected value at [prompt] to ==
        I've got you down for a trip to Mercury, leaving on June 9th
      and returning June 17th.
    Received:
        <speak>I've got you down for a trip to the swift planet, leaving on
        June 9th and returning June 17th.</speak>

      28 | - "Schedule a trip to the swift planet leaving June 9th and
                  returning June 17th":
    > 29 |    - prompt: I've got you down for a
                  trip to Mercury, leaving on June 9th and returning June 17th.

      at test/schedule-trip.test.yml:30:0
      Timestamp:
        2019-05-27T21:55:25.020
```

```
Test Suites: 1 failed, 1 total
Tests:       1 failed, 2 passed, 3 total
Snapshots:   0 total
Time:        1.038s
Ran all test suites.
```

Oh no! The test fails! It expects that the response's output speech to be "I've got you down for a trip to Mercury, leaving on June 9th and returning June 17th" but receives "I've got you down for a trip to the swift planet, leaving on June 9th and returning June 17th." Something is still not quite right. Let's dig deeper into the request to see why.

When given an utterance that says, "Schedule a trip to the swift planet leaving June 9th and returning June 17th," then the "destination" slot will appear like this in the request:

```
"destination": {
  "name": "destination",
  "value": "the swift planet",
  "resolutions": {
    "resolutionsPerAuthority": [
      {
        "authority": "amzn1.er-authority.echo-sdk.{SKILL ID}.PLANETS",
        "status": {
          "code": "ER_SUCCESS_MATCH"
        },
        "values": [
          {
            "value": {
              "name": "Mercury",
              "id": "MERCURY"
            }
          }
        ]
      }
    ]
  },
  "confirmationStatus": "NONE",
  "source": "USER"
}
```

As you can see, the destination property's value property is "the swift planet," exactly as uttered in the request. And, you might recall that the intent handler extracts the value of the destination slot from the request with this line:

```
const destination =
    Alexa.getSlotValue(handlerInput.requestEnvelope, 'destination');
```

The getSlotValue() function will return the value property of the slot, "the swift planet" in this particular case. This phrase is then used to produce the response's speech text. The response is, "I've got you down for a trip to the swift planet..." instead of, "I've got you down for a trip to Mercury..." which is what our test expects.

Looking further in the destination property, you see that the resolutions property carries additional information about the slot's value that comes from resolving the slot's entity, including a name property with "Mercury" as its value. This is precisely what we want. There's a lot to take in when looking at the resolutions property, so let's break it down bit by bit.

resolutionsPerAuthority is an array of entity resolutions that matched what Alexa heard for the slot. Although it is an array, it almost always has a single entry which aligns with the slot type, in this case, PLANETS, as shown in the authority property.

The status property indicates, via the code sub-property, whether or not entity resolution successfully found a match. In this case, the status code is "ER_SUCCESS_MATCH", which means that "the swift planet" successfully resolved to a value. Had it not successfully matched one of the entities in PLANETS, the status code would have been "ER_SUCCESS_NO_MATCH" and there would be no values property in the resolution object.

The values property is an array containing an entry for every entity that matches what Alexa heard for that slot. Each entry will contain both the ID and the name of the matching entity. There is usually only a single matching value, but if there is any ambiguity, the values array may contain two or more entries. If there are multiple matches, the first entry is the closest match and is usually the best one to use.

Now that we know what to expect in the resolutions property, we can create a helper module to extract the resolved entity value from the slot:

```
slots/starport-75/lambda/Helpers.js
const Alexa = require('ask-sdk-core');

const getResolvedSlotValue = (requestEnvelope, slotName) => {
    const slotResolution = Alexa.getSlot(requestEnvelope, slotName)
        .resolutions.resolutionsPerAuthority[0];

    return slotResolution.status.code === 'ER_SUCCESS_MATCH' ?
        slotResolution.values[0].value.name :
        Alexa.getSlotValue(requestEnvelope, slotName);
};

module.exports = getResolvedSlotValue;
```

The function in this handy module extracts the slot resolution from the given request envelope, then considers its status code to decide whether or not to return the values[0].value.name property. If the status is "ER_SUCCESS_MATCH", then the resolved value will be returned. Otherwise, the unresolved slot value (from Alexa.getSlotValue()) will be returned. We could alternatively pivot on ER_SUCCESS_NO_MATCH and respond to the user indicating that we don't know anything of the slot value that they are asking about. Instead, we'll leverage Alexa's support for automatic validation in the next chapter.

Now we can change the intent handler to import the helper module and use its getResolvedSlotValue() function to extract the destination from the intent request:

slots/starport-75/lambda/ScheduleTripIntentHandler.js
```
const getResolvedSlotValue = require('./Helpers');

    . . .

        const destination =
            getResolvedSlotValue(handlerInput.requestEnvelope, 'destination');
```

With this change to the intent handler, we can try our test again:

```
$ bst test --jest.collectCoverage=false schedule-trip.test.yml

BST: v2.6.0  Node: v17.6.0
Use bst speak to interact directly with Alexa.

 PASS  test/schedule-trip.test.yml
  en-US
    Schedule a trip
      ✓ Schedule a trip to Mercury leaving Friday and returning next
        Thursday
    Plan a trip
      ✓ Plan a trip between June 9th and June 17th to visit Mars
    Plan a trip (synonym)
      ✓ Schedule a trip to the swift planet leaving June 9th and
        returning June 17th

Test Suites: 1 passed, 1 total
Tests:       3 passed, 3 total
Snapshots:   0 total
Time:        1.031s
Ran all test suites.
```

It passes! When the user asks to schedule a trip to "the swift planet," Alexa automatically interprets that as the entity we defined as Mercury. From there the intent handler is able to fetch the resolved entity's name rather than the nickname for the planet. Entity resolution has saved the day!

With all tests are passing, now's a good time to deploy the skill (by using git to push the code to AWS CodeCommit) and try it out vocally with an actual device or manually with ask dialog. If you were to use ask dialog to test the skill, the session might look like this:

```
$ ask dialog --locale en-US
User   >   open star port seventy five
Alexa  >   Welcome to Star Port 75 Travel. How can I help you?
User   >   plan a trip to the red planet leaving July 17th and
           returning July 31st
Alexa  >   I've got you down for a trip to Mars, leaving on
           2019-07-17 and returning 2019-07-31.
```

After asking for a trip to "the red planet," a synonym for Mars, Alexa responds by saying that she has reserved a trip to Mars. For fun, feel free to try scheduling a trip to any of the other planets using the synonyms declared in the interaction model.

Handling Multi-Value Slots

Up to this point, the slots we've defined only accept a single value per slot: one destination, one departure date, and one return date. But sometimes you need to collect a list of values in a slot rather than a single slot value. For instance, if you were building a skill for ordering pizza, you might want the user to name several toppings to be used when making a pizza.

With a small tweak to a slot definition, we can specify that a slot is able to accept a list of values. To illustrate how this works, suppose that we want to add an intent to the Star Port 75 skill that lets a user state their favorite planets. Such an intent might be declared in the interaction model like this:

```
{
  "name": "FavoritePlanetsIntent",
  "samples": [
    "my favorite planets are {planets}",
    "i like {planets}",
    "{planets} are my favorite"
  ],
  "slots": [
    {
      "name": "planets",
      "type": "PLANETS",
      "multipleValues": {
        "enabled": true
      }
    }
  ]
},
```

Multi-Value Slots Have Limited Availability

At the time this is being written, Multi-Value Slots are only available in the following locales: en-AU, en-CA, en-UK, and en-US.

For the most part, this intent isn't much different than ScheduleTripIntent, just with a single slot. The "planets" slot, however, has a multipleValues property with an enabled subproperty set to true. This indicates that the slot value may be a list instead of a single item. In fact, the payload of the intent request will include a type property for each slot value that will be either "Simple" for single slot values or "List" for multi-value slot values. For example, for an utterance of "my favorite planets are Mars, Saturn, and Pluto," the "planets" slot will look like this in the intent request:

```
"planets": {
  "name": "planets",
  "confirmationStatus": "NONE",
  "source": "USER",
  "slotValue": {
    "type": "List",
    "values": [
      {
        "type": "Simple",
        "value": "mars",
        "resolutions": { ... }
      },
      {
        "type": "Simple",
        "value": "mercury",
        "resolutions": { ... }
      },
      {
        "type": "Simple",
        "value": "Neptune",
        "resolutions": { ... }
      }
    ]
  }
},
```

Reading the values of a "List" slot requires a different approach than what we used to read the "destinations" slot from the ScheduleTripIntent. The Alexa.getSlot() and Alexa.getSlotValue() functions are remnants of an earlier version of the ASK SDK before multi-value slots were an option. But for multi-value slots, we'll need to revisit the getResolvedSlotValue() function to use two new functions, Alexa.getSlotValueV2() and Alexa.getSimpleSlotValues(), as shown here:

slots/starport-75/lambda/Helpers.js
```
const getResolvedSlotValue = (requestEnvelope, slotName) => {
    const slotValueV2 = Alexa.getSlotValueV2(requestEnvelope, slotName);

    const simpleSlotValue = Alexa.getSimpleSlotValues(slotValueV2);

    return simpleSlotValue.map(sv => {
      if (sv.resolutions) {
        const rpa = sv.resolutions.resolutionsPerAuthority[0];
        return rpa.status.code === 'ER_SUCCESS_MATCH' ?
            rpa.values[0].value.name:
            sv.value;
      } else {
        return sv.value;
      }
    });
  }
```

Alexa.getSlotValueV2() fetches the given slot by name ("planets" in this case), and from that returns the embedded slotValue object. From that, you could examine the type property to determine how to process the rest of the slot. But the Alexa.getResolvedSlotValue() does that for you, returning an array of "Simple" slot values. What's more, it works equally well for "Simple" slots as it does for "List" slots. In the case of "Simple" slots, it still returns an array, but an array of one value.

This new implementation of getResolvedSlotValue() takes the array of "Simple" slot value object and maps them to an array of string values where each value is either the resolved value name, if the status code is "ER_SUCCESS_MATCH", or the value property if not. This means that if the user were to state that their favorite planets are Mars, Saturn, and Pluto, then getResolvedSlotValue() will return ['Mars', 'Saturn', and 'Pluto'].

Putting getResolvedSlotValue() to work, here's how it can be used in an intent handler for FavoritePlanetsIntent:

slots/starport-75/lambda/FavoritePlanetsIntentHandler.js
```
const Alexa = require('ask-sdk-core');
const getResolvedSlotValue = require('./Helpers');

const FavoritePlanetsIntentHandler = {
  canHandle(handlerInput) {
    return Alexa.getRequestType(
            handlerInput.requestEnvelope) === 'IntentRequest'
      && Alexa.getIntentName(
            handlerInput.requestEnvelope) === 'FavoritePlanetsIntent';
  },
  handle(handlerInput) {
    const planets =
        getResolvedSlotValue(handlerInput.requestEnvelope, 'planets');
```

```
    const planetList =
        planets.length ===1 ?
        planets[0] :
        planets.slice(0, -1).join(', ') + ' and ' + planets.slice(-1);
    const speakOutput = `I like ${planetList}, too!`;
    return handlerInput.responseBuilder
        .speak(speakOutput)
        .getResponse();
  }
};

module.exports=FavoritePlanetsIntentHandler;
```

This handler receives the array of planet names return from the call to getResolvedSlotValue() and simply echoes them in the spoken response (after separating them with commas and the word "and").

After making these changes and deploying the skill, we can try this out with the ask dialog command:

```
$ ask dialog --locale en-US
User  > open star port seventy five
Alexa > Welcome to Star Port 75 Travel. How can I help you?
User  > My favorite planets are Mars Saturn and Pluto
Alexa > I like Mars, Saturn and Pluto, too!
```

As you can see, three planets are named in the utterance and those three planets are echoed in the response. But it doesn't need to be three planets listed. Any number of planets can be named and will be included in the "List" slot and ultimately echoed to the user. For example, if the user is a big fan of several planets, they might list six planets:

```
$ ask dialog --locale en-US
User  > open star port seventy five
Alexa > Welcome to Star Port 75 Travel. How can I help you?
User  > my favorite planets are Mercury Earth Mars Saturn Venus and Neptune
Alexa > I like Mercury, Earth, Mars, Saturn, Venus and Neptune, too!
```

Even though more planets were listed, the intent request was handled equally well.

Automatically Testing Multi-Value Slots?

Unfortunately, neither BST nor the Alexa Skill Test Framework directly support multi-value slots. That means that testing intents with multi-value slots requires a more manual or semi-automatic approach.

It's worth noting that although we used getSlot() and getSlotValue() to retrieve the simple "destination" slot in the handler for ScheduleTripIntent, the getSlotValueV2() and getSimpleSlotValues() functions will work as well with single-value slots as it does for multi-value slots.

Wrapping Up

Slots provide a way for Alexa skills to interpret what a user says as parameterized requests. The slot values are extracted from the utterance and provided in the request given to an intent handler.

Each slot has a name and a type. Amazon provides several dozen built-in types to cover many common cases, including dates and times, numbers, city names, movie titles, colors, foods, and sports—to name a few. You can also define your own custom types to cover situations not handled by Amazon's built-in types (such as planets).

When defining a custom slot type, it's also possible to define synonyms for the slot's values. This allows the user to use familiar or alternate terms for slot values in their requests, while Alexa is still able to map those terms to a canonical value for the purposes of handling the intent.

Capturing user input as parameters using slots works well when the user specifies valid and complete information. But when the user leaves out required details (such as a trip's starting date) or provides invalid information (such as a destination not offered), then Alexa will need to ask the user to provide more valid details. In the next chapter, we'll see how to define multi-turn dialogs that enable Alexa to elicit information that the user may have omitted, validate the slot values they give, and ask for confirmation before proceeding.

CHAPTER 4

Creating Multi-Turn Dialogs

"Would you prefer window or aisle?"

"We don't serve Coca-Cola. Is Pepsi okay?"

"Does your order look correct?"

Conversations are often sprinkled with follow-up questions. As humans, we rarely speak our thoughts precisely and completely. We state enough to initiate the conversation and then the other party asks follow-up questions to refine their understanding of what we said. Sometimes that's to elicit additional information we didn't provide. Other times it's to let us know that something we said isn't valid and ask us to supply new information. And in some cases, they just want to confirm that they correctly heard us.

Elicitation, validation, and confirmation are essential elements of human dialog. And, as it turns out, they are also essential to dialog between Alexa and the users of a skill. Unlike visual user interfaces which can present the user with a form made up of specific and finite questions and choices, conversation with an Alexa skill is more open-ended. The user could say almost anything to a skill and Alexa will either need to infer what the user is asking for or ask follow-up questions to refine her understanding.

In this chapter, we'll add dialogs to the trip scheduling intent we created in the previous chapter. The dialog we create will elicit any information that the user leaves out of the request, validate that the slot values provided make sense in the context of planning a planetary excursion, and confirm that Alexa correctly understood the details of the trip. Although we'll write a little code in the intent handler for more advanced cases, most of the work of declaring dialog rules is handled in the interaction model. So that's where we'll start, by elaborating on our understanding of the interaction model as it pertains to declaring dialog rules.

Adding Dialogs and Prompts in the Interaction Model

Up to this point, we've been working with the interaction model as a way to match intents with sample utterances, possibly with slots and custom types. That is, we've focused on a subset of the interaction model known as the language model, as defined within the languageModel property.

But the language model is only one of three parts of a skill's interaction model. In addition to the language model, the interaction model can also define dialog rules and prompts. These are represented in the interaction model JSON structure in the dialog and prompts properties, which are peers to the languageModel property. The following high-level sample of interaction model JSON shows these three properties together:

```
{
  "interactionModel": {
    "languageModel": {
        ...
    },
    "dialog": {
        ...
    },
    "prompts": [
        ...
    ]
  }
}
```

Dialog rules, defined within the dialog property, ensure that the values given in slots are valid and complete. This includes elicitation, validation, and confirmation. Elicitation ensures that all slot values are provided to a handler and, if not, then the user is asked to provide the missing information. Validation ensures that the values given fit what is expected for a slot. And confirmation ensures that the skill heard everything correctly by asking the user to confirm the given values before the skill takes action on the intent.

As Alexa elicits, validates, or confirms slot values, she will need to ask the user for missing or different information or to confirm what she hears. Prompts, declared in the prompts property, are the follow-up questions, cues Alexa will use to obtain missing or incorrect data.

We'll look at validation and confirmation a little later in this chapter. First, let's declare dialog rules to make sure that the user provides everything needed to schedule a trip and the prompts Alexa will speak to collect any missing information.

Eliciting Missing Slot Values

Imagine that a user wants to book a weeklong trip to Mars, leaving on July 17th. If the user were to say, "Schedule a trip to Mars, leaving July 17th and returning July 23rd," then our skill will be happy to oblige, with no further changes to the skill's code.

However, that requires that the user know exactly how to speak to our skill and what slots the intent is expecting. If the user were to leave out any information, how would the skill respond? For example, what if the user were to say, "I want to go to Mars" without specifying departure and return dates? Let's run that through the ask dialog command to see what happens:

```
$ ask dialog --locale en-US
  User  >  open star port seventy five
  Alexa >  Welcome to Star Port 75 Travel. How can I help you?
  User  >  Let's plan a trip to Mars
  Alexa >  I've got you down for a trip to Mars, leaving on undefined and
           returning undefined.
```

As you can see, Alexa had no trouble understanding that the user wants to plan a trip to Mars, but because no dates were specified, she has the user leaving on "undefined" dates. While technically correct based on what the user asked for, "undefined" is probably not what the user intended. It's quite likely that the user expected that Alexa would ask follow-up questions to complete their travel plan. Instead, Alexa used what little information she received and punted on the rest.

But, we can make Alexa ask for missing information by enabling slot elicitation on the slots whose values are required and by declaring prompts which define the follow-up questions. We'll declare the intent and each of its slots for which we're defining dialog rules within the interaction model's dialog property:

```
dialog/starport-75-ations/skill-package/interactionModels/custom/en-US.json
"dialog": {
  "intents": [
    {
      "name": "ScheduleTripIntent",
      "slots": [
        {
          "name": "destination",
          "type": "PLANETS",
          "elicitationRequired": true,
          "prompts": {
            "elicitation": "Slot.Elicitation.ScheduleTrip.Destination"
          }
        },
```

```
      {
        "name": "departureDate",
        "type": "AMAZON.DATE",
        "elicitationRequired": true,
        "prompts": {
          "elicitation": "Slot.Elicitation.ScheduleTrip.DepartureDate"
        }
      },
      {
        "name": "returnDate",
        "type": "AMAZON.DATE",
        "elicitationRequired": true,
        "prompts": {
          "elicitation": "Slot.Elicitation.ScheduleTrip.ReturnDate"
        }
      }
    ]
  }
 ]
},
```

On the surface, this looks almost as if we're repeating the intent definition that we've already declared in languageModel. But it is subtly different. In the list of slots, we still must specify each slot's name and type, both of which must match what was declared in the language model. But instead of defining synonyms or other concepts pertaining to the language model, this is where we should declare dialog rules such as elicitation, validation, and confirmation.

The elicitationRequired property is what enables elicitation on each slot. When it's set to true, Alexa will prompt the user for the missing information if no value for that slot was given. The prompts property is where we define the prompts that Alexa will speak to the user during the dialog. In this case, the elicitation prompt specifies how Alexa will ask the user for missing information if the user fails to specify the destination, departure date, or return date.

The elicitation property does not carry the actual text that Alexa will speak to the user, however. Instead, it contains a reference to a prompt defined in the prompts section of the interaction model. For example, if the return data isn't specified, then Alexa will ask the user to provide the return date by speaking the prompt whose ID is "Slot.Elicitation.ScheduleTrip.ReturnDate". But the actual prompt is one of three prompts we will define in the prompts section of the interaction model:

dialog/starport-75-ations/skill-package/interactionModels/custom/en-US.json
```
"prompts": [
  {
    "id": "Slot.Elicitation.ScheduleTrip.Destination",
```

```
    "variations": [
      {
        "type": "PlainText",
        "value": "Where do you want to go?"
      },
      {
        "type": "PlainText",
        "value": "Which planet would you like to visit?"
      }
    ]
  },
  {
    "id": "Slot.Elicitation.ScheduleTrip.DepartureDate",
    "variations": [
      {
        "type": "PlainText",
        "value": "When do you want to depart?"
      },
      {
        "type": "PlainText",
        "value": "When will your trip start?"
      }
    ]
  },
  {
    "id": "Slot.Elicitation.ScheduleTrip.ReturnDate",
    "variations": [
      {
        "type": "PlainText",
        "value": "When do you want to return?"
      },
      {
        "type": "PlainText",
        "value": "When will your trip end?"
      }
    ]
  }
}
]
```

Notice that each prompt is defined by an ID and a variations property. To make Alexa sound more natural, it's useful to not have her prompt the user exactly the same way each time she asks a follow-up question. The variations property is an array containing one or more variations for Alexa to choose randomly when she prompts the user. For example, if the user fails to specify the departure date, Alexa may ask "When do you want to depart?" or she may ask "When will your trip start?" Both ask for the same thing, but in different ways. For the sake of brevity, the sample only includes two variations of each prompt, but you may declare more. In fact, the more variations you declare, the more natural conversation with your skill will seem.

The type property for all of the prompts is set to "PlainText", in which prompts are specified exactly as-is. The other option is "SSML", which lets you specify richer responses using the Speech Synthesis Markup Language, which we'll look at in Chapter 6, Embellishing Response Speech, on page 131.

Now that we've defined the dialog rules and the prompts to go with them, we're almost ready to test the elicitation rules. But first, we need to tell Alexa that we want her to be responsible for all dialog handling. The simplest way to handle incomplete dialog requests is to configure the intent for automatic dialog delegation, by setting the delegationStrategy property to "ALWAYS" on the intent:

```
"dialog": {
  "intents": [
    {
      "name": "ScheduleTripIntent",
      "delegationStrategy": "ALWAYS",
...
    }
  ]
},
```

"ALWAYS" enables automatic dialog delegation. When dialogs are automatically delegated, Alexa will handle all requests with incomplete slot data, without invoking the fulfillment code until all required slots are available. If a user fails to specify a slot value, she will automatically prompt them for the missing information using one of the prompts associated with that slot. The other option for the delegationStrategy property is "SKILL_RESPONSE" (which is also the default value) and indicates that automatic delegation is off and that one or more intent handlers will be involved in handling the incomplete dialog requests. We'll talk more about how to explicitly handle dialog requests in section Explicitly Handling Dialog Delegation, on page 98.

If your skill has several intents for which you want automatic delegation enabled, you can optionally specify the delegation strategy for the entire dialog rules configuration instead of for each intent:

```
"dialog": {
  "delegationStrategy": "ALWAYS",
  "intents": [
    {
...
    }
  ]
},
```

You can enable automatic delegation globally for all intents by setting the delegationStrategy property to "ALWAYS" at the dialog rules level. From there, you may choose to disable it for individual intents by setting the same property to "SKILL_RESPONSE" on each intent. Whether you declare the delegation strategy individually for each intent or globally for all intents will depend on if you plan to use explicit dialog handling more often or not. In our skill, either way will work fine at this point, as we have no other intents that accept slots and require dialogs.

Now we're ready to test our new elicitation rules. Unfortunately, there's currently no way to automatically test auto-delegated dialogs without deploying the skill using BST or the Alexa Skills Test Framework. Therefore, we'll need to deploy the skill first and then manually test it.

Once deployed, we can use ask dialog or the Alexa developer console to test the skill. Using the Alexa developer console simulator, the conversation might look like this:

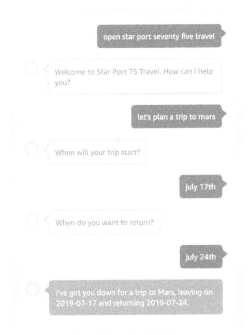

That's a lot better than traveling on some "undefined" dates. As you can see, when the user asked to schedule a trip to Mars, but didn't specify travel dates, Alexa stepped in, using the prompts defined for those missing slots, and asked the user to provide the missing information.

Slot elicitation ensures that the intent is given all of the information it needs to be handled successfully. But what if the values given don't make sense? Let's see how to define slot validation rules.

Validating Slot Values

Suppose that the user asked Alexa to plan a trip, but rather than ask for a trip to one of the planets in our solar system, the user asked for a trip to Chicago. Such a conversation in the simulator might look like this:

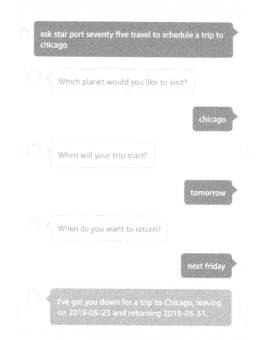

As you can see, even though the destination slot is typed as PLANETS, it didn't stop the user from asking for and scheduling a trip to Chicago. Alexa did stop and ask the user which planet that they'd like to visit, but that was only because "Chicago" isn't one of the planets defined in PLANETS, so she wasn't sure if she should put "Chicago" into that slot. But once she prompted the user for a planet and the user again said "Chicago," she went ahead and used that value as the destination.

To stop the user from offering values that aren't valid, we can define validation rules on the slot. For example, consider the following declaration of the destination slot, with an "isInSet" validation rule to ensure that the given value is one of the planets in our solar system:

dialog/starport-75-ations/skill-package/interactionModels/custom/en-US.json
```
{
  "name": "destination",
  "type": "PLANETS",
  "elicitationRequired": true,
  "prompts": {
    "elicitation": "Slot.Elicitation.ScheduleTrip.Destination"
  },
  "validations": [
    {
      "type": "isInSet",
      "prompt": "Slot.Validation.UnknownDestination",
      "values": ["mercury", "venus", "earth", "mars", "jupiter",
                 "saturn", "uranus", "neptune", "pluto"]
    }
  ]
},
```

The validations property defines one or more validation rules to be applied to
the slot. The one validation rule defined here has a type of "isInSet", If the
value given by the user for the "destination" slot isn't one of the values listed
in the values property, then the "Slot.Validation.UnknownDestination" prompt
will be returned to the user to ask them to supply a different value.

This should do the trick. But doesn't it seem a bit odd to duplicate the list of
planet names, when we've already defined all planets as part of the PLANETS
type? We can get rid of that duplication by replacing the "isInSet" rule with
a new "hasEntityResolutionMatch" rule, as shown here:

```
"validations": [
  {
    "type": "hasEntityResolutionMatch",
    "prompt": "Slot.Validation.UnknownDestination"
  }
]
```

The "hasEntityResolutionMatch" rules considers the slot's type and ensures
that whatever value the user specifies matches one of the values in the type.
If the user were to ask for a trip to anywhere that isn't a member of the PLANETS
type, then validation fails and Alexa will present the user with one of the
variations of the "Slot.Validation.UnknownDestination" prompt.

Speaking of that prompt, here's how "Slot.Validation.UnknownDestination"
may be defined:

dialog/starport-75-ations/skill-package/interactionModels/custom/en-US.json

```json
{
  "id": "Slot.Validation.UnknownDestination",
  "variations": [
    {
      "type": "PlainText",
      "value": "Star Port 75 Travel doesn't offer travel to {destination}.
              Where else would you like to go?"
    },
    {
      "type": "PlainText",
      "value": "{destination} sounds like a wonderful trip. Unfortunately,
              we don't serve that destination. Pick another destination."
    }
  ]
}
```

With this validation rule in place and a corresponding prompt at the ready, we're ready to try out validation on the "destination" slot. Because we're still using automatic dialog delegation, we can't test the dialog with the BST testing tool or the Alexa Skill Testing Framework. But we can deploy it and try it out in the developer console simulator. The conversation might look something like this:

As before, after the user asked for a trip to Chicago, Alexa wasn't sure that "Chicago" should be used for the slot value, so she asked where the user wants to go. But when the user said "Chicago" in response to the elicitation prompt, the validation rule kicked in. Since "Chicago" isn't one of the planets defined in PLANETS, she explained that Chicago isn't one of the destinations served and asked for another destination.

Now, let's say that it doesn't make sense to leave Earth only to travel to Earth. Therefore, while Earth is one of the planets in our solar system, it may not be a valid destination. Fortunately, we can specify more than one validation rule for a slot. To account for that case, let's configure another rule to exclude Earth as a destination:

```
dialog/starport-75-ations/skill-package/interactionModels/custom/en-US.json
"validations": [
  {
    "type": "hasEntityResolutionMatch",
    "prompt": "Slot.Validation.UnknownDestination"
  },
  {
    "type": "isNotInSet",
    "prompt": "Slot.Validation.NoStaycations",
    "values": ["earth"]
  }
]
```

The "isNotInSet" validation rule is the opposite of "isInSet". In this case, "earth" will pass the first validation check, because Earth is one of the planets contained within the PLANETS type. But it will fail this new validation rule, because "earth" is an entry in the "isNotInSet" rule. Therefore, if the user asks for a trip to Earth, Alexa will stop them and prompt them for another choice using the "Slot.Validation.NoStaycations" prompt. That prompt is defined like this:

```
dialog/starport-75-ations/skill-package/interactionModels/custom/en-US.json
{
  "id": "Slot.Validation.NoStaycations",
  "variations": [
    {
      "type": "PlainText",
      "value": "Star Port 75 doesn't specialize in stay-cations. Where else
                would you like to go?"
    },
    {
      "type": "PlainText",
      "value": "Wouldn't you like to get a bit further away? Which other
                planet do you want to visit?"
    }
  ]
}
```

With this new validation and its associated prompts declared, let's give it a try. First, we'll need to deploy the skill (using git commit/git push for Alexa-hosted skills or ask deploy if the skill is AWS Lambda-hosted). Then, in the developer console's simulator, we can test out the validation by planning a trip to Earth as shown in the screenshot on page 94.

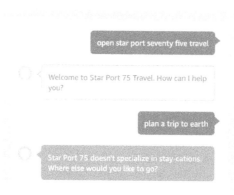

Nice! Although the skill recognizes Earth as a valid planet, it also prohibits it from being chosen as a destination, because traveling from Earth to Earth doesn't make sense for the Star Port 75 Travel skill.

Aside from validating slots whose types are lists, as is the case with the PLANETS type, Alexa also supports many other kinds of validation,[1] including date and number validation to ensure that values fall within a specific range. With that in mind, it might make sense to add validation to the departure and return dates, at very least enforcing that the return date falls after the departure date. But that kind of validation is a bit trickier than it sounds, so let's defer it until section Explicitly Handling Dialog Delegation, on page 98. Instead, let's look at the third kind of dialog rule: confirmation.

Confirming Slots

Confirmation can be thought of as reverse validation. When validating slot values, the skill verifies that the values given by the user meet certain criteria. Confirmation, on the other hand, is checking with the user to make sure that what the skill is about to do meets the user's expectations.

When scheduling a trip, for example, it would be helpful if Alexa repeated the trip details back to the user to make sure that she heard everything correctly before booking the trip. To enable such confirmation for the ScheduleTripIntent, we can simply set the confirmationRequired property on the intent to true and specify the prompt Alexa should use to confirm the trip details:

---

1. https://developer.amazon.com/docs/custom-skills/validate-slot-values.html#use-multiple-validation-rules-for-a-slot

dialog/starport-75-ations/skill-package/interactionModels/custom/en-US.json

```
{
  "name": "ScheduleTripIntent",
  "confirmationRequired": true,
  "prompts": {
    "confirmation": "Confirmation.ScheduleTrip"
  },
  "slots": [
...
  ]
}
```

When the confirmationRequired property is set to true, Alexa will automatically ask for confirmation before submitting the request to the intent handler. As declared here, she will prompt the user for confirmation using the prompt named "Confirmation.ScheduleTrip", which is declared like this:

dialog/starport-75-ations/skill-package/interactionModels/custom/en-US.json

```
{
  "id": "Confirmation.ScheduleTrip",
  "variations": [
    {
      "type": "PlainText",
      "value": "I've got you down for a trip to {destination} leaving on
              {departureDate} and returning {returnDate}. Is that correct?"
    },
    {
      "type": "PlainText",
      "value": "You want to visit {destination} between {departureDate}
              and {returnDate}. Is that right?"
    }
  ]
}
```

Just as with other prompts we've defined, the "Confirmation.ScheduleTrip" prompt has a couple of variations (although it's generally a good idea to have as many variations as you can come up with to make the interaction feel natural). In both variations, the prompt's text has placeholders for the destination and travel dates so that Alexa can present those values to the user to confirm. These placeholders are automatically bound to their corresponding slot values.

Giving this a spin in the developer console's simulator, we can see the confirmation in action as shown in the screenshot on page 96.

You may have noticed that the final message has changed to "You're all set. Enjoy your trip to Mars." Before we added confirmation, it seemed appropriate to repeat all of the trip details in the final message. But if the confirmation message echoes those details, then it's redundant to repeat them again in the final message. Therefore, the intent handler has changed slightly to speak a friendlier message:

```
dialog/starport-75-ations/lambda/ScheduleTripIntentHandler.js
const Alexa = require('ask-sdk-core');
const getResolvedSlotValue = require('./Helpers');

const ScheduleTripIntentHandler = {
  canHandle(handlerInput) {
    const request = handlerInput.requestEnvelope.request;
    return Alexa.getRequestType(
            handlerInput.requestEnvelope) === 'IntentRequest'
      && Alexa.getIntentName(
            handlerInput.requestEnvelope) === 'ScheduleTripIntent'
      && Alexa.getRequest(handlerInput.requestEnvelope)
            .intent.confirmationStatus === 'CONFIRMED';
  },
  handle(handlerInput) {
    const destination =
        getResolvedSlotValue(handlerInput.requestEnvelope, 'destination');
```

```
        const departureDate =
              Alexa.getSlotValue(handlerInput.requestEnvelope, 'departureDate');
        const returnDate =
              Alexa.getSlotValue(handlerInput.requestEnvelope, 'returnDate');

        const speakOutput = handlerInput.t('SCHEDULED_MSG',
              { destination: destination });

        return handlerInput.responseBuilder
          .speak(speakOutput)
          .withShouldEndSession(true)
          .getResponse();
    },
};

module.exports=ScheduleTripIntentHandler;
```

What's more, notice that the canHandle() function checks that the confirmation status is "CONFIRMED". That's so that this request handler will only handle the request if the user said "Yes" or otherwise affirmed the dialog.

On the other hand, if the user says "No" or otherwise denies the dialog, then the confirmation status will be "DENIED". This situation should also be handled, as shown here:

dialog/starport-75-ations/lambda/ScheduleTripIntentHandler_DENIED.js
```
const Alexa = require('ask-sdk-core');

const ScheduleTripIntentHandler_DENIED = {
  canHandle(handlerInput) {
    const request = handlerInput.requestEnvelope.request;
    return Alexa.getRequestType(
            handlerInput.requestEnvelope) === 'IntentRequest'
      && Alexa.getIntentName(
            handlerInput.requestEnvelope) === 'ScheduleTripIntent'
      && Alexa.getRequest(handlerInput.requestEnvelope)
            .intent.confirmationStatus === 'DENIED';
  },
  handle(handlerInput) {
    const destinationSlot =
          Alexa.getSlot(handlerInput.requestEnvelope, 'destination');
    const destinationSlotJSON = JSON.stringify(destinationSlot);

    const speakOutput =
        "Okay, I'll cancel your trip. What can I do for you now?";

    return handlerInput.responseBuilder
        .speak(speakOutput)
        .reprompt("How can I help you?")
        .getResponse();
  },
};

module.exports=ScheduleTripIntentHandler_DENIED;
```

If the user issues a denial, then the dialog will conclude and Alexa will ask the user what she should do next.

Whether it be elicitation, validation, or confirmation, automatically delegated dialogs are great for adding natural conversation around slot gathering. But sometimes your skill's dialog needs are more advanced than what automatic delegation can offer. For those situations, let's have a look at how to write code that steps in during dialog delegation.

Explicitly Handling Dialog Delegation

Earlier in section Validating Slot Values, on page 90, we added validation for the destination slot. But at that time, we deferred validation for the travel date slots. That's because when it comes to travel dates, we will need to ensure that the return date falls after the departure date. And although it is possible to automatically validate dates, it's not so easy to validate two or more slots with how they relate to each other. For that, we'll need to write some explicit validation code that steps in to compare the two dates.

But first, let's add some simple validation for the dates. The "isInDuration" validation rules ensures that a date slot's value falls within a range. The following excerpt from the interaction model's dialog rules shows how to do some basic validation on the two date slots:

dialog/starport-75-delegate/skill-package/interactionModels/custom/en-US.json
```
{
  "name": "departureDate",
  "type": "AMAZON.DATE",
  "elicitationRequired": true,
  "prompts": {
    "elicitation": "Slot.Elicitation.ScheduleTrip.DepartureDate"
  },
  "validations": [
    {
      "type": "isInDuration",
      "prompt": "Slot.Validation.DepartureDateInTheFuture",
      "start": "P1D",
      "end": "P30D"
    }
  ]
},
{
  "name": "returnDate",
  "type": "AMAZON.DATE",
  "elicitationRequired": true,
  "prompts": {
```

```
      "elicitation": "Slot.Elicitation.ScheduleTrip.ReturnDate"
    },
    "validations": [
      {
        "type": "isInDuration",
        "prompt": "Slot.Validation.ReturnDateInTheFuture",
        "start": "P1D",
        "end": "P60D"
      }
    ]
}
```

Both date slots apply the "isInDuration" validation to require that the dates are in the near-ish future. These date ranges are specified in the start and end properties, which are expressed in ISO-8601 duration format.[2] Per ISO-8601 duration format, the "P" stands for "period" and "D" stands for "day". Therefore, "P1D" means 1 day out from the current day, "P30D" means 30 days out, and "P60D" means 60 days out. Therefore, the departure date must be within the next 30 days, after today. And the return date must be within the next 60 days after today.

That's a good start and better than no validation at all. But it still doesn't prevent the user from specifying a return date that is before the departure date. Star Port 75 Travel specializes in space travel, not time travel, so it's important to be sure that the traveler returns after they depart.

In order to do that, we'll need to disable fully-automatic delegation for the ScheduleTripIntent with the following tweak to the intent's entry in the dialog section of the interaction model:

```
"dialog": {
  "intents": [
    {
      "name": "ScheduleTripIntent",
      "delegationStrategy": "SKILL_RESPONSE",
...
    }
  ]
},
```

By setting delegationStrategy to "SKILL_RESPONSE", we can write intent handlers that have a say in the dialog flow. It doesn't make the dialog delegation completely manual—the other dialog rules we defined for automatic delegation will still work. Instead, think of it as semi-automatic, where an intent handler can be part of the dialog flow.

---

2. https://en.wikipedia.org/wiki/ISO_8601#Durations

If the delegation strategy is "SKILL_RESPONSE", a state machine is applied where a dialog has one of three states: "STARTED", "IN_PROGRESS", or "COMPLETED". The following state machine diagram illustrates the states that a dialog goes through on its way to completion:

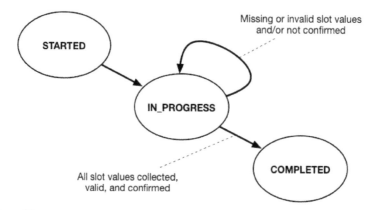

When handling an intent request, we can write code that inspects the dialogState property of the request to know the current state of the dialog. But if we do this in the intent handler's handle() function, we'll end up with a mess of if/else if/else blocks. Instead, it's neater to write two or more distinct intent handlers and check for the dialog state in each intent handler's canHandle() function.

For the purposes of validating departure and return dates, we'll write a new intent handler that handles the ScheduleTripIntent when its dialog is not in "COMPLETED" state (in other words, in "STARTED" or "IN_PROGRESS" state):

dialog/starport-75-delegate/lambda/ScheduleTripIntentHandler_InProgress.js
```
const Alexa = require('ask-sdk-core');

const ScheduleTripIntentHandler_InProgress = {
  canHandle(handlerInput) {
    return Alexa.getRequestType(
            handlerInput.requestEnvelope) === 'IntentRequest'
      && Alexa.getIntentName(
            handlerInput.requestEnvelope) === 'ScheduleTripIntent'
      && Alexa.getDialogState(handlerInput.requestEnvelope) !== 'COMPLETED';
  },
  handle(handlerInput) {
    const currentIntent = handlerInput.requestEnvelope.request.intent;
    const departureString =
        Alexa.getSlotValue(handlerInput.requestEnvelope, 'departureDate');
    const returnString =
        Alexa.getSlotValue(handlerInput.requestEnvelope, 'returnDate');

    if (departureString && returnString) {
      const departureDate = new Date(departureString);
      const returnDate = new Date(returnString);
```

```
      if (departureDate >= returnDate) {
        currentIntent.slots['returnDate'].value = null;
        return handlerInput.responseBuilder
          .speak("Star Port Seventy Five specializes in space travel, " +
              "not time travel. Please specify a return date that is " +
              "after the departure date.")
          .addDelegateDirective(currentIntent)
          .getResponse();
      }
    }

    return handlerInput.responseBuilder
      .addDelegateDirective(currentIntent)
      .getResponse();
  },
};
module.exports=ScheduleTripIntentHandler_InProgress;
```

The canHandle() function looks similar to the canHandle() function we wrote for ScheduleTripIntentHandler, but in addition to inspecting the request type and intent name, it also checks that the dialogState property is not "COMPLETED".

If so, then the handle() function will have a chance to inspect the request further and validate slots or even change slot values. In this case, it first checks to see if both the departure date and return date are specified—if not, then there's no point in applying a comparison validation against them. It then compares the return date with the departure date. If the return date is the same as or earlier than the departure date, then it clears out the "returnDate" slot (so that the user can provide a new value) and adds an appropriate validation message to be spoken by Alexa.

Whether or not the dates are valid, it's important to allow Alexa to continue handling the dialog delegation once the handle() function completes. The call to addDelegateDirective() sends a directive to Alexa, telling her to carry on with automatic dialog delegation—the same as if we had set the delegationStrategy to "ALWAYS".

Although it's optional, we pass the current intent to addDelegateDirective() so that the change we made to the "returnDate" slot carries forward in the dialog. If you don't pass the current intent to addDelegateDirective(), then any changes to the slot values will be lost when the handle() function completes. In the case of ScheduleTripIntentHandler_InProgress, this means that the return date won't be cleared out and the user won't be prompted to provide the return date again.

As with any new intent handler, don't forget to register it with the skill builder:

dialog/starport-75-delegate/lambda/index.js

```
const ScheduleTripIntentHandler_InProgress =
            require('./ScheduleTripIntentHandler_InProgress');

...

exports.handler = Alexa.SkillBuilders.custom()
    .addRequestHandlers(
        HelloWorldIntentHandler,
        ScheduleTripIntentHandler,
        ScheduleTripIntentHandler_InProgress,
        StandardHandlers.LaunchRequestHandler,
        StandardHandlers.HelpIntentHandler,
        StandardHandlers.CancelAndStopIntentHandler,
        StandardHandlers.FallbackIntentHandler,
        StandardHandlers.SessionEndedRequestHandler,
        StandardHandlers.IntentReflectorHandler)
    .addErrorHandlers(
        StandardHandlers.ErrorHandler)
    .addRequestInterceptors(
        LocalisationRequestInterceptor)
    .lambda();
```

ScheduleTripIntentHandler_InProgress is now ready to handle the partially complete ScheduleTripIntent while dialog delegation gathers slot values. But our original intent handler, ScheduleTripIntentHandler, needs its canHandle() function tweaked ever so slightly.

The purpose of ScheduleTripIntentHandler is to handle the complete ScheduleTripIntent once all slot values are gathered and validated—when the dialog state is "COMPLETED". Therefore, to prevent ScheduleTripIntentHandler from handling requests whose dialog state is "STARTED" or "IN_PROGRESS", we must change its canHandle() function to check that the dialog state is "COMPLETED":

dialog/starport-75-delegate/lambda/ScheduleTripIntentHandler.js

```
canHandle(handlerInput) {
  return Alexa.getRequestType(
          handlerInput.requestEnvelope) === 'IntentRequest'
    && Alexa.getIntentName(
          handlerInput.requestEnvelope) === 'ScheduleTripIntent'
    && Alexa.getDialogState(handlerInput.requestEnvelope) === 'COMPLETED';
},
```

Now we're ready to try out our new date validation logic. After deploying the skill, we can test it in the developer console's simulator. Planning a trip to Jupiter with invalid travel dates might look like the screenshot on page 103.

Clearly, June 24th is after June 17th. Thus it's not possible to leave on June 24th for an excursion to Jupiter and return a week earlier. Our new intent

> open star port seventy five travel

> Welcome to Star Port 75 Travel. How can I help you?

> let's plan a trip to jupiter

> When do you want to depart?

> june 24th

> When do you want to return?

> june 17th

> Star Port Seventy Five specializes in space travel, not time travel. Please specify a return date that is after the departure date.

> When will your trip end?

handler catches that case and prevents such a backwards trip from being scheduled.

Wrapping Up

It is rare in human conversation for all details to be given in a single statement. Conversation involves a lot of back and forth, often with one party giving details as the conversation progresses and the other asking for those details. Knowing that one half of an Alexa conversation is human, it's quite likely that the human won't give all of the details up front. This means that Alexa must initiate dialog with the user to collect and validate all slot values.

Alexa dialogs are defined by three essential activities: elicitation, validation, and confirmation. Alexa elicits any missing slot values by prompting the user until all slots are filled. As slot values become available, Alexa applies validation rules to ensure that the values given make sense. Once all slot values are available, Alexa can prompt the user one last time to confirm that she heard correctly what the user said.

For many common cases, Alexa dialogs are handled automatically by the platform, requiring no special intent-handling code in the skill. For some advanced cases, however, it is possible to write an intent handler that steps into the dialog to perform custom validation or even populate or change slot values.

Our skill gathers information for scheduling an interplanetary excursion and does a great job of pretending to schedule the trip. In reality, however, it only logs travel plans and doesn't really schedule anything. We'll fix that in the next chapter as we see how to integrate Alexa skills with external APIs.

CHAPTER 5

Integrating User Data

With many things in this world, there's usually more than meets the eye. When you watch a movie or a TV show, you often think of the actors who play the main characters, but probably don't often think much about those behind the scenes who catered the filming, built the sets, or created the costumes. When you go out to a nice restaurant, you interface with your server and might even acknowledge the chef, but rarely consider the farmer who grew the vegetables or the driver who delivered the unprepared food in their truck. Even this book that you're reading is the product of many more hands than just the one whose name appears on the cover.

Alexa skills are often much the same—there's usually more than meets the ear. You will speak with Alexa and she will respond to your queries based on the skill's programming. But it's not unusual for an Alexa skill to draw on one or more backend services to fulfill its functionality. From the user's perspective, it's just a front end skill that they talk to. But in reality the skill may simply be a voice-enabled facade to a much larger backend system.

In this chapter, we're going to expand the Star Port 75 Travel skill beyond its own perimeter and have it coordinate with services that will make it more complete. We'll start by leveraging a service provided by the Alexa platform itself and then step even further outside of the skill by applying account linking to consume an external, OAuth 2-secured REST API.

Accessing a User's Amazon Info

As people get to know each other, they learn and remember things about each other. We start by getting to know each others' names. Then, when we greet each other in the future, we can be more personable and acknowledge each other by name. As we get to know someone better, we might learn their phone number or email address so that we can contact them later. As the relationship progresses, you may share your address with someone so that they can visit you or maybe send you a birthday or Christmas card.

Although Alexa isn't human, it helps the users of our skill to feel comfortable talking with her if she's able to speak with them on a personal level. If she greets someone by name when a skill is launched, it makes her seem more human and less like a machine. And if she knows useful information such as a user's email address, then the skill can send the user information that they can refer to later when not interacting with the skill.

Alexa offers several services through which a skill can obtain several useful bits of information about a user:

- The user's name (first name or full name)
- The user's email address
- The user's phone/mobile number
- The device's address
- The device's geolocation

Even though these services and the data that they offer are available to any skill, you don't need to worry that every Alexa skill knows too much about you. In order for a skill to use these services, they must provide an authorized access token in their requests to the skills. And the only way a skill is able to provide such an access token is if the user has explicitly granted permission to read that information.

In the Star Port 75 Travel skill, we're going to leverage an Alexa-provided service to fetch the user's name and greet them personally when they launch the skill. Before we can do that, however, we'll need to first configure the skill to be able to read the user's name.

Configuring Skill Permissions

We're going to leverage some of this user information in the Star Port 75 Travel skill to greet a user by name when they launch the skill. Therefore, we need to configure our skill to request permission for the user's given names. To do that, we'll add a new permissions property in the skill's manifest (skill.json) that looks like this:

integration/starport-75-user-info/skill-package/skill.json

```
{
  "manifest": {
    ...
```

```
    "permissions": [
      { "name": "alexa::profile:given_name:read" }
    ]
  }
}
```

Here we're configuring the skill for one permission. The alexa::profile:given_name:
read entry is for permission to read the user's given name. Notice that the
permissions property is an array. Therefore, if your skill needs additional permissions, you can configure more by listing them alongside the alexa::profile:giv-
en_name:read permission under permissions. A few other permissions you might
ask for include the following:

- Full name—alexa::profile:name:read
- Email address—alexa::profile:email:read
- Phone/mobile number—alexa::profile:mobile_number:read
- Device address—alexa::devices:all:address:full:read

For example, our skill only needs the user's given name. Suppose, however,
that your skill needs the user's email address and their phone number in
addition to their first name. You could then configure the permissions property
like this:

```
{
  "manifest": {
    ...
    "permissions": [
      { "name": "alexa::profile:given_name:read" },
      { "name": "alexa::profile:email:read" },
      { "name": "alexa::profile:mobile_number:read" }
    ]
  }
}
```

Although the skill may be configured with one or more permissions, Alexa
won't automatically request those permissions when the skill is launched.
The configuration of the permissions property in the manifest only specifies the
permissions that a skill may request, not that it necessarily will. We'll soon
see how to have the skill request permission. But first, let's assume that
permission has been given and fetch the user's given name.

Requesting User Data

When requesting a user's personal information from Alexa, you'll need three things:

- The Alexa API base URL
- A path to the endpoint for the specific data you want
- An authorized API access token

As it turns out, two out of those three things are readily available to you in the handlerInput object passed into the request handler. From the handlerInput, you can use code like the following to obtain the base URL and the API access token:

```
const apiBaseUrl = handlerInput.context.System.apiEndpoint;
const accessToken = handlerInput.context.System.apiAccessToken;
```

The API base URL may vary depending on the user's location, so Alexa gives the correct one to you via the handlerInput so that you don't have to write code in your skill to figure it out. By appending the appropriate path to the API's base URL, you can use any HTTP client library you like to request any personal information that your skill has permission to read. These are a few API paths you might find useful:

- Full name—/v2/accounts/~current/settings/Profile.name
- Given name—/v2/accounts/~current/settings/Profile.givenName
- Email address—/v2/accounts/~current/settings/Profile.email
- Phone/mobile number—/v2/accounts/~current/settings/Profile.mobileNumber
- Device address—/v1/devices/{deviceId}/settings/address
- Country and postal code—/v1/devices/{deviceId}/settings/address/countryAndPostalCode

For example, if you want to fetch the user's given name, you can create a full URL for the request like this:

```
const givenNameUrl = apiBaseUrl +
    '/v2/accounts/~current/settings/Profile.givenName';
```

That will work as long as you also pass the API access token in the request and as long as the token has been granted permission to access the user's given name. It's an OAuth2 Bearer token—more specifically, a JSON Web Token (JWT)[1]—so you'll need to pass it in the Authorization header.

---

1. https://jwt.io/

Putting it all together and using the node-fetch module,[2] you can fetch the user's given name with the following:

```
const apiBaseUrl = handlerInput.context.System.apiEndpoint;
const accessToken = handlerInput.context.System.apiAccessToken;
const givenNameUrl = apiBaseUrl +
    '/v2/accounts/~current/settings/Profile.givenName';

const givenName = await fetch(
    givenNameUrl,
    {
      method: 'GET',
      headers: {
        'Accept': 'application/json',
        'Authorization': 'Bearer ' + accessToken
      }
    }
);
```

If all of that seems daunting, then you may be delighted to know that ASK has made it much easier for you by providing a ready-to-use client for accessing user information. Instead of extracting the base URL and token from handlerInput, concatenating a path to the base URL, and using them with an HTTP library directly, you can use the UpsServiceClient which gives you easy access to user information more conveniently. The simplified code looks like this:

```
const upsClient = handlerInput
                        .serviceClientFactory.getUpsServiceClient();
const givenName = await upsClient.getProfileGivenName();
```

That's a lot easier! The serviceClientFactory property of handlerInput gives access to a handful of service clients that you might use in your skill's handler code. Among them is the UpsServiceClient, which provides (among other things) the user's given name via the getProfileGivenName() function. Notice that we need to apply the await keyword to the call to getProfileGivenName(). This is because getProfileGivenName() is performed asynchronously via a Javascript promise, but the handler needs to wait on the result of that promise before moving on.

You may be wondering why it's named UpsServiceClient. As it turns out, UpsServiceClient is a service client that aggregates access to two Alexa services in a single client, the Customer Preference Service and the Customer Settings Service. Since this client unifies those two services, Amazon named it the Unified Preference Service, or UPS as an acronym, thus the name UpsServiceClient for the client object.

---

2. https://github.com/node-fetch/node-fetch

In addition to the user's given name, the UpsServiceClient offers a half-dozen other bits of information that you might find useful:

- Full name—getProfileName()
- Email address—getProfileEmail()
- Phone/Mobile number—getProfileMobileNumber()
- Preferred unit of distance—getSystemDistanceUnits(deviceId)
- Preferred unit of temperature—getSystemTemperatureUnit(deviceId)
- Time zone—getSystemTimeZone(deviceId)

Notice that the last three items are device specific and require that the device ID be passed in as an argument. The device ID can be obtained from the handlerInput via the context.System.device.deviceId property.

In order to use the service client factory, we'll need to configure an API client in the skill builder. By default, the serviceClientFactory will be null and of no use in fetching a user's given name (or any other information for that matter). By configuring an API client in the skill builder, we'll have no trouble at all using serviceClientFactory to work with the unified preference service. The following snippet from index.js shows how to configure the default API client:

```
integration/starport-75-user-info/lambda/index.js
exports.handler = Alexa.SkillBuilders.custom()
    .addRequestHandlers(
    ...
        )
    .addErrorHandlers(
        StandardHandlers.ErrorHandler)
    .withApiClient(new Alexa.DefaultApiClient())
    .addRequestInterceptors(
        LocalisationRequestInterceptor)
    .lambda();
```

Now let's apply what we've learned about the service client in the context of the launch request handler's handle() function:

```
integration/starport-75-user-info/lambda/StandardHandlers.js
const LaunchRequestHandler = {
    canHandle(handlerInput) {
        const reqEnvelope = handlerInput.requestEnvelope;
        return Alexa.getRequestType(reqEnvelope) === 'LaunchRequest';
    },
    async handle(handlerInput) {
        const { serviceClientFactory, responseBuilder } = handlerInput;

        let speakOutput = handlerInput.t('WELCOME_MSG');

        try {
            const upsClient = serviceClientFactory.getUpsServiceClient();
```

```
        const givenName = await upsClient.getProfileGivenName();
        speakOutput = handlerInput.t('WELCOME_MSG_PERSONAL',
            {
                givenName: givenName
            });
    } catch (error) {
    }

    return responseBuilder
      .speak(speakOutput)
      .reprompt(speakOutput)
      .getResponse();
  }
};
```

This first thing you'll notice about this new implementation of handle() is that it extracts the responseBuilder and serviceClientFactory objects out of handlerInput to make them more conveniently available later in the function.

Next, the speakOutput variable is set to the default welcome message before attempting to fetch the user's given name. Assuming that we are able to obtain the user's given name, we pass it in an object to the t() function to be used in a more personal welcome message. The more personal "WELCOME_MSG _PERSONAL" message is defined in languageStrings.js as follows:

integration/starport-75-user-info/lambda/languageStrings.js
```
module.exports = {
    en: {
        translation: {
            ...
            WELCOME_MSG_PERSONAL: 'Welcome back to Star Port 75 Travel, ' +
                                  '{{givenName}}! How can I help you?',
            ...
        }
    }
}
```

The handle() function ends by returning the personal greeting in the response.

If an error is thrown while fetching the user's given name—most likely because the skill doesn't have permission—then the catch block does nothing, the generic greeting remains unchanged, and the handler returns the less personal greeting.

Ultimately, it's completely up to the user to decide whether or not to grant the skill permission to access their personal information. The skill shouldn't pester them too much about it unless the information is critical to the function of the skill. On the other hand, even if the desired information isn't critical, you'll want to offer some way to let the user know that your skill wants such permission. Let's see how to prompt the user for permission without being annoying about it.

Asking for Permission

In order for a user to grant your skill permission to access their personal information, they'll need to find your skill in the companion application on their mobile device or in the browser-based companion application.[3] However, because permission is granted out-of-band in a separate device, the user may not be aware that they should go to the companion application to give permission. Therefore, it might be a good idea to prompt them for permission.

Depending on how important the permission is to your skill's functionality, there are four approaches you can take:

- Not prompt the user at all. Let them discover the permissions on their own if and when they explore your skill in the companion application. (Not recommended)

- Passively prompt the user to grant permission in the companion application. They will see that your skill is asking for permission if they open the companion application and can decide whether or not to grant it.

- Actively prompt the user to grant permission in the companion application. This involves having Alexa explicitly ask the user to grant the skill permission via the companion application.

- Demand that permission be granted with a permissions consent card. The skill will not function fully until the user has granted permission in the companion application. (Only recommended if the skill cannot function without the required information.)

At this point, the Star Port 75 Travel skill is not prompting the user for permission in any way. That means, unless they open the companion application, navigate to the skill's configuration, and happen to notice that it is requesting permission to read their given name, they will probably never grant the skill permission and it will always greet them with the generic, impersonal greeting. Therefore, we should consider applying one of the other three approaches to gain permission from the user.

Regardless of which approach we choose, the technique is essentially the same. That is, along with the text we have Alexa speak in the response, we should include a permissions consent card in our response. Doing so involves

---

3.   https://alexa.amazon.com

calling the withAskForPermissionsConsentCard() method on the responseBuilder. For example, if we are explicitly asking the user to grant permission for reading the user's given name, then the handler method might build a response like this:

```
return responseBuilder
    .speak("Please open the Amazon Alexa app and grant me permission "
        + " to access your email address ")
    .withAskForPermissionsConsentCard(
      [
        'alexa::profile:given_name:read'
      ])
    .getResponse();
```

A card is a simple visual representation of a skill response that is displayed in the Alexa companion application on the user's mobile device or in the browser-based companion application website. We'll look at cards in more detail in Chapter 9, Complementing Responses with Cards, on page 213. But for now it's enough to know a permissions consent card is a special card that prompts the user to grant one or more permissions to a skill. When displayed in the iOS companion application, the card will look something like this:

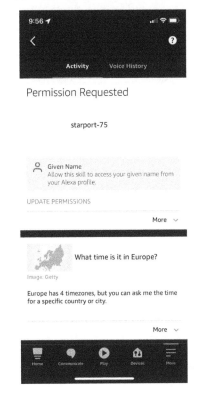

To grant permission, the user will click on the "MANAGE" button which should launch the Skill Permissions screen shown here:

From the skill permissions screen, they can check one or all permissions that they want to grant and click the "SAVE PERMISSIONS" button to submit their changes. Once permission is granted, the skill will be able to read the given name (or whatever information permission was granted for).

A permissions consent card can be returned in response to any request. It is usually best to avoid explicitly asking for permission from a user unless they're trying to use some functionality of the skill that requires that permission.

In the Star Port 75 Travel skill, permission to read the user's given name isn't strictly required. While we'd like to greet the user in a personal way, not being able to will in no way limit the ability of the skill to plan a trip through the solar system. Therefore, it's probably best if we send a permissions consent card in response to the launch request, but not have Alexa vocally request the permission. When the user opens their companion application, they may notice the card and grant the requested permission.

To passively request permission to read the user's given name, we'll add a few lines in the catch block of the launch request handler that calls withAskFor-PermissionsConsentCard():

integration/starport-75-user-info/lambda/StandardHandlers.js

```
try {
  const upsClient = serviceClientFactory.getUpsServiceClient();
  const givenName = await upsClient.getProfileGivenName();
  speakOutput = handlerInput.t('WELCOME_MSG_PERSONAL',
      {
          givenName: givenName
      });
} catch (error) {
➤ if (error.name === 'ServiceError' && error.statusCode == 403) {
➤   responseBuilder
➤     .withAskForPermissionsConsentCard([
➤         'alexa::profile:given_name:read'])
➤ } else {
➤   console.error("Error reading the given name: ", error);
➤ }
}
```

If the user has already granted permission, then the try block will have no problem reading the given name and setting the greeting message to a personal greeting. But if it fails and if the error is a service error indicating that the skill doesn't have permission to read the given name (for example, an HTTP 403 status code), then it will slip a permission consent card into the request. Any other error is simply logged—there's no reason to stop the skill or alert the user if it can't read the given name.

Trying It Out

We're now ready to kick the tires on this new personal greeting and permission consent card. First, deploy the skill. Then launch the skill on your device or in the developer console without granting permission to read the given name. For example using the ask dialog client, the interaction looks like this:

```
$ ask dialog --locale en-US
  User  > open star port seventy five
  Alexa > Welcome to Star Port 75 Travel. How can I help you?
```

As you can see, because the skill doesn't have permission to fetch the user's first name, it produces the generic greeting.

So far, so good. Now open the companion application on your mobile device or visit the companion application website in your web browser to see the permission consent card. Using the companion application, grant the requested permission and try again:

```
$ ask dialog --locale en-US
  User  >  open star port seventy five
  Alexa >  Welcome back to Star Port 75 Travel, Craig! How can I help you?
```

As you can see, the results are quite different. This time, it knows the user's first name and is able to produce a personal greeting.

We could stop here knowing that everything works as expected. But manual testing with ask dialog or an actual device isn't repeatable and prone to human error. Let's see how to write a proper automated test using BST.

Mocking and Testing Alexa Services

Under the covers, the getProfileGivenName() method makes an HTTP request to a REST endpoint provided by Amazon. Therefore, if we're going to test our new friendlier launch request handler, we're going to need a way to mock the request to that endpoint, so that it doesn't try to send a request to the actual endpoint. To do that, we're going to mix a network mocking library called Nock[4] with a feature of bst for filtering requests.

To start, we'll need to install Nock using npm install:

```
$ npm install --prefix=lambda --save-dev nock
```

We'll use Nock in a BST filter to mock the behavior of the given name endpoint. A BST filter[5] is a Javascript module that implements one or more functions that get a chance to review or even change a request sent by a test before it is handed off to the request handler. A filter can intercept test flow for the entire test suite, for a single test, for each request or response, or when the test or test suite ends. To test our new friendlier launch request handler, we're going to write a filter that intercepts requests before they make it to the request handler and uses Nock to mock the given name endpoint.

The filter will only be needed for testing, so we should create it in the test/unit folder and not the lambda folder, so that it won't be packed up and deployed with the rest of our skill code when we deploy the skill. The filter will be in a Javascript module named mock-given-name-filter.js that looks like this:

```
integration/starport-75-user-info/test/unit/mock-given-name-filter.js
const nock = require('nock');

module.exports = {
  onRequest: (test, requestEnvelope) => {
    const mockGivenName = test.testSuite.configuration.givenName;
    const TEST_API_ENDPOINT = 'https://api.amazonalexa.com';
```

4.　https://github.com/nock/nock
5.　https://read.bespoken.io/unit-testing/guide/#filtering-during-test

```
      requestEnvelope.context.System.apiEndpoint = TEST_API_ENDPOINT;
      requestEnvelope.context.System.apiAccessToken = 'API_ACCESS_TOKEN';
      if (mockGivenName) {
        nock(TEST_API_ENDPOINT)
            .get('/v2/accounts/~current/settings/Profile.givenName')
            .reply(200, `"${mockGivenName}"`);
      } else {
        nock(TEST_API_ENDPOINT)
            .get('/v2/accounts/~current/settings/Profile.givenName')
            .reply(403,
                {
                  "code":"ACCESS_DENIED",
                  "message":"Access denied with reason: FORBIDDEN"
                });
      }
    }
};
```

The module declares a single filter method, onRequest(), which will be invoked before every request handled by a skill's handler method when running tests with bst test. It is given a test object that includes details about the test that triggered the request, and a requestEnvelope object that is the request envelope object. We can use these objects in the filter to make decisions and even set or change details of the request before the request is sent to the handler.

The first thing this filter does is extract the value of a givenName property from the test suite's configuration. This is a custom test configuration property that we'll set in our test suite in a moment. The filter checks to see if it is set and, if so, will continue to setup the mock service. If givenName is not set, then it returns an error in the response with an HTTP 403 status as an indication that the skill doesn't have permission to make the request.

In a deployed skill, the base API URL is provided by the platform in the requestEnvelope as context.System.apiEndpoint. When running with bst test, however, the API endpoint is left undefined, so we'll need to set it in the request so that getProfileGivenName() will be able to form the request. Since we'll be mocking the service, the base URL we use in the test isn't important. Nevertheless, we'll set it to "https://api.amazonalexa.com"—the base URL used for skills in the North American region.

Similarly, we'll also need to provide the access token in the request by setting a value on requestEnvelope.context.System.apiAccessToken. Again, the actual value given here is unimportant, but it must be set or else a call to getProfileGivenName() won't even attempt to send a request to the service. In a deployed skill the token is a JWT, but for testing purposes, we'll just set it to "API_ACCESS_TOKEN".

Finally, the filter mocks the endpoint, specifying that if a GET request for
"/v2/accounts/~current/settings/Profile.givenName" is received, then it
should reply with an HTTP status of 200 and a JSON payload consisting of
a simple string, which is the name specified by the givenName property from
the test suite.

Now let's use the filter to test the launch request. As you'll recall from chapter
Chapter 2, Testing Alexa Skills, on page 31, we already have a test for the launch
request handler that asserts the proper output speech when there is no permission to fetch the given name. Here's an updated version of it that applies the
filter to assert that a permissions consent card is sent in the response:

integration/starport-75-user-info/test/unit/standard-handlers-unauthorized.test.yml
```
---
configuration:
  locales: en-US
  filter: mock-given-name-filter.js

---
- test: Launch request
- LaunchRequest:
  - prompt: Welcome to Star Port 75 Travel.
                        How can I help you?
  - response.card.type: AskForPermissionsConsent
```

In the test suite's configuration, we set the filter property to reference the filter
module we created. But since we don't set a givenName property, the filter will
reply to the service request with an HTTP 403 response. Therefore, the skill
response should have the default greeting along with a permissions consent
card, asserted by verifying that response.card.type is "AskForPermissionsConsent".

The more interesting test case is the one where the request for the user's
given name actually returns a value. To test that case, we can make a duplicate of the original test, tweaking it to specify the filter, the given name, and
to assert that the personal greeting is returned. Here's what that test case
will look like:

integration/starport-75-user-info/test/unit/standard-handlers-authorized.test.yml
```
---
configuration:
  locales: en-US
  filter: mock-given-name-filter.js
  givenName: Craig

---
- test: Launch request
- LaunchRequest:
  - prompt: Welcome back to Star Port 75 Travel, Craig! How can I help you?
```

In the test suite's configuration, we set the filter property to reference the filter module we created. And we set the givenName property with "Craig", a name we will expect to see in the personal greeting returned from the launch request. Finally, the test for the launch request asserts that the output speech contains the personal message with the expected name.

Let's run both test suites, standard-handlers-authorized.test.yml and standard-handlers-unauthorized.test.yml, and see how they fare:

```
$ bst test --jest.collectCoverage=false standard-handlers
BST: v2.6.0  Node: v17.6.0
PASS  test/standard-handlers-unauthorized.test.yml
 en-US
   Launch request
     ✓ LaunchRequest

PASS  test/standard-handlers-authorized.test.yml
 en-US
   Launch request
     ✓ LaunchRequest

Test Suites: 2 passed, 2 total
Tests:       2 passed, 2 total
Snapshots:   0 total
Time:        1.077s, estimated 2s
Ran all test suites.
```

It looks like everything passed! Now we have a repeatable test to ensure that our launch request handler will always send a personal greeting to users who have granted it permission to read their given name. And, if they haven't given permission, we have a test that will passively request permission with a permissions consent card.

Although Alexa offers some useful information via the unified preference service, it's not the only service you can use in your skills. We'll see a few more of Alexa's services in later chapters. But for now, let's think outside of the skill and see how to work external services using a technique called account linking.

Linking with External APIs

While some Alexa skills are self-contained, many are actually just a front-end user interface to a larger backend application. This is similar to how many React or Angular applications are just front-ends that integrate with a backend application.

The Star Port 75 Travel skill may provide a lot of functionality on its own, but ultimately it is a user interface to what could be a much larger backend travel planning system. Therefore, we will need to connect our skill to the API of a backend system that handles the actual booking.

Account linking is a means by which an Alexa skill can connect to an API on behalf of a user, using OAuth 2[6] for security between the skill and the API. It involves registering the skill as a client application with the backend API and configuring the skill with the OAuth 2 client details so that Alexa can conduct the authorization process to obtain permission for the skill to make requests to the API.

You do not need to fully understand OAuth 2 to take advantage of account linking, but it might be helpful for you to become familiar with a few of the essentials before diving into account linking.

Rather than take time away from working directly on our Alexa skill while we develop a backend booking system, let's use an existing API to act as a surrogate booking system. Specifically, we'll ask Google Calendar's API to stand in as our travel planning backend service. A travel event is, after all, largely concerned with dates on a calendar, so Google Calendar will do just fine for our needs. The first thing we'll need to do is configure client credentials for our skill to access the Google Calendar API.

Configuring the Skill as an OAuth 2 Client

As with any OAuth 2 client, an Alexa skill involved in account linking must be configured with details about how to obtain an access token from the remote service. Generally, these are the key pieces of information needed:

- Client ID—An identifier for the client

- Client Secret—A secret string that acts as a password for the client

- Authorization URL—A URL to a web page where the user will be prompted to grant permission to the client to access the user's data

- Access Token URL—A URL for a REST endpoint from which the client will obtain an access token that will be used on requests to the API

No matter what backend service you are connecting with, the client ID and secret are typically assigned when registering the client with the service. The authorization and access token URLs are usually available from the service's documentation and often displayed along with the client ID and secret.

6.　https://oauth.net/2/

For Google's Calendar API, you'll need to register your skill as a client application and create credentials. Follow Google's instructions for setting up an OAuth2 client for Google Calendar,[7] and you'll receive a client ID and secret that you can use to setup account linking for the Star Port 75 Travel skill.

To setup account linking, create a JSON file that describes the client details for the backend service. Because the file will contain client secrets and only be used temporarily, the name of the file doesn't matter and you shouldn't commit it to source code control. As for the contents of the file, it should look a little something like this:

```
{
  "accountLinkingRequest": {
    "clientId": "518123456789-00mcp70e9c.apps.googleusercontent.com",
    "clientSecret": "emqj0OpiRkfx5xKZ1RgqKRPi",
    "authorizationUrl": "https://accounts.google.com/o/oauth2/v2/auth",
    "accessTokenUrl": "https://www.googleapis.com/oauth2/v4/token",
    "scopes": [
      "https://www.googleapis.com/auth/calendar.events"
    ],
    "type": "AUTH_CODE",
    "accessTokenScheme": "HTTP_BASIC",
    "domains": [],
    "skipOnEnablement": true
  }
}
```

The actual client ID and secret shown here are fake; you shouldn't try to use them. But the authorization and access token URLs are the actual URLs you'll need. As for the rest of the properties, they are as follows:

- scopes—The scope of permission(s) that a connected skill will have. In this case, the scope allows the skill to create new events on the user's calendar.

- type—Alexa account linking supports two kinds of authorization: authorization code grant and implicit grant (see the OAuth 2 specification for details). In this case, we're using authorization code grant.

- accessTokenScheme—When requesting an access token, a client may pass its own credentials, either using HTTP Basic authentication or as form parameters. For the Google Calendar API, we're specifying HTTP Basic authentication of client credentials.

---

7. https://developers.google.com/calendar/auth

- domain—A list of domains from which the authorization page may fetch data from. For example, if the authorization page loads images from a domain different from that of the authorization URL, then you must specify that domain here.

- skipOnEnablement—When set to true, enables a skill for optional account linking. This allows a user to enable and use your skill without linking accounts first. If set to false, the user will be prompted to link their account upon enabling the skill.

Now that we've defined the account linking metadata, we can use it to enable account linking for our skill. We'll use Alexa's Skill Management API (SMAPI) to setup account linking. SMAPI is a REST API that offers several endpoints for managing the finer details of a skill. Although you can make requests to SMAPI using any HTTP client you like, the ask smapi command is the most convenient way to interact with SMAPI, offering several subcommands that map to the REST API's endpoints. The responses to all ask smapi subcommands are in JSON format.

For purposes of setting up account linking for our skill, we'll use the update-account-linking-info. Assuming that we saved the account linking metadata in a file named linking.json, we can enable account linking like this:

```
$ ask smapi update-account-linking-info \
  --skill-id=amzn1.ask.skill.28e3f37-2b4-4b5-849-bcf4f2e081 \
  --account-linking-request=file:linking.json
```

We must also specify the skill ID with --skill-id. The skill ID shown here is fake, so you'll need to use the actual skill ID for your skill. If you're not sure what the skill ID is, you can find it on the home page of the Alexa Developer Console[8] by clicking the "View Skill ID" link under the skill's name. Alternatively, if you have deployed the skill at least once, you can find it in the .ask/ask-states.json file, by searching for the skillId property:

```
$ more .ask/ask-states.json | grep "skillId"
      "skillId": "amzn1.ask.skill.28e3f37-2b4-4b5-849-bcf4f2e081",
```

Finally, we supply the account linking specification through the --account-linking-request parameter. This parameter can accept raw JSON or, if prefixed with "file:" as shown here, reference a JSON file.

Now that we have enabled account linking for our skill, we can delete the account linking metadata file. We won't be needing it again and because it contains our application's credentials, it shouldn't be checked into source

---

8.   https://developer.amazon.com/alexa/console/ask

code control. If we ever need to recreate it for any reason, we'll need to lookup the credentials from Google's developer site. But for now we're ready to start taking advantage of account linking to post our planned trips to our users' calendars.

Making Authorized Requests

When a user first uses our skill, they will not have yet linked their Google Calendar to the Star Port 75 Travel skill. That means that if they start to plan a trip, we won't be able to save their trip to their calendar. And since we're trying Google Calendar as a surrogate backend travel system, that means that our skill will not be able to do its job of actually booking the trip for the user. Therefore, we need to stop the user from planning a trip until they've linked their account.

To do that, we'll create a new intent handler for ScheduleTripIntent. But unlike our other intent handlers, this one will only be triggered if the user hasn't linked their Google Calendar yet. This new intent handler will be created in a file named ScheduleTripIntentHandler_Link.js and will look like this:

```
integration/starport-75-account-linking/lambda/ScheduleTripIntentHandler_Link.js
const Alexa = require('ask-sdk-core');

const ScheduleTripIntentHandler_Link = {
  canHandle(handlerInput) {
    return Alexa.getRequestType(handlerInput.requestEnvelope)
                                          === 'IntentRequest'
      && Alexa.getIntentName(handlerInput.requestEnvelope)
                                          === 'ScheduleTripIntent'
      && !Alexa.getAccountLinkingAccessToken(handlerInput.requestEnvelope);
  },
  handle(handlerInput) {
    const linkText = handlerInput.t('LINK_MSG');

    return handlerInput.responseBuilder
      .speak(linkText)
      .withLinkAccountCard()
      .getResponse();
  }
};

module.exports=ScheduleTripIntentHandler_Link;
```

As you can see, the canHandle() function is quite similar to the other two intent handlers we've written for ScheduleTripIntent. It checks that the request type is an intent request and that the intent name is ScheduleTripIntent. But then it also tried to fetch the account linking token from the request. If the user has linked their account, the account linking token should have a value; if not, then that means that this intent handler needs to go to work to prompt the user to link their Google Calendar to the skill.

The handle() function is rather simple. The most significant line in handle() is the call to the response builder's withLinkAccountCard() function. This simple line will cause Alexa to send an account linking card to the user's companion application. From there, the user may link their account before trying to plan a trip.

When creating the response, the handle() function also includes a message that Alexa will speak to the user, asking them to link their Google Calendar account to the skill. That message is defined in languageStrings.js with the key "LINK_MSG":

```
integration/starport-75-account-linking/lambda/languageStrings.js
module.exports = {
  en: {
    translation: {
      ...
      LINK_MSG: "You'll need to link the Star Port " +
                "75 Travel skill with your Google Calendar so " +
                "that I can schedule your trip. I've added a " +
                "card in the Alexa app to help you with that.",
      ...
    }
  }
}
```

Since this is a new intent handler, we'll need to remember to register it with the skill builder in index.js:

```
integration/starport-75-account-linking/lambda/index.js
const ScheduleTripIntentHandler_Link =
            require('./ScheduleTripIntentHandler_Link');

...

exports.handler = Alexa.SkillBuilders.custom()
    .addRequestHandlers(
        HelloWorldIntentHandler,
        ScheduleTripIntentHandler_Link,
        ScheduleTripIntentHandler,
        ScheduleTripIntentHandler_InProgress,
        StandardHandlers.LaunchRequestHandler,
        StandardHandlers.HelpIntentHandler,
        StandardHandlers.CancelAndStopIntentHandler,
        StandardHandlers.FallbackIntentHandler,
        StandardHandlers.SessionEndedRequestHandler,
        StandardHandlers.IntentReflectorHandler
        )
```

```
    .addErrorHandlers(
        StandardHandlers.ErrorHandler)
    .withApiClient(new Alexa.DefaultApiClient())
    .addRequestInterceptors(
        LocalisationRequestInterceptor)
    .lambda();
```

Notice that this new intent handler is registered before the other two intent handlers for ScheduleTripIntent. That's because it needs to consider the request before the others and make sure that the user has linked their account before even attempting to walk the user through the trip planning process.

Now, assuming that the user has linked their Google Calendar with our skill, we can use the account linking access token to make requests to the Google Calendar API. More specific to our needs, we can post a new calendar event that represents a planned trip. The following module encapsulates the action of saving a trip to the user's calendar:

integration/starport-75-account-linking/lambda/GoogleCalendarTripSaver.js
```
const Alexa = require('ask-sdk-core');
const fetch = require('node-fetch');

module.exports = {
  async saveTrip(handlerInput, destination, departureDate, returnDate) {
    const accessToken =
        Alexa.getAccountLinkingAccessToken(handlerInput.requestEnvelope);
    const payload = {
        summary: `Trip to ${destination}`,
        description: `Trip to ${destination}`,
        start: { 'date': departureDate },
        end: { 'date': addOneToDate(returnDate) }
    };

    await fetch(
      'https://www.googleapis.com/calendar/v3/calendars/primary/events',
      {
        method: 'POST',
        body: JSON.stringify(payload),
        headers: {
          'Accept': 'application/json',
          'Content-type': 'application/json',
          'Authorization': 'Bearer ' + accessToken
        }
      });
  }
};

function addOneToDate(yyyyMMddString){
    var asDate =  new Date(yyyyMMddString);
    asDate.setDate(asDate.getDate() + 1);
    return [ asDate.getFullYear(),
```

```
            ('0' + (asDate.getMonth() + 1)).slice(-2),
            ('0' + asDate.getDate()).slice(-2)]
        .join('-');
}
```

By keeping all of the Google Calendar specific code in this module, we avoid cluttering up the code in ScheduleTripIntentHandler.js. It will also make it easy to swap out for a more realistic travel system later if we decide to do so.

This module starts by calling Alexa.getAccountLinkingAccessToken() to fetch the account linking access token from the handlerInput. Because the ScheduleTripIntentHandler_Link intent handler should've prevented the user from getting this far without having linked their Google Calendar, we can rest assured that the access token is non-empty.

Next, the request payload is constructed. The only fields required are the calendar event's summary, description, and start and end dates. Because the end date is non-inclusive, the end property is set using a function defined lower in the module to add a day. This way the event will appear in the calendar, spanning from the start date up to and including the end date.

Finally, we use the node-fetch module to POST the payload to the Google Calendar API. Pay specific attention to the Authorization header, which we set to "Bearer" followed by the account linking access token. Without this header, the request will fail for lack of permission.

Notice that the call to fetch() is prefixed with await. That's because fetch() is performed asynchronously and returns a Javascript promise. Without await, it would return the promise immediately. The await keyword causes our code to wait for the request to complete before moving on. And, because we're using await, the saveTrip() function is itself marked as async to indicate that it performs an asynchronous function.

Since we're using the node-fetch module to make HTTP requests, we'll need to be sure to install it using npm:

```
$ npm install --prefix ./lambda node-fetch
```

The last thing we need to do is require the new GoogleCalendarTripSaver module in the ScheduleTripIntentHandler module and use it to save a completely defined trip:

integration/starport-75-account-linking/lambda/ScheduleTripIntentHandler.js
```
const Alexa = require('ask-sdk-core');
const TripSaver = require('./GoogleCalendarTripSaver');
const getResolvedSlotValue = require('./Helpers');
```

```javascript
const ScheduleTripIntentHandler = {
  canHandle(handlerInput) {
    return Alexa.getRequestType(
            handlerInput.requestEnvelope) === 'IntentRequest'
      && Alexa.getIntentName(
            handlerInput.requestEnvelope) === 'ScheduleTripIntent'
      && Alexa.getDialogState(handlerInput.requestEnvelope) === 'COMPLETED';
  },
  async handle(handlerInput) {
    const destination =
        getResolvedSlotValue(handlerInput.requestEnvelope, 'destination');

    const departureDate =
        Alexa.getSlotValue(handlerInput.requestEnvelope, 'departureDate');
    const returnDate =
        Alexa.getSlotValue(handlerInput.requestEnvelope, 'returnDate');

    await TripSaver.saveTrip(
        handlerInput, destination, departureDate, returnDate);

    const speakOutput = handlerInput.t('SCHEDULED_MSG',
        { destination: destination });
    return handlerInput.responseBuilder
      .speak(speakOutput)
      .withShouldEndSession(true)
      .getResponse();
  },
};
```
```javascript
module.exports=ScheduleTripIntentHandler;
```

Notice that the result of the require() call is assigned to a constant named Trip-Saver. Later, if we were to decide to replace Google Calendar with another backend module, we'd only need to change the module included. Everything else in ScheduleTripIntentHandler could remain the same.

Now that we have the new intent handler in place to check for an account linking access token, and a new module for saving a trip being used by ScheduleTripIntentHandler, it's time to take them out for a test drive.

Testing Account Linking

We're going to use ask dialog to try out our new account linking code. Since ask dialog enables us to interact with a deployed skill as if we were talking to an actual device, we'll first need to deploy the skill by committing it to AWS CodeCommit (if Alexa-hosted):

```
$ git add .
$ git commit -m "Add account linking"
$ git push
```

Or, if the skill is hosted in AWS Lambda, then deploy using ask deploy:

```
$ ask deploy
```

Now let's fire up ask dialog and try to plan a trip:

```
$ ask dialog --locale en-US
  User  >  open star port seventy five
  Alexa >  Welcome back to Star Port 75 Travel, Craig! How can I help you?
  User  >  plan a trip to Jupiter
  Alexa >  You'll need to link the Star Port 75 Travel skill with your
           Google Calendar so that I can schedule your trip. I've added
           a card in the Alexa app to help you with that.
  User  >
```

As you can see, everything started out fine. In fact, the skill even greeted the user by name using the code we wrote earlier in this chapter. But then when we asked to plan a trip to Jupiter, it stopped and asked us to link the skill with Google Calendar.

Meanwhile, in the companion application, the account linking card was displayed:

If we are going to successfully schedule a trip, then we'll need to link with Google Calendar. If we click the "LINK ACCOUNT" button, we'll be taken to Google's authorization page (by way of the Google login page if we're not already authenticated) and asked to permit Star Port 75 Travel access to our calendar. Once permitting access, we can try again:

```
$ ask dialog --locale en-US
  User  >  open star port seventy five
  Alexa >  Welcome to Star Port 75 Travel. How can I help you?
  User  >  plan a trip to Jupiter
  Alexa >  When do you want to depart?
  User  >  September 15th
  Alexa >  When do you want to return?
  User  >  September 20th
  Alexa >  I've got you down for a trip to Jupiter leaving on
           2019-09-15 and returning 2019-09-20. Is that correct?
  User  >  yes
  Alexa >  Enjoy your trip to Jupiter!
---------- Skill Session Ended ----------
  User  >
```

This time, it seems to have worked. Because we've linked accounts, the ScheduleTripIntentHandler_Link intent handler is satisfied and allows the trip planning flow to continue as normal. Once we've completed planning our trip to Jupiter, we should expect to see the trip on our calendar like this:

And now our trip to Jupiter is on the books. Time to start packing!

Unfortunately, it is very difficult to automatically test account linking in our skill. We can easily create a BST filter to set an account linking access token and use Nock to mock the request to Google's Calendar API. but because BST doesn't handle dialog flows, we'd also need to write even more filters to test each stage of the flow individually. So, for now, we'll just rely on manual testing with ask dialog to prove that account linking works in our skill.

Wrapping Up

Not all Alexa skills are self-contained applications. Much like many browser-based Javascript applications, Alexa skills might be a front end to one or more backend services.

Among the services offered by the Alexa platform is the unified preference service, a service that provides some essential information about the user and the settings for the device they are using. Using the unified preference service, your skill can fetch a user's name, phone number, or email address—as long as the user grants permission for the skill to do so by responding to a permissions consent card displayed in the Alexa companion application.

Similarly, Alexa skills can consume services hosted outside of themselves, including REST services that are secured with OAuth 2. Account linking enables a skill to prompt the user with an account linking card in the Alexa companion application, with which they can link their external account to their Alexa profile and allow a skill to perform operations in the external service on their behalf.

The Star Port 75 Travel skill is really starting to take shape. With what we applied in this chapter, it now knows its users by name and schedules their interplanetary excursions. It almost feels as if we could really use it to plan our next vacation to Mercury. (Be sure to pack lots of sunscreen!)

In the next chapter, we're going to do something a little different by learning how to apply the Speech Synthesis Markup Language (SSML) to change how Alexa speaks, adding a little personality to her responses and making her seem even less machine-like.

CHAPTER 6

Embellishing Response Speech

If decades of science fiction have taught us anything, it's that when computers or robots talk, they speak in a mechanical tone and staccato voice. Whether it's the robot from *Lost in Space* or the lovable robot from *Wall-E*, most talking machines in science fiction do not speak in natural human tones.

In the real world, however, Alexa has a much more human voice than her sci-fi counterparts. She speaks almost as naturally as most any person you'll meet (possibly better in some cases). Even so, despite her natural voice, Alexa doesn't often speak with a great deal of variation or emotion. Her tone, although human-like, is at best very matter-of-fact, and at worst might even betray her as a machine.

We want the users of our skills to feel comfortable when they speak with Alexa. The more human she seems the more likely that they will continue to use our skills and continue to rely on Alexa as a relatable assistant that can help them with whatever they need.

In this chapter, we're going to explore the Speech Synthesis Markup Language (SSML), using it to gain control over how Alexa speaks responses. We'll use SSML to change the tone, volume, and pitch of Alexa's voice, change how she pronounces words, and even completely change her voice altogether.

To start, let's have a look at a simple SSML example and see how to test it with Alexa's text-to-speech simulator.

Getting to Know SSML

SSML[1] is an XML-based markup language that describes not only what Alexa should say, but how she should say it. Much the same as how HTML describes

---

1. https://www.w3.org/TR/speech-synthesis11/

how text should appear on a webpage, SSML describes how text should sound when spoken. We will apply SSML in our skill's responses to make Alexa sound more natural, and expressive, and to add a little pizzazz.

Not All SSMLs Are the Same

As a W3C specification, SSML defines several elements for crafting voice responses for several voice assistants, including Google Assistant, Siri, and, of course, Alexa. But as with many specifications, each SSML implementation is a little different from the others and different from the specification. As such, not all SSML elements defined in the specification will work with Alexa. And Alexa adds a few custom elements that are not part of the specification.

Before we start adding SSML to our skill responses, let's have a look at a simple SSML document on its own, outside of the context of a skill:

```
<speak>
  Hello world!
</speak>
```

As you can see, the root element of any SSML document is the <speak> element. But you can leave it out in the text passed to speak() and it will be inferred.

Aside from the <speak> element, this example doesn't leverage SSML to alter how Alexa speaks. So let's make a small change to alter how Alexa will say "Hello world":

```
<speak>
  <amazon:effect name="whispered">Hello world</amazon:effect>!
</speak>
```

Now, instead of simply saying "Hello world" in her normal voice, Alexa will whisper the greeting, thanks to the <amazon:effect> element. But don't just assume that to be true; let's actually *hear* her say it using handy text-to-speech simulator provided in the Alexa Developer Console.

Testing SSML with the Text-to-Speech Simulator

The main subject of this chapter is using SSML to modify how responses returned from a skill will *sound*. Unfortunately, simply reading the words on the pages of this book can't compare with actually *hearing* what effect SSML will have on text. Although it's absolutely possible to write automated tests to assert that a skill's response contains an expected SSML response, there's no way to write a test to verify how it sounds.

The most important tool for testing SSML is your own ears. When Alexa speaks a response, you can deploy and interact with your skill, and listen and decide if it sounds the way you expected it and make adjustments if not. Even so, it'd be even better if there were a way to listen to how Alexa will speak an SSML response before you code it into your intent handler's response.

Fortunately, Amazon has provided a useful (and incredibly fun) tool to listen to snippets of SSML. Under the "Test" tab of the developer console, you may have noticed a sub-tab labeled "Voice & Tone". You can find it by opening any skill in the developer console, clicking on the "Test" tab at the top, and then clicking on "Voice & Tone" in the left-hand panel. You should see something like this:

On the left is Alexa's text-to-speech simulator. It provides a text editor, in which you can write or paste in SSML. Once you're ready to hear the results, make sure your volume is turned up and click the "Play" button at the bottom. Alexa will speak whatever the SSML in the text editor says she should speak.

For example, when you first open the text-to-speech simulator, it is already preloaded with this small bit of SSML:

```
<speak>
    I want to tell you a secret.
        <amazon:effect name="whispered">I am not a real human.
        </amazon:effect>.
    Can you believe it?
</speak>
```

If you leave this unchanged, then Alexa will say, in her normal voice, "I want to tell you a secret." Then, she will whisper, "I am not a real human." Finally, she will say, "Can you believe it?" in her normal voice.

Need More Space?

You may find the width of the editor in the text-to-speech simulator to be a bit cramped. Unfortunately, there's no built-in way to widen it by stretching the left-hand panel.

However, if you are using Chrome, you can install the Alexa Skills Kit Console Chrome Extension[a] and be able to resize the panel by dragging the divider that separates the left panel from the right panel. This extension also lets you save and replay frequently used utterances so that you don't have to type or say them when testing your skill.

a. https://github.com/jovotech/ask-console-chrome-extension

When it comes to testing SSML, there's no substitute for actually hearing the results. So you'll definitely want to have the text-to-speech simulator in reach as you work through the examples in this. Be warned, however: you might find yourself having so much fun tinkering with different SSML incantations in the tool that you'll lose hours of time.

We're going to use SSML to add some flair to the Star Port 75 Travel skill's responses. But before we inject any SSML into our skill's code, let's take a tour of some of the ways SSML can change how Alexa speaks. As we work through various SSML examples, use the text-to-speech simulator to try them out. We'll begin our tour with SSML elements that change the sound of Alexa's voice.

Changing Alexa's Voice

Variety is a hallmark of human speech. It's what keeps us from sounding robotic and canned. When asking a question, we might apply a different inflection than when making a statement. When we're excited or disappointed about something, we'll speak with a great deal of emotion, perhaps in a different rate or tone, as compared to our default speech patterns.

Likewise, if Alexa is to be accepted as anything more than a machine, it's important that her responses exhibit some of the same variety as in human speech, exhibiting variations in tone, rate, volume, excitement, and disappointment. With SSML we can adjust all of these things and even change Alexa's voice to a completely different voice.

Let's have a look at how to fine-tune how loudly, quickly, and at what tone Alexa speaks.

Adjusting Prosody

In linguistics, prosody is a term used to describe things such as tone, stress, and rhythm of speech. In SSML, prosody can be specified with the <prosody> tag and is specifically concerned with volume, rate, and pitch.

As an example of using the <prosody> tag, let's say you want Alexa to speak a word or phrase at a different volume than normal. The <prosody> tag's volume attribute can help, as shown in the following SSML snippet:

```
<speak>
    Welcome to <prosody volume="x-loud">Star Port 75 Travel</prosody>!
</speak>
```

The volume attribute accepts one of six predefined values, "x-loud", "loud", "medium", "soft", "x-soft", and "silent" (no sound whatsoever). While none of these values will result in a volume that is dramatically different from Alexa's normal volume, they do have a subtle effect on how loud she speaks.

You can also specify a relative volume that is either greater than or less than the current volume:

```
<speak>
    Welcome to <prosody volume="+6dB">Star Port 75 Travel</prosody>!
</speak>
```

In this case, the value "+6dB" is about twice the volume of the current volume. Similarly "-6dB" would be approximately half the volume of the current volume. Take care; volumes much greater than "+6dB" relative to the default volume might result in distortion in the response.

The <prosody> tag can also alter the rate at which Alexa speaks one or more words. For example, consider the following use of <prosody> to have her speak slower than normal:

```
<speak>
    Welcome to <prosody rate="x-slow">Star Port 75</prosody> Travel!
</speak>
```

If you were to paste this into the text-to-speech simulator, Alexa would speak most of the sentence at a normal rate, but would slow down significantly when saying, "Star Port 75."

Like the volume attribute, the rate attribute accepts a handful of predefined values, including "x-slow", "slow", "medium", "fast", and "x-fast". But you can also specify a relative value as a percentage of the current rate, where "100%" is equal to the current rate. For example, to have her speak "Star Port 75" twice as fast as normal, set the rate attribute to "200%":

```
<speak>
    Welcome to <prosody rate="200%">Star Port 75</prosody> Travel!
</speak>
```

On the other hand, if you want Alexa to slow down significantly when saying, "Star Port 75," you can set the rate to "20%", which is the minimum allowed value:

```
<speak>
    Welcome to <prosody rate="20%">Star Port 75</prosody> Travel!
</speak>
```

One other attribute of prosody that can be controlled is pitch. Pitch specifies how high or low Alexa's voice is when she speaks. For example, if you want her to speak in a rather low tone, you can set the pitch attribute to "x-low":

```
<speak>
    Welcome to <prosody pitch="x-low">Star Port 75</prosody> Travel!
</speak>
```

In addition to predefined pitch values—"x-low", "low", "medium", "high", and "x-high"—you can specify a relative pitch as a positive or negative percentage (where "+0%" is normal pitch):

```
<speak>
    Welcome to <prosody pitch="-33.3%">Star Port 75</prosody> Travel!
</speak>
```

In this case, setting pitch to "-33.3%" is the minimum allowed value and is equivalent to setting it to "x-low". Similarly, "+50%" is the maximum allowed value and is the same as setting pitch to "x-high".

You are welcome to mix and match volume, rate, and pitch as you see fit for some interesting effects. The following snippet of SSML, for instance, has Alexa saying "Star Port 75" in an amusingly low, slow, and loud voice:

```
<speak>
  Welcome to
  <prosody pitch="-33.3%"
           rate="20%"
           volume="x-loud">Star Port 75</prosody> Travel!
</speak>
```

You'll definitely want to paste this example into the text-to-speech simulator and give it a try. It should give you some idea of how to alter Alexa's voice to make her sound as if she may have had too much to drink.

While the <prosody> tag gives you near complete control over volume, rate, and pitch, these attributes are often used in combination to apply emphasis to a word or phrase. For simplicity's sake, the <emphasis> tag can be used to control rate and volume in a simpler way when emphasis is the desired outcome:

```
<speak>
  Welcome to
  <emphasis level="strong">Star Port 75</emphasis> Travel!
</speak>
```

Here, a strong emphasis is applied, resulting in a slower rate and increased volume, much as a parent might speak to a child when they're in trouble. On the other hand, setting level to "reduced" will have Alexa speak quicker and at a lower volume, much like a teenager might speak when telling their parent that they've wrecked the family car.

While prosody can add some dramatic effects to the words that Alexa speaks, it has its limits. Meanwhile, language is filled with brief words or phrases that express a great deal of emotion beyond what prosody can handle. Let's see how Alexa can speak with excitement and disappointment with interjections.

Adding Interjections

Imagine you are watching your favorite sports team compete in the championship game. The competition is down to the final moments and the score is tied. It's clear that the coach must put in his star players. They're the only ones who can pull out a win. Inexplicably, however, the coach calls in a rookie who hasn't seen any game time all season long. In response, you yell "Boo!" with a tone of judgmental negativity. As you continue to watch the game and the timer ticks down to the final seconds, the unseasoned rookie shocks everyone when they score, winning the game for the team! Everyone jumps to their feet and shouts "Yay!" enthusiastically.

Now, imagine that same scenario, only with the words "boo" and "yay" said in an emotionless, deadpan tone. If you can imagine it, you realize that those words, as insignificant as they may seem, carried a lot more value when they were said with emotion than when said without.

Certain words and phrases are expected to be said with excitement or disappointment. "Boo" and "yay" are two such words. "Holy smokes," "aw man," and "Great Scott" are a few more. These are interjections, usually used as an exclamation in speech, that just sound wrong when said flat and without emotion.

Although it is possible to have Alexa speak interjections without any special SSML handling, she'll say them in a matter-of-fact tone, without any emotion or expression. For example, try the following SSML in the text-to-speech simulator:

```
<speak>
  Great Scott!
</speak>
```

Despite the exclamation mark, Alexa will simply say the words without any feeling. But by applying SSML's <say-as> tag, we can liven up the phrase:

```
<speak>
  <say-as interpret-as="interjection">Great Scott!</say-as>
</speak>
```

The interpret-as attribute indicates that the contents of the <say-as> tag should be read as an interjection, more expressively than without the <say-as> tag.

It's important to understand that officially, there are only so many words and phrases that can be used as interjections. These are referred to as *speechcons* in Alexa's documentation.[2] Even so, you might find other phrases that sound good when wrapped with <say-as> as interjections, so feel free to experiment as much as you like.

Prosody and speechcons help give more character to Alexa's natural voice. But we can take it further. Let's see how to make Alexa speak with excitement or disappointment.

Applying Emotion

Imagine that you're developing a game skill and want to cheer on the user, congratulating them on doing well. If you were to have Alexa simply say, "Way to go! That was awesome!" it would come out kind of flat and emotionless. Similarly, if you want Alexa to console the player when things don't go well, you might have her say, "Aw, that's too bad." But without emotion, it will seem insincere.

As a computerized voice assistant, there's not much you can do to make Alexa actually feel excitement or disappointment. But with the <amazon:emotion> tag, you can make her sound as if she's excited or bummed out.

---

2.   https://developer.amazon.com/docs/custom-skills/speechcon-reference-interjections-english-us.html

Applying the <amazon:emotion> tag, we can have her congratulate the user like this:

```
<amazon:emotion name="excited" intensity="medium">
  Way to go! That was awesome!
</amazon:emotion>
```

Or, to express a sincere feeling of disappointment when things don't work out, you can use the <amazon:emotion> tag like this:

```
<amazon:emotion name="disappointed" intensity="medium">
  Ah, that's too bad.
</amazon:emotion>
```

In either case, the intensity attribute can be used to adjust how excited or disappointed Alexa speaks the text. If, after trying the <amazon:emotion> tag, you feel as if Alexa could be even more excited or disappointed (or perhaps less so), then you can adjust the intensity of the emotion by setting the intensity attribute to either "low", "medium", or "high".

Apply Domain-Specific Speech

Have you ever noticed how the anchorpersons on the news often speak in a peculiar tone that despite not sounding natural, is clearly recognizable as the "news voice"? Or how the radio DJ on the local Top 40 station speaks with an energetic voice that hypes up the music to be played?

While Alexa's native voice could be used to read news articles or announce the next hit song on the radio, it wouldn't express the same tone we've come to expect from newscasters and radio DJs.

To put Alexa into those roles, you can use the <amazon:domain> tag. This tag has a single name attribute that specifies the desired voice domain, either "news", "music", "long-form", "conversational", or "fun". Each of these domain-specific voice styles give a unique twist on how Alexa says the given text.

For example to have Alexa read a news article in a voice like that of a newscaster, you can use <amazon:domain> like this:

```
<amazon:domain name="news">
  This just in: A local resident reported that he was frightened by a
  mysterious bright light shining through the trees behind his home.
  Officers responded, relying on their extensive training, and
  determined that the offending light source was not an alien spacecraft
  as originally suspected, but was, in fact, the earth's moon.
</amazon:domain>
```

The "news" domain can be combined with the <voice> tag for a few of the alternate voices, including Matthew, Joanna, and Lupe. Joanna's voice sounds particularly good when reading the news clip:

```
<voice name="Joanna">
  <amazon:domain name="news">
    This just in: A local resident reported that he was frightened by a
    mysterious bright light shining through the trees behind his home.
    Officers responded, relying on their extensive training, and
    determined that the offending light source was not an alien spacecraft
    as originally suspected, but was, in fact, the earth's moon.
  </amazon:domain>
</voice>
```

Similarly, if you set the name attribute to "music", her tone will make her sound like she is announcing the next song on the local radio station's rush hour playlist:

```
<amazon:domain name="music">
  That was "Immigrant's Song" by Led Zeppelin. We've got songs by Ozzy
  Osbourne, Van Halen, and Scorpions coming up for your drive home. But
  first, here's "Highway Star" by Deep Purple on the Rockin' 98.1 FM.
</amazon:domain>
```

Unfortunately, the "music" domain is incompatible with the <voice> tag. If used together, the <amazon:domain> tag will have no effect.

Another domain that Alexa may speak in is the "long-form" domain. This is useful when she is reading a lengthy span of text, such as if she's reading a passage from a book. For example, here's how to use the "long-form" domain to read the first paragraph from Moby Dick:

```
<amazon:domain name="long-form">
  Call me Ishmael. Some years ago - never mind how long precisely - having
  little or no money in my purse, and nothing particular to interest
  me on shore, I thought I would sail about a little and see the
  watery part of the world. It is a way I have of driving off the
  spleen and regulating the circulation.
</amazon:domain>
```

As with the "music" domain, you can't combine <voice> and <amazon:domain> when the domain name is "long-form".

The "conversational" domain causes Alexa to speak in a relaxed voice, as if she's speaking with friends. Try the following SSML, both with and without the <amazon:domain> tag and see if you can hear the difference:

```
<voice name="Matthew">
  <amazon:domain name="conversational">
    Have you read any good books lately? I just finished a
```

```
        book about anti-gravity. I couldn't put it down.
    </amazon:domain>
</voice>
```

Per Amazon's documentation, the "conversational" domain must be used with either Matthew's or Joanna's voice. But even if you try it with Alexa's natural voice, there's still a noticeable difference.

There's one more domain that you can try. The "fun" domain causes Alexa to speak in a friendly and animated tone. It can be used like this:

```
<lang xml:lang="ja-JP">
  <amazon:domain name="fun">
    今日はこれまでで最高の日です！
  </amazon:domain>
</lang>
```

Unfortunately, the "fun" domain only works with Japanese skills. Even if you set the language to "ja-JP", if the skill's manifest does not designate this as a Japanese skill, then the <amazon:domain name="fun"> tag will have no effect. Also, the "fun" domain cannot be mixed with the <voice> tag.

All of the SSML tricks we've seen this far make subtle changes to Alexa's tone. Even so, maybe you'd rather your responses be in a completely different voice than Alexa's. Let's see how to swap out Alexa's voice for one of several alternate voices.

Switching to an Alternate Voice

In addition to Alexa, Amazon has several other voice-related projects, including an interesting one called Polly.[3] Polly employs machine learning to synthesize voices that sound very natural and realistic, including voices suited for a number of languages and voices with specific accents associated with a locale.

Using SSML's <voice> tag, we can tap into a select subset of Polly voices and use them in responses from our Alexa skills as a direct replacement for Alexa's voice.

For example, suppose that we would like our skill to greet users with the voice of a young boy. In that case, we can apply the voice of Justin, one of the Polly voices supported by Alexa:

```
<speak>
  <voice name="Justin">Welcome to Star Port 75 travel!</voice>
</speak>
```

---

3. https://aws.amazon.com/polly/

Similarly, we can use the voice of Amy to hear the greeting spoken as if by a British woman:

```
<speak>
  <voice name="Amy">Welcome to Star Port 75 travel!</voice>
</speak>
```

Not all Polly voices are supported by Alexa. There are, however, over two dozen voices, both female and male, spanning several languages and locales.[4] It's also important to know that the <voice> tag can be used in combination with all other SSML tags except <say-as> when using interjections.

Even if you're happy with how Alexa's voice sounds, you may need to adjust how she pronounces words. Let's look at a few ways to guide Alexa's pronunciation.

Adjusting Pronunciation

Among the most peculiar quirks of human language, especially in English, is how the same arrangement of letters can form a word that has different meaning or even pronunciation depending on context, locale, or merely the quirks of the person speaking. George and Ira Gershwin wrote a whole song that played on this concept, identifying several pairs of conflicting pronunciations of words like tomato, potato, neither, and pajamas.

Most of the time, Alexa is pretty good about figuring out the correct way of saying a word based on its context. For example, if she were to say, "The storm is getting close," the "s" in "close" would be a soft "s" sound. However, if she were to say, "You should close the windows," the "s" would have a harder sound, much like the sound of a "z."

On the other hand, if she were reciting the Gershwin tune, and said "You like tomato and I like tomato," then the whole charm of the song would be missed because she would say "tomato" exactly the same both times. In cases like this, a little SSML can help her say words differently than she would normally say them.

Let's start by looking at how to adjust Alexa's pronunciation of words based on locale-specific variation.

Using Locale-Specific Pronunciation

It's common for a word to be pronounced differently due to locale variations. For example, the word "route" is often pronounced differently in the United

---

4. https://developer.amazon.com/docs/custom-skills/speech-synthesis-markup-language-ssml-reference.html#voice

States than it is in other English-speaking countries. It is usually pronounced to rhyme with "cow" in the U.S. But, it is pronounced with a long "u" sound and sounds like "root" in Great Britain.

Normally, Alexa pronounces words using the locale that the user's device is configured with. Using the <lang> element in SSML, however, will direct Alexa to speak a word in a specific locale. For example, consider the following SSML example:

```
<speak>
  The most direct <lang xml:lang="en-US">route</lang> is to the left.
  Turn right if you want to take the scenic
  <lang xml:lang="en-GB">route</lang>.
</speak>
```

When Alexa reads this SSML, she will use the U.S. pronunciation in the first use of the word "route" and the British pronunciation when "route" is said the second time.

The <lang> tag isn't limited to single words and may, in fact, be used to wrap an entire response to apply a locale-specific pronunciation to all words in the response. Also, <lang> may be nested within other <lang> tags to override the outer tag's pronunciation. For example, the following SSML applies U.S. pronunciation to the entire text, overriding the second use of "tomato" with a British pronunciation:

```
<speak>
  <lang xml:lang="en-US">
  You like tomato. I like <lang xml:lang="en-GB">tomato</lang>.
  </lang>
</speak>
```

In the U.S. pronunciation, "tomato" has a long "a" sound. But, the "a" sounds like the word "awe" in the British pronunciation.

Applying Alternate Pronunciation

Even within a given locale, a word may have different meanings and with each meaning a different pronunciation. For example, consider the following SSML:

```
<speak>
  When they complimented her bow she took a bow.
</speak>
```

If you were to play this SSML in the text-to-speech simulator, Alexa would pronounce both instances of the word "bow" the same, with a long "o" sound.

However, the second "bow" actually rhymes with "cow" so it should be pronounced differently.

To fix this, we can use the <w> tag like this:

```
<speak>
  When they complimented her bow she took a
  <w role="amazon:SENSE_1">bow</w>.
</speak>
```

The <w> tag's role attribute indicates the role of the word in the sentence, as either a noun (amazon:NN), a simple verb (amazon:VB), a past participle (amazon:VBD), or as shown in this example, the non-default sense of the word (amazon:SENSE_1).

Many times, Alexa is able to figure out the correct pronunciation without the <w> tag, based on the context of its use. For example, Alexa will pronounce each use of the word "lead" different in the following SSML:

```
<speak>
  They got the lead out and took the lead.
</speak>
```

Therefore, before using the <w> tag, you should test your text in the text-to-speech simulator without the tag to see if Alexa will figure it out on her own.

Interpreting Numeric Phrases

Numbers can be especially tricky when it comes to how they should be pronounced. A 10-digit phone number, for example, could be misspoken as a cardinal number:

```
<speak>
  For technical support, give us a call at 5555933033.
</speak>
```

In this case Alexa will pronounce the phone number as "five billion, five hundred fifty five million, nine hundred thirty three thousand, thirty three." While that is technically correct, it's not how phone numbers are typically said out loud. To have her read the phone number as a phone number, you can either introduce dashes between the area code, exchange, and line number or you can use the <say-as> tag to indicate that this is a phone number:

```
<speak>
  For technical support, give us a call at
  <say-as interpret-as="telephone">5555933033</say-as>.
</speak>
```

By setting the interpret-as attribute to "telephone", we direct Alexa to say, "five five five, five nine three, three zero three three."

In addition to phone numbers, the <say-as> tag offers several other ways to interpret numbers, including the following valid values for the interpret-as attribute:

- ordinal—Interpret as an ordinal number (for example, "fifty-third").
- cardinal—Interpret as a cardinal number (for example, "fifty-three").
- digits—Say each digit individually, with no pauses.
- fraction—Speak the number as a fraction (for example, "one twentieth").
- unit—Speak the number and a unit of measure (for example, "12 mg" will be said as "12 milligrams").
- date—Speak the number as a date in YYYYMMDD format, or a format specified by the format attribute.
- time—Speak the number as a measurement of time (for example, 1'20" will be said as "one minute, twenty seconds").
- address - Interpret the number as a part of an address.

Setting interpret-as to "date" is especially interesting. Normally, Alexa is really good at interpreting dates without the <say-as> tag when they are presented in a format that suggests that a date. For example, "2019-11-12" and "11-12-2019" will both be interpreted automatically as dates by Alexa and spoken as "November twelfth twenty nineteen." The phrase "20191112", however, will be spoken as "twenty million one hundred ninety one thousand one hundred twelve." Using <say-as> we can coerce Alexa into speaking it as a date:

```
<say-as interpret-as="date">20191112</say-as>
```

You can also use question marks (?) as placeholders in a date for parts of a date you don't know or don't want Alexa to speak. For example, the following SSML snippet causes Alexa to say, "November twenty nineteen":

```
<say-as interpret-as="date">201911??</say-as>
```

Even when a date is formatted, it might be ambiguous as to what date format is to be used. For example, consider the following SSML excerpt:

```
<say-as interpret-as="date">1/10/71</say-as>
```

In this case, Alexa will say, "January tenth nineteen seventy one," because she will assume that the date format is month-day-year (or "mdy"). But what if the intention was for her to say, "October first nineteen seventy one"? In that case, you an use the format attribute to guide her in saying the date:

```
<say-as interpret-as="date" format="dmy">1/10/71</say-as>
```

Any combination of "m", "d", and "y" in the format attribute will help her understand the arrangement of date components. You can even specify only one or two components in format to have her speak the partial date:

```
<say-as interpret-as="date" format="dm">1/10/71</say-as>
```

Here, Alexa will say "October first" but will not speak the year.

Applying Phonetics

Although tags like <w> and <lang> are helpful in guiding Alexa to speak words with alternate pronunciation, they may still not offer the exact pronunciation we want.

For example, the seventh planet from the sun in our solar system, Uranus, has two commonly used pronunciations—one where the "a" makes the schwa sound (that odd upside-down "e" that makes an "uh" sound) and another where it has a long "a" sound. Although one of those pronunciations may sound a little crude, both are technically correct.[5] By default, Alexa uses the schwa pronunciation of "Uranus" and there's no obvious way to have her say it the other way. By applying phonetics, however, we can have her pronounce Uranus (or any other word, for that matter) in any way we like.

The <phoneme> tag can be wrapped around words to provide a very specific pronunciation, based on the values given in the alphabet and ph attributes. The alphabet attribute specifies the phonetic alphabet to use and may either be "ipa" (for International Phonetic Alphabet) or "x-sampa" (for the X-SAMPA alphabet). The ph attribute specifies the phonetic spelling of the word.

Applying the <phoneme> to the word "Uranus", we can specify that Alexa speak either form of the word:

```
<speak>
  You say <phoneme alphabet="ipa" ph="jʊərənəs">Uranus</phoneme>,
  I say <phoneme alphabet="ipa" ph="jʊreɪnəs">Uranus</phoneme>
</speak>
```

In this case, we're using the IPA alphabet in both cases. In the first case, she says "Uranus" with the schwa-pronunciation (which is also the default pronunciation). But in the second case, she says it with a long "a" sound.

Alternatively, you could use X-SAMPA spelling to achieve the same effect:

---

5. https://www.universetoday.com/18943/how-should-you-pronounce-uranus/

```
<speak>
  You say <phoneme alphabet="x-sampa" ph="jUr\@n@s">Uranus</phoneme>,
  I say <phoneme alphabet="x-sampa" ph="jUr\ein@s">Uranus</phoneme>
</speak>
```

Unless you're a linguistics fanatic, you'll probably find phonetic spelling and its strange set of characters incredibly difficult to grasp. Fortunately, you won't likely need to use phonetic spelling often in responses from your Alexa skills. And when you do, you can usually find the IPA spelling on the Wikipedia page for the word you need to spell and just copy-and-paste it into your SSML.

Inserting Breaks in Speech

When you listen to music, you'll notice that the instruments and voices are not constantly producing tones. There are short pauses between most notes and longer breaks every so often. In musical notation, those longer breaks when the instrument makes no sound are called rests. Rests are just as important in music as the times when the instruments are playing notes because they help establish the proper rhythm of the song.

When we speak, we place rests or brief pauses between words, phrases, and sentences. The breaks in speech help the listener understand what we're saying better, help establish mood or add a dramatic flair, or at very least keep us all from sounding like auctioneers.

Written word has similar pauses inferred by spaces and punctuation. A single space helps break words apart, commas add a brief pause between phrases, and periods add a longer pause between sentences. When we need an even more significant break in thought, a new paragraph—perhaps separated by a blank line—breaks the previous thought from the next thought.

In SSML, Alexa honors many of the punctuational pauses we use in written form and automatically interprets them as spoken pauses when she speaks. For example, consider the following SSML:

```
<speak>
  Welcome to Star Port 75 Travel, your out of this world travel agent.
  We specialize in travel to all points in the Earth's solar system.

  Where would you like to go?
</speak>
```

When Alexa speaks the text in that SSML document, she will put a brief pause between "Travel" and "your" and a longer pause between "agent" and "We". And, because there's a blank line between "system" and "Where", she'll pause even longer. In other words, she will speak those two sentences in much the same way that you might hear it in your head when you read it for yourself.

While Alexa honors punctuational pauses, you might want more explicit control over those breaks in speech. SSML offers three elements to help with that. The <s> element can be used around one or more words to identify the text as a sentence. And the <p> element is used much the same was to identify a chunk of text as a paragraph. Using these two elements, we can rewrite the SSML from before like this:

```
<speak>
  <p>
    <s>Welcome to Star Port 75 Travel, your source for out-of-this-world
      adventures</s>
    <s>We specialize in travel to all points in the Earth's solar system</s>
  </p>
  <p><s>Where would you like to go?</s></p>
</speak>
```

In most cases, it's easier to use punctuation and whitespace to identify breaks for paragraphs and sentences. But as we'll see later, inserting line breaks can be tricky in JavaScript and impossible when SSML is written in a YAML file such as a skill's interaction model. In those cases, the <p> and <s> tags are much easier to use.

You can also use the <break> element for more control over the length of the pause. For example, let's suppose you need a longer break than what <p> or <s> offer. Using the <break> tag, you can define a break several seconds long:

```
<speak>
  I'll give you a moment to decide.
  <break time="10s"/>
  What is your decision?
</speak>
```

In this example, Alexa will pause for 10 seconds after the first sentence before continuing to the next sentence. Notice that the value is qualified in units of seconds with "s". Although it's unusual to need finer-grained control, you may also choose to use "ms" to define the break's length in milliseconds:

```
<break time="10000ms"/>
```

The time attribute also accepts a handful of predefined values, including "none", "x-weak", "weak", "medium", "strong", and "x-strong". Both "none" and "x-weak" create no break whatsoever. Both "weak" and "medium" insert a break equivalent to the break created by a comma. Giving time a value of "strong" inserts a break that is the same as using a period or <s>. And "x-strong" is the equivalent of <p>.

We've seen several ways to alter how Alexa speaks. Now let's have a look at how SSML can be used to add sound effects and music.

Adding Sound Effects and Music

Although Alexa SSML is primarily concerned with voice and how Alexa speaks and utters words, nothing adds pizazz to a skill's response quite like a little music or a sound effect. In a trivia game skill, for instance, you might play a bell sound just before Alexa announces that the answer is correct, or a buzzer before she says that the answer is wrong. Or if you're building a skill for some well-known brand, you might launch the skill with a brief snippet of that brand's theme song.

SSML's <audio> tag can be used to add small sound clips to a response. And to help you get started, Amazon offers a vast library of ready-to-use sound effects for you to use in your skills.[6] Once you've found a sound clip you like, you can add it to your SSML by copying the URL into the src attribute of the <audio> tag like this:

```
<speak>
  Welcome to Star Port 75 Travel, your source for <audio src=
  "soundbank://soundlibrary/scifi/amzn_sfx_scifi_small_zoom_flyby_01"/>
  out-of-this world adventures.

  Where do you want to blast off to?
</speak>
```

In this particular example, the sound of a futuristic vehicle plays in the middle of the first sentence.

You can also play custom sounds with <audio>. The sounds must be encoded as MP3 files (MPEG version 2), no longer than 240 seconds, with a bit rate of 48kbps and a sample rate of 22050Hz, 24000Hz, or 16000Hz. You can use any audio tool, such as Audacity[7] or ffmpeg[8] to create the file. You'll also need to host your MP3 file at an HTTPS endpoint whose SSL certificate is signed by an Amazon-approved certificate authority. Amazon S3 is an easy option that meets this requirement.

---

6. https://developer.amazon.com/docs/custom-skills/ask-soundlibrary.html
7. https://www.audacityteam.org/
8. https://ffmpeg.org/

For example, suppose that Star Port 75 were a recognized brand and that their television and radio advertisements have resulted in a well-recognized musical branding. If we were hosting an MP3 of that musical branding on Amazon S3, then we could have Alexa play it at the start of the launch response like this:

```
<speak>
  <audio src="https://starport75.dev/audio/SP75.mp3"/>
  Welcome to Star Port 75 Travel, your source for <audio src=
  "soundbank://soundlibrary/scifi/amzn_sfx_scifi_small_zoom_flyby_01"/>
  out-of-this world adventures.

  Where do you want to blast off to?
</speak>
```

Notice that you can use multiple <audio> tags in a single SSML response, as long as the total length of all sound clips and music does not exceed 240 seconds.

You've probably had a lot of fun trying out the various SSML tags in the text-to-speech simulator. As much fun as that can be, at some point we need to inject the SSML we've crafted into the responses from our skill. So, for now, playtime is over and it's time to see how to use SSML in our skill code.

Applying SSML in Skill Responses

There are two places where you'll likely use SSML in a skill:

- In a request handler's response, through the response builder's speak() or reprompt() methods

- In the interaction model as one of the values defined in the prompts section

And even though automated tests can't possibly verify how SSML sounds, you'll probably want your tests to assert that the SSML returned is what you expect.

In the Star Port 75 skill, we're going to add SSML in the response from the launch handler to include some audio clips to the launch message. And for fun we'll also throw a few interjections into the validation prompts in our interaction model.

First, let's tweak the default response from the launch request handler to include SSML. The new "WELCOME_MSG" string in languageStrings.js will look like this:

```
ssml/starport-75/lambda/languageStrings.js
WELCOME_MSG:
'<speak>' +
'<p><audio src="https://starport75.dev/audio/SP75.mp3"/> ' +
'Welcome to Star Port 75 Travel, your source for <audio src= ' +
'"soundbank://soundlibrary/scifi/amzn_sfx_scifi_small_zoom_flyby_01"/> ' +
'out-of-this world adventures.</p> ' +
'<p>Where do you want to blast off to?</p> ' +
'</speak>',
```

As you can see, the SSML returned here is quite similar to the SSML we created when learning about the <audio> tag. The tricky part is including multiline
SSML as we define a JavaScript variable. Although JavaScript offers several
options for working with multiline text, it gets complicated when we try to
mirror that multiline value in our YAML-based BST tests. So instead of fum-
bling around with multiline string of SSML, we'll just assign a single line of
SSML to speakOutput, but split it across multiple lines of JavaScript with string
concatenation.

Meanwhile, in the test specification, we can assert that the launch request
returns that chunk of SSML with the following test:

```
ssml/starport-75/test/unit/launch-request-unauthorized.test.yml
---
configuration:
  locales: en-US
  filter: mock-given-name-filter.js

---
- test: Launch request
- LaunchRequest:
  - prompt:
      <speak><p>
      <audio src="https://thetalkingapp.s3.amazonaws.com/SP75.mp3"/>
      Welcome to Star Port 75 Travel, your source for <audio src=
      "soundbank://soundlibrary/scifi/amzn_sfx_scifi_small_zoom_flyby_01"/>
      out-of-this world adventures.</p>
      <p>Where do you want to blast off to?</p></speak>
  - response.card.type: AskForPermissionsConsent
```

Notice how the prompt property in the test specification appears to be a multiline
chunk of SSML. In reality, this is interpreted as a single line of SSML that
matches the SSML returned from the launch request handler. You can prove
it by running the tests:

```
$ bst test --jest.collectCoverage=false launch-request-unauthorized
BST: v2.6.0  Node: v17.6.0
Remember, you can always contact us at https://gitter.im/bespoken/bst.
 PASS  test/launch-request-unauthorized.yml
   en-US
     Launch request
       ✓ LaunchRequest (409ms)

Test Suites: 1 passed, 1 total
Tests:       1 passed, 1 total
Snapshots:   0 total
Time:        1.22s, estimated 2s
```

Much like JavaScript, YAML offers several ways of declaring multiline values, but it can be very difficult to write multiline SSML in a YAML test specification that matches multiline SSML expressed in JavaScript. It's often just easier to flatten the SSML to a single line string.

We can also use SSML in prompts defined in our skill's interaction model. For example, we can use the <say-as> tag in some of the validation prompts to liven them up a bit:

```
{
  "id": "Slot.Validation.UnknownDestination",
  "variations": [
    {
      "type": "SSML",
      "value": "<speak><say-as interpret-as="interjection">huh?</say-as>
        Star Port 75 Travel doesn't offer travel to {destination}.
        Where else would you like to go?</speak>"
    },
    {
      "type": "SSML",
      "value": "<speak><say-as interpret-as="interjection">d'oh!</say-as>
        {destination} sounds like a wonderful trip. Unfortunately, we
        don't serve that destination. Pick another destination.</speak>"
    }
  ]
}
```

Now, whenever a user tries to plan a trip to a destination that isn't one of the planets defined in the PLANETS type, Alexa will either begin her response confused by saying "Huh?" or reply in a manner not unlike Homer Simpson.

Don't Break JSON Strings

 It's very important to understand that although the preceding snippet of interaction model JSON appears to show multiple lines for the value property, it must be written as a single line. It was necessary to split those lines so that they'd fit within the margins of the printed page, but JSON does not support splitting values across multiple lines. When you write SSML into your skill's interaction model, be sure to write it into a single line without any line breaks.

Escaping Reserved Characters

One very important thing that you should be aware of when working with SSML is that SSML is an XML-based language. As such, certain characters have special meaning and are reserved. Specifically, the characters in the following table cannot be used in the content of an SSML without escaping them first:

Name	Character	Escape Code
Less than	<	<
Greater than	>	>
Ampersand	&	&
Quote	"	"
Apostrophe	'	'

For example, the following SSML is invalid due to three unescaped reserved characters:

```
<speak>
  When she entered the five & dime, she noted that the sale price was < the
  regular price, but still > than the discount store across town.
</speak>
```

By replacing the reserved characters with their escaped equivalents, we get the following valid SSML:

```
<speak>
  When she entered the five &amp; dime, she noted that the sale price was &lt;
  the regular price, but still &gt; than the discount store across town.
</speak>
```

This is especially important to realize when your skill injects values it receives from a database or some external service into the SSML. There's no way to trust that the data you receive won't include reserved characters, so you'll need to escape those values before applying them to SSML.

For example, suppose that instead of Star Port 75, you are creating a skill that locates nearby restaurants. In that case, you might have a string in lan-guageStrings.js with the following SSML:

```
FOUND_RESTAURANT: '<speak>You should have dinner at ' +
  '<audio src="soundbank://soundlibrary/musical/amzn_sfx_bell_timer_01"/>' +
  '{{restaurant}}</speak>',
```

Meanwhile, in your intent handler, you might have the following snippet to inject a found restaurant name into the text:

```
const restaurantName = ...; // get restaurant from database or some service
const speakOutput = handlerInput.t('FOUND_RESTAURANT',
    {restaurant: restaurantName});
```

This will work fine if the restaurant name is something like "Burger Barn". But suppose that the found restaurant's name is something like "Burgers & Brews". The resulting SSML will look like this:

```
<speak>
  You should have dinner at
  <audio src="soundbank://soundlibrary/musical/amzn_sfx_bell_timer_01"/>
  Burgers & Brews
</speak>
```

The ampersand makes the SSML invalid. To fix this, you can add the following function to your fulfillment code:

```
const escapeForSsml = (inString) => {
  return inString.replace(/&/g, '&amp;')
                 .replace(/</g, '&lt;')
                 .replace(/>/g, '&gt;')
                 .replace(/"/g, '&quot;')
                 .replace(/'/g, '&apos;');
};
```

And then, change the call to handlerInput.t() to call the escapeForSsml() function as it creates the SSML parameter object:

```
const restaurantName = ...; // get restaurant from database or some service
const speakOutput = handlerInput.t('FOUND_RESTAURANT',
    {restaurant: escapeForSsml(restaurantName)});
```

This will ensure that any special characters in the parameters are escaped before being injected into the SSML. The resulting SSML will now look like this:

```
<speak>
  You should have dinner at
  <audio src="soundbank://soundlibrary/musical/amzn_sfx_bell_timer_01"/>
  Burgers &amp; Brews
</speak>
```

SSML is a very powerful way to give character and a unique sound to Alexa's responses. But as we've seen, SSML markup can result in lengthy string values. Let's take a look at a way to simplify SSML markup by using Speech Markdown.

Writing Responses with Markdown

Speech Markdown[9] is a community-led project that makes it possible to write your speech responses using a variation of the popular Markdown[10] text-processing tool.

As a simple example of Speech Markdown's capabilities, consider the following SSML that has an interjection:

```
<speak>
  <say-as interpret-as="interjection">Great Scott!</say-as>
</speak>
```

Using Speech Markdown, this same response could be written like this:

```
(Great Scott!)[interjection]
```

While the SSML document may have been a bit more clear in purpose, the Speech Markdown snippet is a clear winner when it comes to brevity.

Aside from interjections, Speech Markdown offers full parity with all of SSML, including Alexa-specific tags such as <amazon:effect> and <amazon:emotion>. The Speech Markdown reference documentation[11] describes Speech Markdown in full detail. Even so, let's take a moment to explore some of the essentials of working with Speech Markdown.

---

9. https://www.speechmarkdown.org/
10. https://daringfireball.net/projects/markdown/
11. https://www.speechmarkdown.org/basics/

Speech Markdown Essentials

Modifying speech with Speech Markdown involves using elements that are either in standard format or short format. For example, suppose that you want to apply emphasis to a word in a sentence. Rather than use the SSML's <emphasis> tag, you can apply the Speech Markdown modifier like this:

```
This is (very)[emphasis:"strong"] important.
```

This is an example a Speech Markdown standard format element. Standard format elements take the form of some text in parenthesis, followed by one or more modifiers in square braces.

Some (but not all) modifiers have a corresponding short format. The emphasis modifier has a handful of short formats, depending on the strength of the emphasis desired. Strong emphasis, for example, uses two plus-signs on each side of the emphasized text like this:

```
This is ++very++ important.
```

Moderate emphasis uses only a single plus-sign on each side of the text:

```
This is +somewhat+ important.
```

On the other end of the spectrum, a minus-sign on each side of the text indicates reduced emphasis:

```
This -isn't very- important.
```

Another example of the short format is when applying breaks in the text. In SSML, you'd use the <break> tag to add a pause in the spoken text. Using SSML, you can use the break modifier to achieve the same thing:

```
I'll give you a moment to decide. [break:"10s"] What is your decision?
```

But the break element also offers a short format in which you can specify the pause time without the break keyword:

```
I'll give you a moment to decide. [10s] What is your decision?
```

But again, not all Speech Markdown elements have a short format. Nevertheless, all of Speech Markdown's elements are more concise than their SSML counterparts. And many of the elements can be combined in a single modifier block. For example, the following Speech Markdown shows how to combine the pitch, rate, and volume elements:

```
Welcome to (Star Port 75)[pitch:"x-low";rate:"x-slow";volume:"x-loud"] Travel.
```

It's important to understand, however, that although most of Speech Markdown's elements can be combined like this, the SSML they produce may not be supported by Alexa. The volume and emphasis elements, for example, can be combined in Speech Markdown like this:

```
Welcome to (Star Port 75)[volume:"x-low";emphasis:"strong"] Travel.
```

But the SSML that this Speech Markdown translates to is not supported by Alexa.

One other thing you can do with Speech Markdown modifiers is to apply them to a longer section of text, rather than a short excerpt. This is done by applying the modifier to a Markdown section marker (#) like this:

```
#[voice:"Joanna";newscaster]
This just in: A local resident reported that he was frightened by a
mysterious bright light shining through the trees behind his home.
Officers responded, relying on their extensive training, and
determined that the offending light source was not an alien spacecraft
as originally suspected, but was, in fact, the earth's moon.

#[voice:"Matthew"]
That was an interesting bit of news
```

Here, the voice and newscaster elements are used to enable Joanna's news voice. That setting remains in effect until the next section changes it to Matthew's regular voice. It translates to the following SSML:

```
<speak>
  <amazon:domain name="news">
    <voice name="Joanna">
      This just in: A local resident reported that he was frightened by a
      mysterious bright light shining through the trees behind his home.
      Officers responded, relying on their extensive training, and
      determined that the offending light source was not an alien spacecraft
      as originally suspected, but was, in fact, the earth's moon.
    </voice>
  </amazon:domain>
  <voice name="Matthew">
    That was an interesting bit of news
  </voice>
</speak>
```

With the basics of Speech Markdown out of the way, let's see how to apply it in the Star Port 75 skill.

Adding Speech Markdown to a Skill Project

Speech Markdown comes in the form of a JavaScript library. Much like any other library, adding Speech Markdown to your skill project starts by adding the library to the skill project:

```
$ npm install --prefix lambda speechmarkdown-js
```

This adds the library dependency to the skill's package.json file in the lambda directory. With the library in place, you can now use require() to bring it into the JavaScript code like this:

```
ssml/starport-75/lambda/index.js
const smd = require('speechmarkdown-js');
```

Here, Speech Markdown is being assigned to the smd constant, from which it can be used anywhere you need to convert Speech Markdown to SSML. For instance, the following snippet shows how the library is used:

```
const speechMarkdown = new smd.SpeechMarkdown({platform: 'amazon-alexa'});
const ssml = speechMarkdown.toSSML("(Hello)[volume:'x-soft'] ++World++!")
```

This creates a new instance of the Speech Markdown library targeting Alexa. From there, it calls toSSML(), passing in some Speech Markdown text, to generate the equivalent SSML.

You might be wondering about the platform property passed into the SpeechMarkdown constructor. Speech Markdown can be used to create SSML for other voice assistants. Although this book is focused on Alexa skill development, other voice assistants like Google Assistant and Samsung Bixby also support some variant of SSML and can take advantage of Speech Markdown.

When creating the SpeechMarkdown instance, you can set the platform property to specify the platform that SSML should be generated for. The valid options are "amazon-alexa", "google-assistant", "samsung-bixby", and "microsoft-azure". Speech Markdown will do its best to generate SSML fitting for the target platform, approximating tags that may not be supported on all platforms, or simply not applying any tags in many cases.

For example, given the following Speech Markdown text...

```
(Be very very quiet)[whisper]
```

...then the SSML emitted will be as follows when the target platform is "amazon-alexa":

```
<speak>
<amazon:effect name="whispered">Be very very quiet</amazon:effect>
</speak>
```

On the other hand, if platform is set to "google-assistant" or "samsung-bixby", then the resulting SSML looks like this:

```
<speak>
<prosody volume="x-soft" rate="slow">Be very very quiet</prosody>
</speak>
```

That's because neither Google Assistant nor Samsung Bixby support Alexa's <amazon:effect> tag. Speech Markdown instead produces SSML using the <prosody> tag to approximate the whisper effect.

You can also call the toText() function on the Speech Markdown instance to strip away all Speech Markdown and produce a plain-text response:

```
// results in "Hello World!"
const text = speechMarkdown.toText("(Hello)[volume:'x-soft'] ++World++!")
```

This can be useful when you are using Speech Markdown to produce SSML responses for Alexa to speak, but also need a non-SSML response when populating text on visual elements such as cards and Alexa Presentation Language documents (which we'll cover in Chapter 9, Complementing Responses with Cards, on page 213 and Chapter 10, Creating Visual Responses, on page 223).

While you could remember to call speechMarkdown.toSSML() in every one of your skill's request handlers, it's a lot easier to set up an interceptor that will do that for you. We already have a LocalisationRequestInterceptor that we added in Chapter 1, Alexa, Hello, on page 1 to enable us to work with response text from the languageStrings module using a t() function. The following modified version of that interceptor processes the text using Speech Markdown:

```
ssml/starport-75/lambda/index.js
const LocalisationRequestInterceptor = {
    process(handlerInput) {
        i18n.init({
            lng: Alexa.getLocale(handlerInput.requestEnvelope),
            resources: languageStrings
        }).then((t) => {
            handlerInput.t = (...args) => {
                const speech =
                    new smd.SpeechMarkdown({platform: 'amazon-alexa'});
                return speech.toSSML(t(...args));
            };
        });
    }
};
```

Now, all you need to do is modify the languageStrings module to use Speech Markdown instead of SSML. For example, the following excerpt from the languageStrings module shows how you might use Speech Markdown in the response for a launch request:

```
ssml/starport-75/lambda/languageStrings.js
WELCOME_MSG: "![['https://starport75.dev/audio/SP75.mp3'] " +
'Welcome to Star Port 75 Travel, your source for ' +
"![['soundbank://soundlibrary/scifi/amzn_sfx_scifi_small_zoom_flyby_01'] " +
'out-of-this-world adventures. ' +
'Where do you want to blast off to?',
```

Aside from replacing the previously more verbose SSML response that used SSML's <audio> tag to add sound effects to a response, the response given here uses the more succinct Speech Markdown ![] format to specify sound effects.

Wrapping Up

Although Alexa has a lovely and very natural voice, we can apply Speech Synthesis Markup Language (SSML) in our skill's responses to alter the way she speaks, pronounces words, and even change her voice to a different voice altogether.

Using the text-to-speech simulator in the Alexa developer console, we can try out snippets of SSML and hear how they will sound before adding them to our skill's fulfillment code. Once it's ready, we can inject the SSML as text to be returned in the response or as prompts in the interaction model. Applying this to the Star Port 75 Travel skill, we were able to add sound effects and music in the response to the launch request as well as spice up validation prompts with a few interjections (known as "speechcons" in Alexa terminology).

While SSML is very powerful, it can also be quite verbose. Speech Markdown offers a more terse approach, enabling you to write rich speech responses using a variant of the popular Markdown text processor to produce SSML responses.

SSML can do amazing things to add emotion, personality, sound effects, and customize how Alexa speaks. In the next chapter, we will take the sounds and speech produced by SSML and returned from Alexa skills to the next level by applying the Alexa Presentation Language for Audio to combine speech, sound, and music into layered and rich audio responses.

CHAPTER 7

Mixing Audio

Whether you realize it or not, a lot of your favorite movies and TV shows aren't recorded in a single consecutive session. A scene in a movie or a TV show may be one clip chosen by the producer from multiple takes. What's more, they probably aren't even captured in the same order that you view them. And most likely, sound effects and soundtrack music are mixed in later during the production process. And yet, once it has all been combined together into the final product, it is seamless and coherent.

When creating responses from a skill's request handlers, the easy thing to do is to just return plain-text for Alexa to speak. Or, if you want to add a little more flavor to the response, SSML can be used. But both of those options are limited on their own. You can't pick from multiple responses, mix it with background sounds and music, nor easily sequence different sounds and speech into a rich and immersive response.

In this chapter, we'll look at the Alexa Presentation Language for Audio (commonly referred to as APL-A), a way of combining sound and speech—both plain-text and SSML—into vivid and inviting audio to be played on a user's Alexa-enabled devices.

Introducing APL for Audio

APL-A is a JSON-based language that gives Alexa skill developers the power of a mixing board to create audio responses that are simply not possible with SSML alone. Using APL-A, you can play multiple sounds simultaneously or one after another. You can also choose from a selection of sounds to play randomly or based on model data provided to the APL-A templates. By applying filters, you can control the volume and length of audio to fit your needs.

APL-A defines only a handful of components and filters, which makes it relatively easy to learn. Despite its short list of components, however, when combined they provide a powerful toolset for creating virtually any audio response you can dream of.

We'll see how to use each of these components and filters and we'll use them to create some responses for the Star Port 75 Travel skill. To get started, however, let's take a look at the APL-A editor, a useful tool for authoring and testing APL-A templates in the developer console. We'll use the APL-A editor throughout this chapter to test our audio creations.

Authoring APL-A Templates

The best way to get started with APL-A is to use the APL-A authoring tool in the developer console. Go to your skill project in the developer console and click on "Multimodal Responses" in the left-hand menu. This will bring up the APL authoring tool where you can create APL-A templates and APL visual templates (which we'll learn more about in Chapter 10, Creating Visual Responses, on page 223:

If you've ever created and saved an APL-A template for the skill in the authoring tool before, you'll see a list of previously created APL-A templates. If this is to be your first APL-A template, however, you'll see "No Saved Audio

Responses" and be presented with a "Create Audio Response" button. Click the button to enter the APL-A editor, shown here.

On the left-hand side of the APL-A editor, you'll notice two buttons labeled "APLA" and "Data". Clicking these buttons will switch between the APL-A editor and a separate editor in which you can define some sample model data. Ultimately, the model data given to an APL-A template will be provided by a skill's request handler. But for purposes of testing an APL-A in the editor, you can setup some test data after clicking the "Data" button.

When you first create a new APL-A template, the editor will be pre-populated with a sample APL-A template that highlights many commonly used APL-A components. Feel free to explore the sample template, tweak it, and test it out by clicking the "Preview" button at the bottom. When you click the "Preview" button, it will be replaced with three buttons for refreshing the audio, playing the audio, and looping. If you make changes to the template, you'll need to click the refresh button for the new APL-A template to be processed before clicking the play button.

When you're ready to create your own custom APL-A template, delete all of the text in the editor and start with the following essential APL-A skeleton template:

```
{
  "type": "APLA",
  "version": "0.9",
  "mainTemplate": {
    "item": {

    }
  }
}
```

Aside from some template metadata, such as the type of document and version, the main thing to notice is the mainTemplate entry. This is where you'll define much of the custom sounds and speech you want included in your response. Inside of mainTemplate, you'll have either an item entry whose value is a single APL-A component, or an items entry whose value is an array of components.

If you choose to use items and specify multiple components in the array, know that only the first component in the array whose when clause evaluates to true will be evaluated. All others will be ignored. We'll see how to use when in section Conditionally Selecting Sounds, on page 174.

At this point, the item property in the barebones template is empty. Therefore, this template won't actually do anything. In fact, if you click the refresh button in the APL-A editor, you'll get an error saying that the document has no content to render. As we test-drive some of APL-A's components, we'll fill it in. Let's do that now, starting with some of the sound-making APL-A components.

Making a Sound

Ultimately, the goal of producing an APL-A template is to produce some speech or sounds that will be returned as part a skill response. For this purpose, APL-A offers two fundamental components that make sound—Speech and Audio—and a third component that intentionally doesn't make any sound. These components are:

- Speech—Causes Alexa to speak some given text or SSML

- Audio—Plays an sound effect from Alexa's soundbank or a custom MP3 from a given URL

- Silence—Pauses silently for a given duration of time

The Speech component works much like the speak() method on the response builder in a request handler, accepting either plain-text for Alexa to speak or SSML to customize how Alexa speaks. The Audio component, on the other hand, plays music or sound effects files, similar to SSML's <audio> tag.

The Silence component works much like SSML's <break> tag to pause for a specified amount of time. This can be used to space out sounds and speech in an APL-A template.

Let's see how these components work, starting with the Speech component.

Rendering Speech

In its simplest form, Speech can simply cause Alexa to say whatever text you provide. For example, here's a very simple APL-A template that causes Alexa to speak a welcome message:

```
{
  "type": "APLA",
  "version": "0.9",
  "mainTemplate": {
    "item": {
      "type": "Speech",
      "content": "Welcome to Star Port 75 Travel!"
    }
  }
}
```

The structure of the Speech element is typical of all APL-A components. It is a JSON object that has a type property to specify which APL-A component you want (in this case Speech). And it includes one or more other properties to specify how the component should work. In this case, the content property contains the text you want Alexa to speak.

Feel free to try out this template (and all others we create in this chapter) in the APL-A editor to see how it sounds.

While plain-text speech is easy enough, you might want to produce something a bit richer. In the previous chapter, we learned how to use SSML to embellish and alter the way that Alexa speaks. You can use SSML in the content, as shown in the following example:

```
{
  "type": "APLA",
  "version": "0.9",
  "mainTemplate": {
    "item": {
      "type": "Speech",
      "contentType": "SSML",
      "content":
        "<speak><say-as interpret-as='interjection'>Awesome!</say-as></speak>"
    }
  }
}
```

This uses the SSML <say-as> tag to say "Awesome" as an interjection, which gives it a bit more character than if it were in plain-text. But you can use any of SSML's tags in the content property, so long as you set the contentType property to "SSML". The contentType property is required for SSML, but is optional when sending plain-text. If you would rather be explicit about the content type when using plain-text, you can set it to "PlainText".

It's common to pass model data from the request handler to an APL-A template so that the spoken text dynamically includes content specific to the current task. For example, let's say that the user has just scheduled a trip to Jupiter. You wouldn't want to hard-code the content property to mention Jupiter, because that would not apply if another user plans a trip to Mars or some other destination.

Instead, you can put a placeholder expression in the APL-A template that will be filled with the destination. For example:

```
{
  "type": "APLA",
  "version": "0.9",
  "mainTemplate": {
    "parameters": [
      "payload"
    ],
    "item": {
      "type": "Speech",
      "content": "Enjoy your trip to ${payload.trip.destination}!"
    }
  }
}
```

Notice the addition of parameters under "mainTemplate". This is used to bind model data to the template. In this case, the entire model data object will be bound to the name "payload". This is then used in the content property whose value "${payload.trip.destination}" references the model data passed to APL-A from the request handler. We'll see how to do this in the request handler's response in section Returning APL-A Responses, on page 189. For now, though, if you want to try out this template in the APL-A editor, click on the "Data" button and add the following JSON in the Data editor:

```
{
  "trip": {
    "destination": "Jupiter"
  }
}
```

When the model data is bound to a parameter named payload, it will contain the entire model data object passed to the APL-A template. But you can also bind subsets of the model data object by specifying parameters whose names match the top-level properties of the model data. Given the trip model data described previously, you could write the APL-A template like this:

```
{
  "type": "APLA",
  "version": "0.9",
  "mainTemplate": {
    "parameters": [
      "trip"
    ],
    "item": {
      "type": "Speech",
      "content": "Enjoy your trip to ${trip.destination}!"
    }
  }
}
```

Notice that in this example only the trip property of the model data is bound to the APL-A template. As a consequence, the reference in the Speech component is now shortened to "${trip.destination}".

As you're trying this out, feel free to change the value of the destination property. When you do, be sure to refresh the audio, and then click the play button to see how APL-A inserts the value of the destination property into the produced audio.

Now let's look at APL-A's other sound-making component: Audio.

Playing Music and Sound Effects

As we saw in the previous chapter, using sound effects and music in a response adds some flair beyond just speech. APL-A's Audio component serves that purpose, as shown here:

```
{
  "type": "APLA",
  "version": "0.9",
  "mainTemplate": {
    "item": {
      "type": "Audio",
      "source":
          "soundbank://soundlibrary/scifi/amzn_sfx_scifi_small_zoom_flyby_01"
    }
  }
}
```

Here, the source property is set to reference one of the many sounds in the ASK sound library.

Although the ASK sound library has a vast selection of sound effects, you can also provide your own by supplying a URL to an MP3 file in the source property, as shown in the following APL-A template:

```
{
  "type": "APLA",
  "version": "0.9",
  "mainTemplate": {
    "item": {
      "type": "Audio",
      "source": "https://starport75.dev/audio/SP75.mp3"
    }
  }
}
```

It's important that the given URL is accessible by the fulfillment code that backs your Alexa skill. It also must be an HTTPS URL because HTTP URLs will not work.

If you're hosting your audio files in Amazon S3, then you'll either need to open up the security on the S3 bucket to allow access to the audio files or, even better, leave them locked down, but use a pre-signed S3 URL. To help you obtain a pre-signed URL, the util.js module that you got when initializing the skill project provides a getS3PreSignedUrl() function.

While you can't use the getS3PreSignedUrl() function in the APL-A template itself, you can call it from your fulfillment code and then pass the resulting URL as a parameter to the APL-A template.

We'll look at how to pass parameters from the fulfillment code in section Returning APL-A Responses, on page 189. But to give some idea of how you might pass a pre-signed S3 URL to the APL-A template, consider the following snippet of fulfillment code:

```
const Util = require('./util');

...

const LaunchRequestHandler = {
  canHandle(handlerInput) { ... },
  handle(handlerInput) {
    ...
```

```
    const mySoundUrl = Util.getS3PreSignedUrl('Media/sounds/my-sound.mp3');
    return responseBuilder
        .addDirective({
          "type": "Alexa.Presentation.APLA.RenderDocument",
          "document": {
            "type": "Link",
            "src": "doc://alexa/apla/documents/welcome"
          },
          "datasources": {
            "sounds": {
              "mySoundUrl": mySoundUrl
            }
          }
        })
      .getResponse()
  }
};
```

The URL returned from getS3PreSignedUrl() includes token information to get through the S3 bucket's security. But it is only valid for about one minute, which is plenty of time for the response to be sent to the device. Do not try to assign it to a module-level constant, though, because it will expire before it can be used.

You may be wondering why you'd use the Audio component instead of just using the Speech component to return SSML with the <audio> tag. While you could do that, it limits how the audio is presented in relation to speech and other sounds. As we'll see in section Mixing Sounds, on page 179, the Audio component can be mixed with Speech or other Audio components such that they play at the same time, effectively offering background audio.

But before we get to that, let's take a quick look at the silent partner of the Speech and Audio components: the Silence component.

Taking a Moment of Silence

If you know how to read music, you're probably familiar with rest notes. In sheet music, rest notes indicate when the instrument should make no sound for a defined period of time. Without rest notes, music would just run together and be unpleasant.

The same is true in audio responses from Alexa. Whether it be for dramatic effect or because you need to sync up one bit of audio with another, a moment of silence can be very useful.

We saw in the previous chapter how to use SSML's <break> tag to put a pause in an Alexa response. In APL-A, the Silence component meets that same purpose. Here's a snippet of APL-A (not a complete template) that shows how the Silence component can be used:

```
{
  "type": "Silence",
  "duration": 10000
}
```

The duration property specifies how long, in milliseconds, that the silence should last. In this case, the silence lasts 10 seconds.

The Silence component can't be used alone in an APL-A template. And, in fact, it doesn't make much sense to send a response in which Alexa doesn't say anything or play any sounds whatsoever. But where Silence shines is when you combine multiple sounds and speech in an APL-A template. So now that we've covered the sound-making (and silence-making) APL-A components, let's see how they can be combined in an APL-A template.

Combining Sounds

Most of the music you hear on the radio, television, or your favorite music streaming service is a carefully orchestrated mix of voices and instruments, not recorded live in one take, but recorded in separate sessions. It's not uncommon for the instrumentalists to record their tracks in the absence of each other and the vocalists. It's not until those tracks are mixed during production that the final product is created.

With APL-A, you get to sit at the mixing board and combine multiple sounds effects, musical pieces, and/or speech to produce a polished and professional sounding response. How you arrange the sounds is up to you. But APL-A provides you with three components for mixing sounds and speech:

- Sequencer—Plays one or more child components in the order specified

- Selector—Plays a single component from a list of child components, chosen either randomly or based on some condition

- Mixer—Plays one or more child components simultaneously

These components are commonly referred to as multi-child components, because while they do not make sounds themselves, they bring together one or more child components.

As we begin our exploration of APL-A's multi-child components, let's start with the most basic of the three: Sequencer.

Sequencing Audio

The Sequencer component's job is to play one or more child components, one after the other, in the order specified. For example, consider the following APL-A template that uses Sequencer to play some spoken text, followed by a sound effect:

```
{
  "type": "APLA",
  "version": "0.9",
  "mainTemplate": {
    "items": [
      {
        "type": "Sequencer",
        "items": [
          {
            "type": "Speech",
            "content": "To the guy who invented zero, thanks for nothing."
          },
          {
            "type": "Audio",
            "source":
              "soundbank://soundlibrary/musical/amzn_sfx_drum_comedy_01"
          }
        ]
      }
    ]
  }
}
```

The items property of Sequencer is used to specify the children components that are played one after another. In this case, the children are Speech and Audio components. But any of APL-A's components, including Silence, can be children of Sequencer. By placing Silence between two Audio or Speech components as children of Sequencer, you can get a brief pause, as shown in this sample APL-A template:

```
{
  "type": "APLA",
  "version": "0.9",
  "mainTemplate": {
    "items": [
      {
        "type": "Sequencer",
        "items": [
          {
            "type": "Speech",
            "content": "I'll give you a moment to decide."
          },
```

```
          {
            "type": "Silence",
            "duration": 10000
          },
          {
            "type": "Speech",
            "content": "What is your decision?"
          }
        ]
      }
    ]
  }
}
```

Another interesting way to use Sequencer is to loop through several entries in a data array. To illustrate how this works, consider the following APL-A template that lists the planets in our solar system:

```
{
  "type": "APLA",
  "version": "0.9",
  "mainTemplate": {
    "parameters": [
      "payload"
    ],
    "item": {
      "type": "Sequencer",
      "items": [
        {
          "type": "Speech",
          "content": "The planets in our solar system are"
        },
        {
          "type": "Sequencer",
          "item": {
            "type": "Speech",
            "content": "${index+1}. ${data}"
          },
          "data": "${payload.solarSystem.planets}"
        },
        {
          "type": "Speech",
          "content": "Yes. I consider Pluto to be a planet."
        }
      ]
    }
  }
}
```

In this example, there are two Sequencer components in play. The first and outermost Sequencer isn't much different from other Sequencer examples we've seen. It plays its children, one after another. But one of those children is another Sequencer that has only one Speech component as a child. But its data property is set to "${payload.solarSystem.planets}", which is expected to be an array of planet names.

When this template is rendered, the inner Sequencer will list off each of the entries in the data array, speaking its index (plus one, since the index is zero-based) and then the value of the entry.

To try this example template in the APL-A editor, open the data editor and add the following model data:

```
{
  "solarSystem": {
    "planets": [
        "Mercury",
        "Venus",
        "Earth",
        "Mars",
        "Jupiter",
        "Saturn",
        "Uranus",
        "Neptune",
        "Pluto"
    ]
  }
}
```

After refreshing the audio and clicking the play button, you should hear Alexa speak the following:

- The planets in our solar system are
- One. Mercury
- Two. Venus
- Three. Earth
- Four. Mars
- Five. Jupiter
- Six. Saturn
- Seven. Uranus
- Eight. Neptune
- Nine. Pluto
- Yes. I consider Pluto to be a planet.

Playing sounds in a sequence is just one way to combine them in an audio response. You may want to selectively play certain sounds instead of playing them all. For that, let's have a look at the Selector component.

Conditionally Selecting Sounds

The Selector component, like the Sequencer component, has one or more child components. But instead of playing them all one after another, the Selector component only plays one of its children, either randomly or based on some criteria.

This can be especially useful when you want Alexa to respond differently to a request so that it doesn't seem like she has canned responses. For example, after a user has scheduled a trip, you want Alexa to tell them to have a great time, but you may want her to say it in different ways each time. The following APL-A document uses Selector to randomly pick one of a few possible responses:

```
{
  "type": "APLA",
  "version": "0.9",
  "mainTemplate": {
    "parameters": [
      "payload"
    ],
    "items": [
      {
        "type": "Selector",
        "strategy": "randomItem",
        "items": [
          {
            "type": "Speech",
            "content": "Enjoy your trip to ${payload.trip.destination}!"
          },
          {
            "type": "Speech",
            "content": "Have a great time on ${payload.trip.destination}!"
          },
          {
            "type": "Speech",
            "content": "I think ${payload.trip.destination} will be amazing!"
          }
        ]
      }
    ]
  }
}
```

The strategy property is set to "randomItem" to specify that you want APL-A to randomly select an item from the items array. If you try this template in the APL-A editor, be sure to create the necessary model data in the data editor. The child item is chosen randomly each time you click the refresh button.

The "randomItem" strategy is just one of a few strategies supported by Selector. The default strategy is "normal", which picks the first child in the "items" array that matches some criteria. To illustrate how the "normal" strategy works, have a look at the following APL-A template:

```
{
  "type": "APLA",
  "version": "0.9",
  "mainTemplate": {
    "parameters": [
      "payload"
    ],
    "items": [
      {
        "type": "Selector",
        "items": [
          {
            "type": "Speech",
            "content": "Enjoy your trip to ${payload.trip.destination}!",
            "when": "${payload.trip.destination == 'Jupiter'}"
          },
          {
            "type": "Speech",
            "content": "Have a great time on ${payload.trip.destination}!",
            "when": "${payload.trip.destination == 'Mars'}"
          },
          {
            "type": "Speech",
            "content": "I think ${payload.trip.destination} will be great!"
          }
        ]
      }
    ]
  }
}
```

Here, the when property is applied to two of the three children. If the destination is Jupiter, then the first child will be chosen and Alexa will say, "Enjoy your trip to Jupiter!" She'll say, "Have a great time on Mars" if Mars is the destination. The third child has no when property, effectively making it the fallback choice for any destination that isn't Mars or Jupiter.

The when property can be used on any APL-A component, even when the component isn't a child of Selector. No matter where the when property is used, the component is conditionally rendered, depending on whether the expression given evaluates to true or false.

Another strategy you might apply is "randomData". The "randomData" strategy is similar to "randomItem", except that instead of randomly selecting a child component, a random entry from a collection of data items is chosen and made available to be used in the child component.

For example, suppose that you want Alexa to respond randomly the same as we did with "randomItem", but instead of having three distinct Speech components as children, you just want to swap out the adjective used to wish them a good trip. Here's an APL-A template that uses "randomData" to do that:

```
{
  "type": "APLA",
  "version": "0.9",
  "mainTemplate": {
    "parameters": [
      "payload"
    ],
    "items": [
      {
        "type": "Selector",
        "strategy": "randomData",
        "data": [
          {
            "article": "an",
            "adjective": "amazing"
          },
          {
            "article": "a",
            "adjective": "great"
          },
          {
            "article": "an",
            "adjective": "awesome"
          },
          {
            "article": "an",
            "adjective": "outstanding"
          },
          {
            "article": "a",
            "adjective": "stellar"
          }
        ],
        "items": [
```

```
      {
        "type": "Speech",
        "content": "Have ${data.article} ${data.adjective} time on
                    ${payload.trip.destination}!"
      }
    ]
  }
 ]
}
}
```

The data property lists a handful of possible adjectives that can be used to describe a trip, along with an article (either "a" or "an") to accompany the adjective. When the template is rendered, one of the data entries is chosen randomly and the article and adjective are inserted in place of "${data.article}" and "${data.adjective}" in the Speech element's content property. As a consquence, Alexa could say any one of the following responses for a trip to Saturn:

- Have an amazing trip to Saturn!
- Have a great trip to Saturn!
- Have an awesome trip to Saturn!
- Have an outstanding trip to Saturn!
- Have a stellar trip to Saturn!

Maybe you like how "randomData" works, but you still want the ability to have different sentence structures like what "randomItem" offers. In that case, you might want to use the "randomItemRandomData" strategy. The following APL-A template demonstrates how "randomItemRandomData" is used:

```
{
  "type": "APLA",
  "version": "0.9",
  "mainTemplate": {
    "parameters": [
      "payload"
    ],
    "items": [
      {
        "type": "Selector",
        "strategy": "randomItemRandomData",
        "data": [
          {
            "article": "an",
            "adjective": "amazing"
          },
```

```
        {
          "article": "a",
          "adjective": "great"
        },
        {
          "article": "an",
          "adjective": "awesome"
        },
        {
          "article": "an",
          "adjective": "outstanding"
        },
        {
          "article": "a",
          "adjective": "stellar"
        }
      ],
      "items": [
        {
          "type": "Speech",
          "content": "Have ${data.article} ${data.adjective} time on
                      ${payload.trip.destination}!"
        },
        {
          "type": "Speech",
          "content": "I hope your trip to ${payload.trip.destination}
                      is ${data.adjective}!"
        }
      ]
    }
  ]
}
}
```

Here, the data property has the same array of article/adjective pairs as before. But the items property has two possible sentence structures that could be used. Because we're using the "randomItemRandomData" strategy, both the data item and the child Speech component will be randomly chosen. Consequently, Alexa could speak any combination of sentence structure and adjective:

- Have an amazing trip to Saturn!
- Have a great trip to Saturn!
- Have an awesome trip to Saturn!
- Have an outstanding trip to Saturn!
- Have a stellar trip to Saturn!
- I hope your trip to Saturn is amazing!
- I hope your trip to Saturn is great!

- I hope your trip to Saturn is awesome!
- I hope your trip to Saturn is outstanding!
- I hope your trip to Saturn is stellar!

The Selector component is arguably one of the most useful of APL-A's multi-child components. Even if you don't need some of the power that other APL-A components offer, Selector will no doubt prove useful anytime you just want to make Alexa seem more human by having her speak a different random response.

But where Selector is perhaps the most useful multi-child component, the Mixer component may just be the most awesome. Let's have a look at how to use Mixer.

Mixing Sounds

The Mixer component does something that no other APL-A component or SSML markup can do: it plays two or more sounds simultaneously.

As an example of the Mixer component's power, imagine that you want Alexa to speak a welcome message while some sound effect plays in the background. The following APL-A template uses Mixer to do exactly that:

```
{
  "type": "APLA",
  "version": "0.9",
  "mainTemplate": {
    "items": [
      {
        "type": "Mixer",
        "items": [
        {
          "type": "Audio",
          "source":
          "soundbank://soundlibrary/musical/amzn_sfx_musical_drone_intro_02"
        },
        {
          "type": "Speech",
          "content": "Welcome to Star Port 75 Travel"
        }]
      }
    ]
  }
}
```

Just like other multi-child components, the child components are specified in the items property. But where Sequencer plays the children one at a time and

Selector plays only one child component, Mixer plays all of the children all together.

If you try this template in the APL-A editor, you'll hear Alexa welcoming you to Star Port 75 Travel along with a musical sound in the background. At least that's the intent. But the audio is a bit loud and at times drowns out the greeting being spoken. Fortunately, there's a way to adjust the volume of any component by using filters. Let's see how to use filters, including the Volume filter to make this example APL-A template sound a little better.

Applying Filters

APL-A provides a handful of filters that can be applied to any of APL-A's components to make adjustments to how they sound. The available filters include:

- Volume—Sets the audio volume. This is especially useful when two or more sounds are used with Mixer to set the volume lower for sounds intended to be in the background.

- FadeIn and FadeOut—Enables sounds to fade in and out rather than start or stop abruptly

- Repeat—Specifies how many times that an audio clip should repeat

- Trim—Starts or stops an audio clip at specified times

One or more filters can be applied to a component via the filters property. You'll probably find the filters most useful when applied to the Audio component, but they can be used on any of APL-A's components, including Speech or the multi-child components. Let's see how to apply filters, starting with the Volume filter.

Adjusting Volume

As we've seen (or heard) with the previous example, a sound that plays too loudly might overpower another sound playing concurrently when using the Mixer component. Or when using Sequencer, some child components may have a higher volume and feel out of place from sounds that are more subtle. These are the kinds of problems that the Volume filter was made to address.

The Volume filter lets you set the playback volume of any component, whether it be sound and speech components or one of the multi-child components. By default, the volume of a component is considered to be 100%, but using the Volume filter, you can adjust the volume relative to the component's full volume.

For example, to soften the volume on the sound clip in the previous example, we can use the Volume filter like this:

```
{
  "type": "APLA",
  "version": "0.9",
  "mainTemplate": {
    "items": [
      {
        "type": "Mixer",
        "items": [
        {
          "type": "Audio",
          "source":
          "soundbank://soundlibrary/musical/amzn_sfx_musical_drone_intro_02",
          "filters": [
            {
              "type": "Volume",
              "amount": "25%"
            }
          ]},
          {
            "type": "Speech",
            "content": "Welcome to Star Port 75 Travel"
          }
        ]
      }
    ]
  }
}
```

The Volume filter's amount property specifies how loud the sound should be played, relative to its default volume. In this case, we've asked that it be played at 25% of full volume. Meanwhile the Speech component doesn't have a Volume filter, so it plays at full volume.

The amount property can be set as a percentage or as a number. Either way, the value given in amount will be multiplied against the full volume to arrive at the volume that the sound should be played at. Thus, another way to specify 25% volume is to set amount to 0.25, as shown in this snippet:

```
"filters": [
  {
    "type": "Volume",
    "amount": 0.25
  }
]
```

You can also set "amount" to values greater than 1, resulting in the sound being played at a volume louder than full volume. For example, the following snippet shows how to play sound at 150% of full volume:

```
"filters": [
  {
    "type": "Volume",
    "amount": 1.5
  }
]
```

There is no upper limit on the amount property, though it's best to keep the number reasonably low. Extremely high values result in distorted sounds that may be unpleasant.

Fading Sound In and Out

Maybe you don't need to alter the volume for an entire time a sound or speech component is playing, but just need it to fade in at the beginning or fade out at the end. A sound clip that starts or ends abruptly may be jarring for the user. By using the FadeIn and FadeOut filters you can ease them into the sound, as shown here:

```
{
  "type": "APLA",
  "version": "0.9",
  "mainTemplate": {
    "items": [
      {
        "type": "Audio",
        "source":"soundbank://soundlibrary/weather/rain/rain_03",
        "filters": [
          {
            "type": "FadeIn",
            "duration": 3000
          },
          {
            "type": "FadeOut",
            "duration": 3000
          }
        ]
      }
    ]
  }
}
```

The sound effect chosen here is almost eight seconds long and starts and stops abruptly without the FadeIn and FadeOut filters. But with a three-second fade-in and fade-out, specified by the duration property, the sound clip is easier on the ears.

Trimming Audio

Sometimes an audio file may be too long for your needs. Or maybe you only need a small section of the audio from the middle. Using the Trim filter, you can cut an audio clip down to just the bit you need.

For example, the sound effect used in the following template is 9.14 seconds long. If you only need five seconds of audio, then you can use the Trim filter like this:

```
{
  "type": "APLA",
  "version": "0.9",
  "mainTemplate": {
    "items": [
      {
        "type": "Audio",
        "source":
          "soundbank://soundlibrary/backgrounds_ambience/traffic/traffic_06",
        "filters": [
          {
            "type": "Trim",
            "end": 5000
          }
        ]
      }
    ]
  }
}
```

By setting the filter's end property to 5000, you are asking that the sound should play from the beginning and stop playing after 5000 milliseconds, or five seconds.

Now let's say that you don't want the first two seconds of audio, but still want a five-second sound. Then you can use the start and end properties together like this:

```
{
  "type": "APLA",
  "version": "0.9",
  "mainTemplate": {
    "items": [
      {
        "type": "Audio",
```

```
        "source":
          "soundbank://soundlibrary/backgrounds_ambience/traffic/traffic_06",
        "filters": [
            {
                "type": "Trim",
                "start": "2000",
                "end": 7000
            }
        ]
      }
    ]
  }
}
```

This combination of start and end trim off the first two seconds of audio, plays the next five seconds, and then stops playing at the seven-second mark of the original audio.

Repeating Sounds

Trimming sounds to make them shorter is easy enough. But what if you need a sound to be longer? The Repeat filter can play a sound (or even spoken text) on repeat. It is especially effective when the sound is used as ambient background sound.

For example, let's say you want to use the sound of rain in your skill. The ASK sound library has several rain sounds, including soundbank://soundlibrary/nature/amzn_sfx_rain_on_roof_01, which sounds exactly like what you need. The only problem is that it is only 2.15 seconds long and you need it to be at least 20 seconds long. Using the Repeat filter, you can extend it like this:

```
{
  "type": "APLA",
  "version": "0.9",
  "mainTemplate": {
    "items": [
      {
        "type": "Audio",
        "source": "soundbank://soundlibrary/nature/amzn_sfx_rain_on_roof_01",
        "filters": [
            {
                "type": "Repeat",
                "repeatCount": 9
            }
        ]
      }
    ]
  }
}
```

The repeatCount property specifies how many times the sound should repeat in addition to the first time. By setting it to 9, the sound will be played 10 times, totalling 21.5 seconds. If you test this in the APL-A editor, however, you may notice that although the repeated sound clip is long enough, the audio drops out approximately every 2.15 seconds between each repeated iteration. That's because the sound has built-in fade-in and fade-out.

To fix that, we'll need to do some clever mixing of Repeat with Trim, as show in the following APL-A template:

```
{
  "type": "APLA",
  "version": "0.9",
  "mainTemplate": {
    "items": [
      {
        "type": "Audio",
        "source": "soundbank://soundlibrary/nature/amzn_sfx_rain_on_roof_01",
        "filters": [
          {
            "type": "Trim",
            "start": 500,
            "end": 1900
          },
          {
            "type": "Repeat",
            "repeatCount": 14
          }
        ]
      }
    ]
  }
}
```

Here, the Trim filter is used to cut the first 500 milliseconds and the last 215 milliseconds off of the source clip. That leaves 1.4 seconds that, when repeated 14 times gives 21 seconds of continuous rain sounds with no dropouts.

Note that it's important that the Trim filter come before the Repeat filter, so that it gets applied first. If Repeat comes before Trim, then the longer repeated sound will be what is trimmed, resuling in a short 1.4-second sound clip.

One challenge you may encounter when deciding how long a sound should be comes when you use the Mixer component to put a sound in the background of some spoken text. Precisely matching the length of the repeated audio clip with the length of the spoken text can be challenging. And even if you get it right, you'll need to readjust should you change what Alexa is speaking.

But this becomes less challenging by setting repeatCount to -1 and using the duration property on the Audio component that plays the background sound, as shown in the following APL-A template:

```
{
  "type": "APLA",
  "version": "0.9",
  "mainTemplate": {
    "item": {
      "type": "Mixer",
      "items": [
        {
          "type": "Audio",
          "source":
              "soundbank://soundlibrary/nature/amzn_sfx_rain_on_roof_01",
          "filters": [
            {
              "type": "Trim",
              "start": 500,
              "end": 1900
            },
            {
              "type": "Repeat",
              "repeatCount": -1
            },
            {
              "type": "Volume",
              "amount": 0.5
            }
          ],
          "duration": "trimToParent"
        },
        {
          "type": "Speech",
          "content": "Today's forecast calls for buckets of rain"
        }
      ]
    }
  }
}
```

When repeatCount is set to -1, the audio will repeat infinitely (or up to the maximum content length). This is much longer than how long it takes for Alexa to say, "Today's forecast calls for buckets of rain." To trim it back down to the length of the audio produced by the Speech component, the "duration" has been set to "trimToParent". This automatically trims the sound produced by Audio to be no longer than the longest child of the Mixer component. Now, no matter what text is spoken as a result of the Speech component, the length of rain sounds will match perfectly.

Now that we've seen how to create all kinds of sounds and speech, mix them, and apply filters to them, let's see how we can package them in custom components that can be reused anytime we need them.

Defining Custom Components

What if you want to reuse that same arrangement of rain sounds and filters over and over for several different excerpts of spoken text. While you could copy-and-paste the APL-A and tweak the content property of the Speech component, a much cleaner option is to capture multiple components into a single, easy-to-use custom component.

The following APL-A template defines a custom RainyDayTalk component that makes it really easy to put rain sounds in the background of anything Alexa may say:

```
{
  "type": "APLA",
  "version": "0.9",
  "compositions": {
    "RainyDayTalk": {
      "parameters": [
        {
          "name": "speechContent",
          "type": "string"
        }
      ],
      "item": {
        "type": "Mixer",
        "items": [
          {
            "type": "Audio",
            "source":
              "soundbank://soundlibrary/nature/amzn_sfx_rain_on_roof_01",
            "filters": [
              {
                "type": "Trim",
                "start": 500,
                "end": 1900
              },
              {
                "type": "Repeat",
                "repeatCount": 8
              },
```

```
          {
            "type": "Volume",
            "amount": 0.5
          }
        ],
        "duration": "trimToParent"
      },
      {
        "type": "Speech",
        "content": "${speechContent}"
      }
    ]
  }
},
"mainTemplate": {
  "item": {
    "type": "RainyDayTalk",
    "speechContent": "Today's forecast calls for a little bit of rain."
  }
}
}
```

The compositions property is where custom components are defined. In this example, there is only one custom component, the RainyDayTalk component. It has all of the Audio and Speech components that our previous example employed, along with the filters we used to make the rain sounds sound good in the background. But instead of hard-coding the spoken text, the RainyDayTalk references a "${speechContent}" parameter, which could contain any text that we want to put into it when using RainyDayTalk.

Meanwhile, the item property of mainTemplate references a single component of type RainyDayTalk, whose speechContent specifies the text we want Alexa to speak while the rain pours in the background.

Unfortunately, there currently isn't a way to define custom components external to an APL-A template and then reuse the component across multiple templates. But the Alexa team has an item in their backlog to enable this, so hopefully it will be possible soon.

We've seen many ways of using APL-A components and filters to mix sound and speech into custom arrangements. And we've used the APL-A editor to test them and hear how they sound. But ultimately, the goal of creating APL-A templates is to return them as the result of a skill's request handler. Let's use what we've learned so far about APL-A to create a response from the Star Port 75 Travel skill.

Returning APL-A Responses

Up until this point, anytime we want Alexa to speak anything to the user in response to a request, we have used the speak() function on the response builder, like this:

```
return handlerInput.responseBuilder
    .speak("Hello world!")
    .getResponse();
```

But now we're going to ask Alexa to send back audio rendered from an APL-A template, so we'll need to do something a little different. Instead of calling speak(), we'll return a directive that tells Alexa to send audio from a given template. The code to build your response builder will change to look something like this:

```
return handlerInput.responseBuilder
    .addDirective({
        "type": "Alexa.Presentation.APLA.RenderDocument",
        "document": {
          // APL-A document goes here ...
        },
    })
    .getResponse();
```

The addDirective() function sends a directive, given as a function parameter, to the user's device. A directive can be thought of as a lower-level API for interacting with an Alexa-enabled device in order to control the device in some way or request state from the device. In this case, the directive sent is Alexa.Presentation.APLA.RenderDocument, which causes an APL-A template to be rendered as audio.

When sending APL-A via addDirective(), the audio produced from the APL-A template plays immediately in response to the handled intent. But you can also send APL-A as a reprompt to be played if the user doesn't respond to a question asked by Alexa. To send APL-A as a reprompt, sent it via addDirectiveToReprompt() like this:

```
return handlerInput.responseBuilder
    .addDirective({
        "type": "Alexa.Presentation.APLA.RenderDocument",
        "document": {
          // APL-A document goes here ...
        },
    })
    .addDirectiveToReprompt({
        "type": "Alexa.Presentation.APLA.RenderDocument",
        "document": {
```

```
        // Reprompt APL-A document goes here ...
    },
})
.getResponse();
```

Regarding the Newness of APL-A Reprompts...

The ability to send APL-A as a reprompt is a relatively new feature. In fact, the addDi-rectiveToReprompt() function isn't even available in older versions of the ASK SDK. If you want to take advantage of this feature, you'll want to be sure that the lambda/package.json file refers to ask-sdk-core version 2.11.0 or higher.

The document property of the directive specifies the APL-A template you want rendered. How you fill in that property will vary slightly based on where you want the APL-A template to reside.

As you were working in the APL-A editor, you no doubt noticed the floppy-disc and download icons in the upper right corner. These icons offer two ways of saving your APL-A template:

- The floppy-disc icon saves the template in the APL-A editor. This is known as a "saved template". This allows you to come back and work on the same template later. But it also makes it possible to reference your template when returning a response from the skill's request handler.

- The download icon downloads the APL-A document to your local filesystem. From there, you can copy the JSON file into your skill project and reference it from there when returning a response from the skill's request handler.

Either option is valid and offers its own set of benefits. As you make your decision, consider the following pros and cons of each option:

- If you save the template in the APL-A editor using the floppy-disc icon, then you'll enjoy a more streamlined way of editing and deploying the template directly in the editor. But you'll be sacrificing the ability to manage it in a version control system.

- If you choose to download the template to your local filesystem, you'll be able to save the template and manage it in the same version control system alongside the rest of your skill's code. But every time you edit the template, you'll need to download the freshest version and copy it over the previous version before deploying your skill.

Once you've decided which option you'll use to save your APL-A template, you'll need to edit the request handler in your skill to return the directive that references that skill. We'll start by seeing how to return a saved template from a request handler.

Returning Saved Templates

If you chose to use a saved template (for example, by clicking the floppy-disc icon in the editor), then filling in the directive's document property is as simple as adding two sub-properties: type to tell the directive that you'll be referencing the APL-A template as a link, and src to give the document URL for the template.

For example, suppose you want to use the welcome template we created in section Mixing Sounds, on page 179 in the response for a launch request. And, suppose that you had saved that template in the APL-A editor with the name "welcome". In that case, the launch request handler would return the directive as shown here:

apl-a/starport-75/lambda/StandardHandlers.js

```
    return responseBuilder
      .addDirective({
        "type": "Alexa.Presentation.APLA.RenderDocument",
        "document": {
          "type": "Link",
          "src": "doc://alexa/apla/documents/welcome"
        }
      })
      .getResponse();
```

When referencing saved templates, the type property should always be "Link". As for the src property, it always takes the form of doc://alexa/apla/documents/_TEM-PLATE NAME_. If the template was saved with the name "welcome", then the complete URL is doc://alexa/apla/documents/welcome.

If you need to send model data to the template as parameters, then you'll need to specify a datasources property in the directive. For example, let's say that you want to return one of the templates we created in section Condition-ally Selecting Sounds, on page 174 to tell the user to enjoy their trip. Those templates referenced the trip's destination with the "${payload.trip.destination}" expression.

Assuming that you saved the template with the name "enjoyYourTrip", then you can pass the destination from the request handler to the APL-A template with a directive that looks like this:

apl-a/starport-75/lambda/ScheduleTripIntentHandler.js

```
    return handlerInput.responseBuilder
      .addDirective({
```

```
        "type": "Alexa.Presentation.APLA.RenderDocument",
        "document": {
          "type": "Link",
          "src": "doc://alexa/apla/documents/enjoyYourTrip"
        },
        "datasources": {
          "trip": {
            "destination": destination
          }
        }
    })
  .getResponse();
```

Notice that payload doesn't appear in the datasources property. That name is the template-local name for the object set to the datasources property.

One very important thing that you should know about using saved templates is that if you ever change your template, you'll need to rebuild the interaction model after saving your changes. Until the interaction model is rebuilt, the APL-A changes won't be picked up and the previous version will still be active.

Now let's see how to send a directive for APL-A templates that you have downloaded from the APL-A editor.

Rendering Downloaded Templates

As it turns out, the document property of the directive is actually intended to hold the entire APL-A template. While linking to a saved template as shown in the previous section helps avoid a lengthy and messy copy-and-paste of APL-A into a skill's request handlers, it is absolutely possible to include the entire APL-A template as the value of the document property. The following snippet shows how this might look:

apl-a/starport-75/lambda/StandardHandlers.js
```
  return responseBuilder
  .addDirective({
    "type": "Alexa.Presentation.APLA.RenderDocument",
    "document": {
      "type": "APLA",
      "version": "0.9",
      "mainTemplate": {
        "item": {
          "type": "Speech",
          "content": "Welcome to Star Port 75 Travel!"
        }
      }
    }
  })
  .getResponse();
```

This may not seem all that bad at first glance. But this is also using a very simple APL-A template. Imagine what this might look like if it were a richer and more interesting APL-A template. Suffice it to say that it would make the request handler code more difficult to read and would be essentially littering handler logic with presentation code.

Rather than hard-code the document directly in the request handler, a better way is to copy the downloaded APL-A template into your skill project somewhere under the lambda directory alongside the skill fulfillment code. To keep it separate from the rest of the fulfillment code, you could create a subdirectory under lambda named apl-a and place your APL-A templates there.

For example, had you downloaded the welcome template and placed it in lambda/apl-a/welcome.json, then you could use the require() function to insert it into the rendering directive like this:

apl-a/starport-75/lambda/StandardHandlers.js
```
    return responseBuilder
      .addDirective({
        "type": "Alexa.Presentation.APLA.RenderDocument",
        "document": require('./apla/welcome.json')
      })
      .getResponse();
```

This way, the two concerns of request-handling and presentation remain separate. Moreover, the request handler code remains relatively clean and easy to read.

Passing model data as parameters to a downloaded template that is pulled in using require() is no different than if it were a saved template. Here's how you'd use require() to reference a downloaded enjoyYourTrip.json template, passing in the destination as model data:

apl-a/starport-75/lambda/ScheduleTripIntentHandler.js
```
    return handlerInput.responseBuilder
      .addDirective({
          "type": "Alexa.Presentation.APLA.RenderDocument",
          "document": require('./apla/enjoyYourTrip.json'),
          "datasources": {
            "trip": {
              "destination": destination
            }
          }
        })
      .getResponse();
```

You may be wondering if it's possible to use both the speak() function and return the Alexa.Presentation.APLA.RenderDocument directive in the same response. In short, yes you can, as shown in the following example:

```
return handlerInput.responseBuilder
  .addDirective({
      "type": "Alexa.Presentation.APLA.RenderDocument",
      "document": require('./apla/enjoyYourTrip.json'),
      "datasources": {
        "trip": {
          "destination": destination
        }
      }
    })
  .speak("Thanks for planning your trip with Star Port 75 Travel!")
  .getResponse();
```

Although it doesn't make much sense to mix speak() with APL-A, it does work. If you use both together, the text given to the speak() function will be spoken first. Then, the audio produced by the APL-A template will follow.

Wrapping Up

Alexa Presentation Language for Audio is a JSON-based template language that offers a powerful way to craft rich, layered, and professional sounding audio responses from an Alexa skill.

APL-A achieves this with a half-dozen components for playing sound and speech and combining them with mixers, sequencers, and selectors. Filters empower you to apply simple effects to audio and speech, including fading in and out, trimming to length, setting the volume, and repeating audio clips.

Returning APL-A from a skill involves sending a directive in place of the typical speak() function, passing in model data that can be rendered dynamically into the reponse audio.

Coming up in the next chapter, we're going to expand the reach of our skill beyond U.S. English, seeing how to customize Alexa's interaction model and responses to better serve users who live in other countries and/or speak different languages.

CHAPTER 8

Localizing Responses

While it's easy to start on a new skill focusing on a single language, eventually you'll reach a point where you'll want to expand your skill's exposure to a larger audience, including users in locations who speak languages different than your skill's first language. It's unreasonable to expect everyone to conform to your skill's language; in fact, most people would probably just not use your skill at all if it isn't available in their native tongue.

In this chapter, we're going to see how to add support for additional languages to an Alexa skill, adding support for Spanish to the Star Port 75 Travel skill. We'll also see how to test localized skills and use SSML to help Alexa properly pronounce non-English words. Let's start by translating our interaction model so that Alexa can hear and understand what a user says to her, even if spoken in another language.

Translating the Interaction Model

As we've developed the Star Port 75 Travel skill, we've defined the skill's interaction model—utterances, slots, dialogs, and prompts—in the skill-package/interactionModels/custom/en-US.json file. As implied by its name, that interaction model is specifically for devices configured for U.S. English. Now, as we are ready to expand to other locales and languages, we need to create additional interaction model files.

Alexa does not support all languages or locales. Chinese, for instance, isn't supported yet, nor are any Chinese locales such as Hong Kong, Taiwan, and Singapore. Nevertheless, Alexa does support nine languages in over a dozen different locales:

- Arabic/Saudi Arabia (ar-SA)
- German/Germany (de-DE)
- English/Australia (en-AU)
- English/Canada (en-CA)
- English/United Kingdom (en-GB)
- English/India (en-IN)
- English/US (en-US)
- Spanish/Spain (es-ES)
- Spanish/Mexico (es-MX)
- Spanish/US (es-US)
- French/Canada (fr-CA)
- French/France (fr-FR)
- Hindi/India (hi-IN)
- Italian/Italy (it-IT)
- Japanese/Japan (ja-JP)
- Portuguese/Brazil (pt-BR)

Supporting additional locales and languages involves creating new interaction model files in the skill-package/interactionModels/custom directory, one for each language-locale pair you wish to support. Each interaction model JSON file will adhere to the same format we used for U.S. English, translating the utterances, prompts, and synonyms to match the language.

Since we already have an interaction model for English-speaking users in the United States, we can quickly add support for all other English-speaking locales by simply copying the en-US.json file to en-AU.json, en-CA.json, en-GB.json, and en-IN.json. We'd only need to change those files if any utterances, prompts, or synonyms are to use any locale-specific colloquialisms.

Alternatively, the ASK CLI offers the ask smapi clone-locale command that can be used to clone a skill's locales:

```
$ ask smapi clone-locale \
  --skill-id amzn1.ask.skill.68a3c3b3-63f5-40b0-b1ad-57636ac4067d \
  --source-locale en-US \
  --target-locales en-AU,en-CA,en-GB,en-IN
```

Locale clones can only be created from an existing locale with the same language. In this case, we are cloning the en-US locale to the other English locales. You can't, however, clone an English locale into a different language.

Locale cloning is asynchronous, so the command will return immediately, but may take a little longer to complete the cloning process. You can check on the status using the ask smapi get-clone-locale-status command:

```
$ ask smapi get-clone-locale-status \
  --skill-id amzn1.ask.skill.68a3c3b3-63f5-40b0-b1ad-57636ac4067d \
  --stage development \
  --clone-locale-request-id 0d34c78d-7de3-4478-be7e-580338e29b05 \
  --profile default
```

The --clone-locale-request-id parameter required to check the cloning status (as well as the other parameters) are available in the response to the ask smapi clone-locale command.

Once the cloning has completed successfully, you'll need to fetch the locale-specific interaction model files using ask smapi get-interaction-model. For example, to fetch the interaction model JSON file for "en-GB", you can use the ASK CLI like this:

```
$ ask smapi get-interaction-model \
  --skill-id amzn1.ask.skill.68a3c3b3-63f5-40b0-b1ad-57636ac4067d \
  --locale en-GB > skill-package/interactionModels/custom/en-GB.json
```

Although cloning locales using the ASK CLI like this is explicit in its purpose, you'll probably find it much simpler to just make a copy of the en-US.json file for each of the other locales.

By simply replicating the English interaction model across all English locales, our skill suddenly works with two-thirds of language-locale pairs supported by Alexa. For the others, we can copy the existing model JSON files for each language-locale we want to support, and then edit each JSON file, translating the utterances, prompts, and synonyms to the target language.

In this chapter, we're going to expand Star Port 75 Travel to three additional locales by creating new interaction model files for each of the three locales that serve Spanish-speaking travelers. You are welcome to add additional language and locale support for other languages if you wish, following the same approach we'll use for Spanish.

We'll start by copying the contents of en-US.json to es-ES.json and translating its content to Spanish. Once we've finished the translation in es-ES.json, we'll copy it for the other two Spanish-speaking locales.

Do I Need to Support All Languages and Locales?

While it's often a great idea to extend the reach of your Alexa skill to as many users as possible, regardless of where they live or what language they speak, translating your interaction model and skill responses can be quite an undertaking, even with the help of translation services like Google Translate. It is not required that your skill support all languages and locales and, depending on your target audience, it may not be desirable to bother with translation to all languages. If you're building a skill for a business that is only available in Canada, then it's best to focus your attention on English and French translations. You can always expand your skill to other languages and locales later as the business expands.

After creating es-ES.json from en-US.json, open the es-ES.json file in your text editor. Our first bit of translation work will be with the invocation name. Typically, the invocation name will need to be translated to the target language, unless it is a brand name that is well-recognized without translation. For Star Port 75, we will translate the invocation name to Spanish like this:

locale/starport-75/skill-package/interactionModels/custom/es-ES.json
```
{
    "interactionModel": {
        "languageModel": {
            "invocationName": "puerto estrella setenta y cinco",
        ...
}
```

Next, we'll need to translate sample utterances in the skill's intent declarations. The skill's main intent is ScheduleTripIntent, which when translated to Spanish, looks like this:

locale/starport-75/skill-package/interactionModels/custom/es-ES.json
```
{
  "name": "ScheduleTripIntent",
  "samples": [
    "programar un viaje a {destination} dejando {departureDate} y
        regresando {returnDate}",
    "planifique un viaje entre {departureDate} y {returnDate} para
        visitar {destination}",
    "programar un viaje a {destination}",
    "planear un viaje entre {departureDate} y {returnDate}"
  ],
  "slots": [
    {
      "name": "destination",
      "type": "PLANETS"
    },
```

```
    {
      "name": "departureDate",
      "type": "AMAZON.DATE"
    },
    {
      "name": "returnDate",
      "type": "AMAZON.DATE"
    }
  ]
}
```

Notice that the intent's name and the names of its slots don't need to be translated. They must remain the same so that the fulfillment code can continue to reference them by those names. But the utterances in the samples property must be changed to match how a Spanish-speaking user may ask to plan a trip. The key is to only change the things that a user may say or hear.

We must also change the values and synonyms of our custom PLANETS type. Here is the PLANETS type with all of its entries translated to Spanish:

locale/starport-75/skill-package/interactionModels/custom/es-ES.json
```
"types": [
  {
    "name": "PLANETS",
    "values": [
      {
        "id": "MERCURY",
        "name": {
          "value": "Mercurio",
          "synonyms": [
            "el mas cercano al sol",
            "el planeta veloz"
          ]
        }
      },
      {
        "id": "VENUS",
        "name": {
          "value": "Venus",
          "synonyms": [
            "la estrella de la mañana",
            "la estrella de la tarde"
          ]
        }
      },
      {
        "id": "EARTH",
        "name": {
          "value": "Tierra",
```

```json
      "synonyms": [
        "el planeta azul",
        "el gran mármol azul",
        "la tercera roca del sol"
      ]
    }
  },
  {
    "id": "MARS",
    "name": {
      "value": "Marte",
      "synonyms": [
        "el planeta rojo"
      ]
    }
  },
  {
    "id": "JUPITER",
    "name": {
      "value": "Júpiter",
      "synonyms": [
        "el Grande",
        "el planeta gigante",
        "el que tiene un ojo"
      ]
    }
  },
  {
    "id": "SATURN",
    "name": {
      "value": "Saturno",
      "synonyms": [
        "el planeta anillado"
      ]
    }
  },
  {
    "id": "URANUS",
    "name": {
      "value": "Urano",
      "synonyms": [
        "el gigante de hielo"
      ]
    }
  },
  {
    "id": "NEPTUNE",
    "name": {
      "value": "Neptuno",
```

```
          "synonyms": [
            "el planeta azul"
          ]
        }
      },
      {
        "id": "PLUTO",
        "name": {
          "value": "Plutón",
          "synonyms": [
            "el planeta enano"
          ]
        }
      }
    ]
  }
]
```

The type's name and each entry's id property must remain untranslated. But the name and synonyms are things that a user may say in the destination slot when planning a trip, so those must be translated.

There's one more bit of translation needed in the interaction model. The dialogs section doesn't include anything a user may say or hear; no translation is required. But the prompts section contains mostly things a user may hear, so we'll definitely need to translate all of those prompts.

For now, let's focus on the prompts that elicit values for the destination, departure date, and return date slots. Here are the elicitation prompts, with each of their variations translated to Spanish:

locale/starport-75/skill-package/interactionModels/custom/es-ES.json
```
"prompts": [
  {
    "id": "Slot.Elicitation.ScheduleTrip.Destination",
    "variations": [
      {
        "type": "PlainText",
        "value": "¿A donde quieres ir?"
      },
      {
        "type": "PlainText",
        "value": "¿Qué planeta te gustaría visitar?"
      }
    ]
  },
  {
    "id": "Slot.Elicitation.ScheduleTrip.DepartureDate",
```

```
    "variations": [
      {
        "type": "PlainText",
        "value": "¿Cuándo quieres partir?"
      },
      {
        "type": "PlainText",
        "value": "¿Cuándo comenzará tu viaje?"
      }
    ]
  },
  {
    "id": "Slot.Elicitation.ScheduleTrip.ReturnDate",
    "variations": [
      {
        "type": "PlainText",
        "value": "¿Cuándo quieres volver?"
      },
      {
        "type": "PlainText",
        "value": "¿Cuándo terminará tu viaje?"
      }
    ]
  },
  ...
]
```

As with the other elements of the interaction model, we only need to translate the variations of each prompt. We must leave the prompt IDs unchanged, as those are referenced from the dialogs section.

You are welcome to translate the remaining prompts on your own. When finished, we'll have created a Spanish translation of the interaction model for the Spain locale. By copying es-ES.json to es-US.json and es-MX.json, we will have fully covered all supported Spanish-speaking locales in our interaction model.

But the interaction model is only half of the translation work. We also must translate the messages that Alexa speaks in responses from our intent handlers. Let's turn our attention to the fulfillment implementation to finish the translation work.

Localizing Spoken Responses

In Chapter 1, Alexa, Hello, on page 1, as we began work on the Star Port 75 Travel skill, we added a LocalisationRequestInterceptor object in index.js and registered it with the skill builder. As a reminder, here's what LocalisationRequestInterceptor looks like:

```
locale/starport-75/lambda/index.js
const LocalisationRequestInterceptor = {
    process(handlerInput) {
        i18n.init({
            lng: Alexa.getLocale(handlerInput.requestEnvelope),
            resources: languageStrings
        }).then((t) => {
            handlerInput.t = (...args) => t(...args);
        });
    }
};
```

The ASK SDK gives us the option of registering one or more request inter-cepters in the skill. Such interceptors may inspect and modify the handlerInput object before giving it to a request handler. In this case, the LocalisationRequestIn-terceptor initializes the i18next module with the locale from the request and the source of the strings that will be spoken in responses. Then, LocalisationRequestIn-terceptor adds a new t() function to the handlerInput that will lookup localized string values.

We've been using that t() function throughout this book to fetch response messages by name from lambda/languageStrings.js. Up to this point, however, there hasn't been much benefit in this mechanism. Had we simply hard-coded those strings in each intent handler and dispensed with the i18next module, languageStrings.js, and the interceptor, our code would've been much simpler.

But now that we're ready to support additional languages in our skill, keeping response text separate from the intent handlers is about to pay off.

You'll recall that the languageStrings.js file defines a map object where the top-level keys are two-character language codes. Currently, we only support English, so the only top-level key is en. Within the en entry is a map of English strings that are returned by the skill's intent handlers. As a reminder, here's what it looks like:

```
locale/starport-75/lambda/languageStrings.js
module.exports = {
  en: {
    translation: {
      WELCOME_MSG:
        '<speak>' +
        '<p><audio src="https://starport75.dev/audio/SP75.mp3"/> ' +
        'Welcome to Star Port 75 Travel, your source for ' +
        '<audio src="soundbank://soundlibrary/scifi/' +
        'amzn_sfx_scifi_small_zoom_flyby_01"/> ' +
        'out-of-this world adventures.</p> ' +
        '<p>Where do you want to blast off to?</p> ' +
        '</speak>',
```

```
WELCOME_MSG_PERSONAL:
  'Welcome back to Star Port 75 Travel, {{givenName}}! ' +
  'How can I help you?',
HELLO_MSG: 'Have a stellar day!',
SCHEDULED_MSG: "You're all set. Enjoy your trip to {{destination}}!",
DATE_VALIDATION_ERROR:
  'Star Port Seventy Five specializes in space travel, ' +
  'not time travel. Please specify a return date that is ' +
  'after the departure date.',
LINK_MSG:
  "You'll need to link the Star Port " +
  "75 Travel skill with your Google Calendar so " +
  "that I can schedule your trip. I've added a " +
  "card in the Alexa app to help you with that.",
HELP_MSG: 'You can say hello to me! How can I help?',
GOODBYE_MSG: 'Goodbye!',
REFLECTOR_MSG: 'You just triggered {{intentName}}',
FALLBACK_MSG: 'Sorry, I don\'t know about that. Please try again.',
ERROR_MSG:
  'Sorry, I had trouble doing what you asked. Please try again.'
  }
}
```

In order to add Spanish or any other language to our skill's responses, we must duplicate the en entry. The new entry's key should be changed to es, the two-letter language code for Spanish. And, its contents should be translated to Spanish. After such a translation, the es entry in languageStrings.js will look like this:

locale/starport-75/lambda/languageStrings.js

```
module.exports = {
  en: {
    ...
  },
  es: {
    translation: {
      WELCOME_MSG:
        '<speak>' +
        '<p><audio src="https://starport75.dev/audio/SP75.mp3"/> ' +
        'Bienvenido a Star Port 75 Travel, su fuente de ' +
        '<audio src="soundbank://soundlibrary/scifi/' +
        'amzn_sfx_scifi_small_zoom_flyby_01"/> ' +
        'aventuras fuera de este mundo.</p> ' +
        '<p>¿A dónde quieres volar?</p> ' +
        '</speak>',
      WELCOME_MSG_PERSONAL:
        '¡Bienvenido de nuevo a Star Port 75 Travel, {{givenName}}! '+
        '¿Como puedo ayudarte?',
      HELLO_MSG: '¡Que tengas un día estelar!',
```

```
    SCHEDULED_MSG:
      'Estás listo. ¡Disfruta tu viaje a {{destination}}!',
    DATE_VALIDATION_ERROR:
      'Star Port Seventy Five se especializa en viajes espaciales, ' +
      'no en viajes en el tiempo. Especifique una fecha de regreso ' +
      'posterior a la fecha de salida.',
    ACCOUNT_LINKING_MSG:
      "Tendrá que vincular la habilidad de viaje Star Port 75 " +
      "con su Google Calendar para que pueda programar su viaje. " +
      "Agregué una tarjeta en la aplicación Alexa para ayudarte " +
      "con eso.",
    HELP_MSG: '¡Puedes saludarme! ¿Cómo puedo ayudar?',
    GOODBYE_MSG: '¡Adiós!',
    REFLECTOR_MSG: 'Acabas de activar {{intentName}}',
    FALLBACK_MSG: 'Lo siento, no sé sobre eso. Inténtalo de nuevo.',
    ERROR_MSG:
      'Lo siento, tuve problemas para hacer lo que me pediste. ' +
      'Inténtalo de nuevo.'
  }
}
```

As you can see, the es and en properties are quite similar. The key difference is that the entries in en are in English, while those in es are in Spanish. If later we decide to support another language, all we'll need to do is copy and paste either the en or es block and change the key to the appropriate language code and translate the string values.

In some cases, you may want to define a region-specific response. In that case, you can define the region-specific language strings in languageStrings.js using the full locale definition instead of the two-letter language abbreviation. For example, suppose that you wanted to have Alexa say something unique as a goodbye statement for English-speaking users in the United Kingdom. To do that, you would add this entry to languageStrings.js:

locale/starport-75/lambda/languageStrings.js
```
"en-GB": {
  translation: {
    GOODBYE_MSG: 'Cheerio!'
  }
},
```

Notice that only the unique region-specific string had to be defined. The i18next library will fallback to the broader language strings when no region specific string is provided.

With the response strings translated to Spanish (along with an English variation for the United Kingdom), let's test our new bilingual skill.

Testing Localization

You may recall that every one of the BST test specifications we've written have started with a configuration block that includes a locales property:

```
---
configuration:
  locales: en-US
```

Up until now, we've only been working with U.S. English, so the locales property in all of our test specifications has been set to "en-US". But now that we're ready to test for other locales, we will set it so that our tests will cover all of the new locales and languages we've extended our skill to support. That's easily done by listing all locales you want to test for, comma-delimited in the locales property.

For example, here's the specification that tests the launch request for an authorized user:

```
---
configuration:
  locales: en-US, en-GB, en-CA, en-AU, en-IN, es-ES, es-MX, es-US
  filter: mock-given-name-filter.js
  givenName: Craig

---
- test: Launch request
- LaunchRequest:
  - prompt: Welcome back to Star Port 75 Travel, Craig!
                        How can I help you?
```

When this specification is run, each of its tests (in this case, there's only one) will be run once for each locale listed in locales. Given the locales we're testing for, the "Launch request" test will be run eight times, each time for a different locale, but asserting the same response.

The problem, however, is that the SSML assertion is in English while three of the eight locales listed are Spanish. That means that it will fail three times when the Spanish response doesn't match the English assertion.

Fortunately, we can extract assertion messages from our tests in a way similar to how we extract the spoken test strings in our fulfillment code. All we need to do is create a new locales directory under the test directory and create YAML files for each language that will hold the assertion messages. To get started, here's the English-specific assertions file:

```
locale/starport-75/test/unit/locales/en.yml
welcomeMessagePersonal: |
    Welcome back to Star Port 75 Travel, Craig!
    How can I help you?
```

The file is named en.yml to indicate that it contains English strings that we'll use in our tests. If our strings differed for the individual English locales, we could be more locale-specific by naming it en-US.yml and creating different files for en-GB.yml, en-CA.yml, and the other English-speaking locales. But a single file for English strings is fine for our needs.

Similarly, we can create a file of Spanish strings in es.yml:

```
locale/starport-75/test/unit/locales/es.yml
welcomeMessagePersonal: |
        ¡Bienvenido de nuevo a Star Port 75 Travel, Craig!
        ¿Como puedo ayudarte?
```

Now that we've extracted the assertion string into separate language-specific files, we can use it in our test by replacing the assertion string with the name "welcomeMessagePersonal":

```
locale/starport-75/test/unit/launch-request-authorized.test.yml
---
- test: Launch request
- LaunchRequest:
  - prompt: welcomeMessagePersonal
```

By applying this same technique to all of our tests, we can add multi-locale test coverage to our skill. For now, though, let's run the launch-request-authorized.yml spec to see if it works:

```
$ bst test --jest.collectCoverage=false launch-request-authorized

BST: v2.6.0  Node: v17.6.0
bst test lets you have a complete set of unit tests using a simple YAML
format. Find out more at https://read.bespoken.io.

 PASS  test/launch-request-authorized.yml
  en-US
    Launch request
      ✓ LaunchRequest (682ms)
  en-GB
    Launch request
      ✓ LaunchRequest (4ms)
  en-CA
    Launch request
      ✓ LaunchRequest (2ms)
  en-AU
    Launch request
      ✓ LaunchRequest (2ms)
```

```
en-IN
  Launch request
    ✓ LaunchRequest (2ms)
es-ES
  Launch request
    ✓ LaunchRequest (2ms)
es-MX
  Launch request
    ✓ LaunchRequest (2ms)
es-US
  Launch request
    ✓ LaunchRequest (2ms)

Test Suites: 1 passed, 1 total
Tests:       8 passed, 8 total
Snapshots:   0 total
Time:        2.064s
Ran all test suites.
```

Awesome! As you can see, the "LaunchRequest" test ran eight times, once for each of our supported locales. And, what's more, they all passed!

Although we could rest happy knowing that our localization work passes the tests, this is one of those cases where it's better to hear what Alexa says and not just trust that she says it correctly. So let's take a moment and make sure that she not only speaks Spanish responses, but also pronounces them correctly.

Fixing Language Pronunciation

If you were to deploy the skill at this point and try it out, either with an actual device or through the testing tool in the developer console, you might be amused at how Alexa pronounces some of the Spanish words. When Alexa speaks the text in the response, she assumes wrongly that all of the words are English words and tries to say them using English pronunciation. The result can be kind of bizarre.

As a small example of how Alexa may mispronounce Spanish words, try out the following SSML in the text-to-speech simulator in the developer console:

```
<speak>
    Manzanas y naranjas
</speak>
```

What you'll hear is Alexa pronounce the first "a" in "manzanas" as a short "a", pronounce "y" as "why", and pronounce the "j" in "naranjas" as a hard "j". What you should've heard, however, when properly pronounced is the "a" pronounced as "aw", the "y" as "e", and the "j" should have an "h" sound.

We can help Alexa by adding a little SSML. The <lang> tag can be used to wrap text to tell Alexa to pronounce words for a different locale. Applying the <lang> tag to the "Manzanas y naranjas" example, we get:

```
<speak>
  <lang xml:lang="es-ES">
    Manzanas y naranjas
  </lang>
</speak>
```

The xml:lang attribute specifies the locale that Alexa should use for pronunciation. In this case, "es-ES" tells Alexa to pronounce the words as Spanish words. Not all locales are supported by the <lang> tag, but the following are valid choices:

- en-US
- en-GB
- en-IN
- en-AU
- en-CA
- de-DE
- es-ES
- hi-IN
- it-IT
- ja-JP
- fr-FR

Although not all Spanish locales are supported, "es-ES" will work fine even if the user's locale is "es-MX" or "es-US".

Now try the new <lang>-wrapped SSML in the text-to-speech simulator. Comparing the results to the original SSML should be like comparing apples and oranges. Alexa will properly pronounce the Spanish words and will sound a lot less bizarre.

We can apply the <lang> tag the same way in all of our translated text used in our skill. In languageStrings.js, for example, the WELCOME_MSG_PERSONAL string could be wrapped with SSML and the <lang> tag like this:

```
locale/starport-75/lambda/languageStrings.js
WELCOME_MSG_PERSONAL:
  '<speak><lang xml:lang="es-ES">' +
  '¡Bienvenido de nuevo a Star Port 75 Travel, {{givenName}}! '+
  '¿Como puedo ayudarte?' +
  '</lang></speak>',
```

Even though the <lang> tag helped Alexa pronounce the Spanish words much more correctly, she still doesn't have a Spanish accent and she uses English sounds to pronounce the Spanish words. As a result, her pronunciation may still be a little off for some words. Before we wrap up the localization of our skill, let's look at a way to change Alexa's voice so that she speaks as if she's a native Spanish speaker.

Using Language-Specific Voices

Most languages have special sounds that other languages don't have, at least not directly. For example, consider the following SSML sample:

```
<speak>
  <lang xml:lang="es-ES">
    Gatos y perros
  </lang>
</speak>
```

This Spanish phrase, which means "cats and dogs", employs a special Spanish sound in the word "perros". The double-"r" should be made with a slight tongue roll. Instead, even with the <lang> tag, Alexa will pronounce it with a simple "r" sound. That's because Alexa's voice is based on English sounds, which do not include the rolled-"r" sound.

In the previous chapter, we looked at the <voice> tag, using it to swap out Alexa's voice for that of Justin and Amy. While both of those voices are very different than Alexa's native voice, they are still English voices and are still unable to speak other languages properly. However, Alexa supports several Polly voices suited for several locales:

- *U.S. English (en-US)*—Ivy, Joanna, Joey, Justin, Kendra, Kimberly, Matthew, Salli

- *AustralianEnglish (en-AU)*—Nicole, Russell

- *British English (en-GB)*—Amy, Brian, Emma

- *IndianEnglish (en-IN)*—Aditi, Raveena

- *German (de-DE)*—Hans, Marlene, Vicki

- *American Spanish (es-US)*—Penelope, Lupe, Miguel

- *Castilian Spanish (es-ES)*—Conchita, Enrique, Lucia

- *Mexican Spanish (es-MX)*—Mia

- *Hindi (hi-IN)*—Aditi

- *Italian (it-IT)*—Carla, Giorgio, Bianca

- *Japanese (ja-JP)*—Mizuki, Takumi

- *French (fr-FR)*—Celine, Lea, Mathieu

- *French Canadian (fr-CA)*—Chantal

- *Portuguese Brazilian (pt-BR)*—Vitoria, Camila, Ricardo

Not only do each of these voice possess a unique tone and personality, they are also based on their respective languages and are able to produce language-specific sounds.

For Spanish, we have the choice of either Conchita and Enrique. For example, try applying Conchita's voice to the cats-and-dogs SSML:

```
<speak>
  <voice name="Conchita">
    <lang xml:lang="es-ES">
      Gatos y perros
    </lang>
  </voice>
</speak>
```

When tested in the text-to-speech simulator, you'll hear a Spanish-speaking woman's voice correctly pronouncing the phrase, including the rolled-"r" in "perros".

If you'd like, you may apply these voices to the Star Port 75 Travel skill by sprinkling <voice> tags in our skill's responses. The WELCOME_MSG_PERSONAL message, for instance, might employ Enrique's voice if changed to look like this:

```
locale/starport-75/lambda/languageStrings.js
WELCOME_MSG_PERSONAL:
  '<speak><voice name="Enrique"><lang xml:lang="es-ES">' +
  '¡Bienvenido de nuevo a Star Port 75 Travel, {{givenName}}! '+
  '¿Como puedo ayudarte?' +
  '</lang></voice></speak>',
```

Polly voices such as Enrique and Conchita may not be a good fit for all skills, as they introduce a new personality that might be jarring to some users who are accustomed to Alexa's voice. But they certainly do help a skill's responses sound more natural when using non-English languages.

Wrapping Up

Even though you'll probably start developing your skill for a single language, eventually you may want to expand your reach and open up your skill to other languages. From the very beginning, our skill has been using the i18next library to externalize response string from intent handlers, establishing a foundation upon which to build support for multiple languages.

What Alexa says is only half of the localization story, however. We also must customize our interaction model to support other languages so that she can hear and understand utterances in other languages. And, while translating our interaction model's utterances, we can also translate the prompts that Alexa will speak as part of a dialog.

The BST testing tool enables us to test multi-language support by extracting the expected response text into locale-specific mappings, referring to those mappings in a locale-agnostic way. When the tests are run, BST will execute each test multiple times, once for each supported locale.

Finally, using SSML's <lang> and <voice> tags, we can fine-tune our skill's responses so that Alexa correctly pronounces non-English words or even apply a completely different voice that speaks that language natively.

We've spent the past few chapters focusing on sound and how Alexa speaks. But while Alexa applications are meant to be voice-first, they can also provide visual complements to voice-first interactions. In the next chapter, we're going to look at how to return visual feedback using cards, simple components that are displayed in the Alexa companion application that are installed on a user's mobile device.

CHAPTER 9

Complementing Responses with Cards

Do you know anyone who talks with their hands? It's such a common behavior, that a word was created to describe it: gesticulate. Some people like showing or drawing pictures to complement what they're saying. And some people will interject the phrase "You just have to see it for yourself" when talking to someone.

Voice is the primary means of human communication, but it's not the only way we communicate. Similarly, Alexa skills offer a voice-first form of user interface, but not necessarily a voice-only user interface. Pictures and text are great companions to spoken words, giving the listener additional material to consider as they hear what is spoken.

In this chapter, we're going to look at cards, one way to add a visual complement to voice responses from Alexa skills.

Embellishing Responses with Cards

A card is a simple representation of a response that is rendered into the Alexa companion application. It appears as a rectangular container with a title and textual content. We've already seen a couple of examples of cards in Chapter 5, Integrating User Data, on page 105 where cards were used to prompt the user to grant our skill access to their given name and to authorize the skill to access the user's calendar.

The screenshot on page 214 shows a few more examples of cards, as they might appear in the iOS Alexa companion application:

In this image, there are three cards displayed. New cards arrive at the top of the list, pushing down older cards. Thus the card that informs about the airspeed of unladen swallows is the most recently received card.

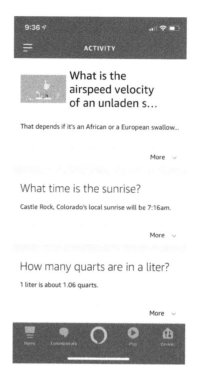

All three of these cards are designed to simply display the query as the title and the spoken response as the content, but the first card also has an image displayed along with the content. In fact, these are examples of two different kinds of cards:

- *Simple cards*—Have only a title and textual content
- *Standard cards*—Have a title, textual content, and an image

The card that deals with unladen swallows is an example of a standard card, because it has an image. The other two are simple cards that only have a title and textual content.

Let's add a few cards to the Star Port 75 Travel skill, starting with a simple card returned in response to the AMAZON.HelpIntent.

Returning Simple Cards

In a desktop or web application there are visual cues to help a user figure out what their options are. The user can see icons, buttons, and menu items and make reasonable guesses about how an application works. But in a voice application, there aren't many visual cues and the user may need to ask for help. That's where the built-in AMAZON.HelpIntent intent comes into play.

When the user says "help," the skill's handler for the AMAZON.HelpIntent will be invoked and respond with some hints for what the user can say to use the skill. Using cards, we can also provide help in their companion application. We'll start by adding a simple card to the response returned from the intent handler for AMAZON.HelpIntent that displays the same text that Alexa will speak:

visual/starport-75/lambda/StandardHandlers.js

```
return handlerInput.responseBuilder
    .speak(speakOutput)
    .reprompt(speakOutput)
➤   .withSimpleCard("How to use this skill", speakOutput)
    .getResponse();
```

Cards aren't returned in every response. But by calling withSimpleCard() on the response builder, we're asking for the response to include a card whose title is "How to use this skill" and whose content is "You can say hello to me! How can I help?" When displayed in the companion application, it might look like this:

That's a good start, but it's not very helpful. Even though it will respond to an utterance of "hello," that's far from all our skill will do. The skill's main function is to schedule interplanetary travel. Therefore, the response—both spoken and displayed in the card—should be more appropriate to scheduling space travel.

Before we make changes to the intent handler, let's add expectations about the card to the test for the help intent:

visual/starport-75/test/unit/index.test.yml

```
---
- test : Launch and ask for help
- LaunchRequest : welcomeMessage
- AMAZON.HelpIntent :
  - prompt : helpMessage
➤ - cardTitle : helpCardTitle
➤ - cardContent : helpCardContent
```

Here we're using the cardTitle and cardContent properties to express what we expect for the card in the response. Because the test is multi-locale, the actual expected values are externalized in locale-specific files. For instance, here are the English values for helpCardTitle and helpCardContent in locales/en.yml:

```
visual/starport-75/test/unit/locales/en.yml
helpMessage: |
    You can ask me to plan a trip to any planet in our solar
    system. For example, you can say "Plan a trip to Jupiter. What
    do you want to do?
➤ helpCardTitle: How to use this skill
➤ helpCardContent: |
➤   Ask me to plan a trip to any planet in our solar
➤   system.\nFor example, you could say:\n"Plan a trip to Jupiter".
➤   "Schedule a trip to Mars"\n"Plan a trip to Venus leaving next
➤   Monday"
```

Similarly, the Spanish values will need to be added to locales/es.yml:

```
visual/starport-75/test/unit/locales/es.yml
helpMessage: |
    Pídeme que planee un viaje a cualquier planeta
    de nuestro sistema solar. Por ejemplo, podría decir
    Planifique un viaje a Júpiter". ¿Qué quieres hacer?
➤ helpCardTitle: Cómo usar esta habilidad
➤ helpCardContent: |
➤   Pídeme que planee un viaje a cualquier planeta
➤   de nuestro sistema solar. Por ejemplo, podría decir
➤   Planifique un viaje a Júpiter".
```

Notice that in addition to adding locale-specific strings for the card title and content, we've also changed the expected helpMessage string to be more fitting for planning a trip through the solar system.

You should also note that the spoken text will be different from what is displayed on the card. Cards are quite useful for offering additional information beyond what is spoken. In this case, the card offers more examples than the spoken text.

In order to make those tests pass, we'll need to change the intent handler to return those messages in a simple card. First, we'll edit languageStrings.js, changing the value for HELP_MSG and adding entries for the card title and content:

```
visual/starport-75/lambda/languageStrings.js
module.exports = {
  en: {
    translation: {
      ...
      HELP_MSG: 'You can ask me to plan a trip to any planet in our solar ' +
        'system. For example, you can say "Plan a trip to Jupiter." What ' +
        'do you want to do?',
```

```
      HELP_CARD_TITLE: 'How to use this skill',
      HELP_CARD_MSG: 'Ask me to plan a trip to any planet in our solar ' +
        'system.\nFor example, you could say:\n"Plan a trip to Jupiter"' +
        '\n"Schedule a trip to Mars"\n"Plan a trip to Venus leaving ' +
        'next Monday"',
      ...
    }
  },
  es: {
    translation: {
      ...
      HELP_MSG: 'Pídeme que planee un viaje a cualquier planeta ' +
        'de nuestro sistema solar. Por ejemplo, podría decir ' +
        'Planifique un viaje a Júpiter". ¿Qué quieres hacer? ',
      HELP_CARD_TITLE: 'Cómo usar esta habilidad',
      HELP_CARD_MSG: 'Pídeme que planee un viaje a cualquier planeta ' +
        'de nuestro sistema solar. Por ejemplo, podría decir:\n'+
        '"Planifique un viaje a Júpiter"\n"Programe un viaje a Marte"' +
        '\n"Planifique un viaje a Venus que saldrá el próximo lunes".',
      ...
    }
  }
}
```

Now we just need to tweak the intent handler to use those strings in the call
to withSimpleCard():

```
visual/starport-75/lambda/StandardHandlers.js
const cardTitle = handlerInput.t('HELP_CARD_TITLE');
const cardContent = handlerInput.t('HELP_CARD_MSG');

return handlerInput.responseBuilder
    .speak(speakOutput)
    .reprompt(speakOutput)
➤   .withSimpleCard(cardTitle, cardContent)
    .getResponse();
}
```

After deploying the skill, invoke it by saying, "Alexa, open Star Port Seventy
Five Travel," and then say "help." Alexa should speak the new, more relevant
help message. But also, if you open the companion application on your phone,
you'll see the help card. On the iOS companion application, it might look like
the screenshot on page 218.

Our help intent handler is much more useful now. And, if the user opens
their companion application, they'll be shown a card with additional help
information. Let's add another card to our skill, but this time with an image.

How to use this skill
starport-75

Ask me to plan a trip to any planet in our solar system.

For example, you could say:

"Plan a trip to Jupiter"

"Schedule a trip to Mars"

"Plan a trip to Venus leaving next Monday"

More ⌄

Rendering Images on Cards

It's been said that a picture is worth a thousand words. It wouldn't be a great idea to have a card with a thousand words in it, but adding an image to a card could carry just as much value.

For example, suppose that we want to return a card in response to scheduling a trip. The card could include text describing the planned trip and be informative. But including an image of the destination along with that information will provide an enormous amount of visual value to the card.

We'll start by adding new language-specific strings for the new card's title and content to languageStrings.js:

```
visual/starport-75/lambda/languageStrings.js
module.exports = {
  en: {
    translation: {
      ...
      SCHEDULED_CARD_TITLE: 'Enjoy your trip!',
      SCHEDULED_CARD_MSG: "You're all set for a trip to {{destination}}, " +
        "leaving {{departureDate}} and returning {{returnDate}}!",
      ...
    }
  },
  es: {
    translation: {
      ...
```

```
    SCHEDULED_CARD_TITLE: 'Enjoy your trip!',
    SCHEDULED_CARD_MSG: "You're all set for a trip to {{destination}}, " +
      "leaving {{departureDate}} and returning {{returnDate}}!",
    ...
    }
  }
}
```

Speaking of the card, we'll need to use a standard card instead of a simple card if we want the card to include an image. Recall that simple cards only carry a title and some text, and standard cards let us include an image. To add a standard card to the response, we'll call WithStandardCard() on the response builder:

```
visual/starport-75/lambda/ScheduleTripIntentHandler.js
const ScheduleTripIntentHandler = {
  ...
  async handle(handlerInput) {
  ...
    const cardTitle = handlerInput.t('SCHEDULED_CARD_TITLE');
    const cardContent = handlerInput.t('SCHEDULED_CARD_MSG',
    {
      destination: destination,
      departureDate: departureDate,
      returnDate: returnDate
    });
    const baseUrl = 'https://starport75.dev/images/planets/';
    const smallImageUrl = baseUrl + destination.toLowerCase() + '_sm.jpg';
    const largeImageUrl = baseUrl + destination.toLowerCase() + '_lg.jpg';

    return handlerInput.responseBuilder
      .speak(speakOutput)
      .withStandardCard(cardTitle, cardContent, smallImageUrl, largeImageUrl)
      .withShouldEndSession(true)
      .getResponse();
  },
```

Before building the response, the card's title and content are retrieved by calling the t() function on handlerInput. In the case of SCHEDULED_CARD_MSG, we pass an object with the destination and travel dates to fill in placeholders in the string.

As for the image, there are two image URLs, one for a small version of the image (approximately 720 pixels by 480 pixels) and one for a large version (approximately 1200 pixels by 800 pixels). The images for each destination are served from Amazon's S3 storage service and are named such that we can construct the S3 URLs by using the destination name normalized to lowercase. Only one of the images will be displayed, depending on the capabilities of the device viewing the card.

With the card's title, content, and image URLs prepared, we simply call With-StandardCard() on the handlerInput to include the card in the response. Note that both image parameters are optional. If both are left off, the card will appear as a simple card. If only one image is given, it will be assumed to be the small image and will be scaled up if displayed on a device with a high resolution. Therefore, it's best to include both images to avoid potential image quality issues that might result from scaling the small image.

After deploying our changes, we can see what the card will look like by planning a trip and the viewing the card in the companion application. For example, if we were to schedule a trip to Saturn, the resulting card might look like this:

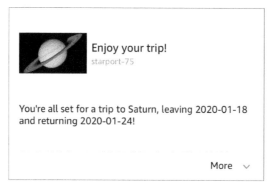

Adding an image of the planet to the card adds a little pizzazz and makes it clear that this card has something to do with a trip to Saturn.

Cards are typically viewed in the Alexa companion application. But they may also appear on the screen of a screen-enabled device such as an Echo Show or Fire TV. For example, if we were to plan a trip to Saturn on an Echo Show, the card would be displayed like the image on the device's screen at the end of the scheduling process as shown on page 221.

Notice that the card is a bit more spread out due to the fact that it has more screen resolution to work with. Even so, it's still the same card that was shown in the companion application, just formatted differently.

Wrapping Up

Voice-first applications are not necessarily voice-only. By complementing the spoken response from our skill with visual components, we enhance the experience for our users.

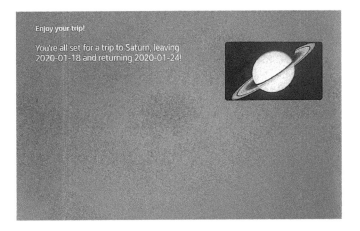

Cards are visual components that appear in the Alexa companion application as well as on the screen of a screen-enabled device such as an Echo Show. Cards are simple in design and limited in how much they can show, but they are equally simple to implement with a call to a single method on the response builder.

Cards are rigid and limited in how much you can customize their design. But in the next chapter, we're going to look at the Alexa Presentation Language, a much more flexible approach to creating rich visual content for screen-enabled devices.

CHAPTER 10

Creating Visual Responses

Think back to the time when you enjoyed nothing more than busting out a box of crayons and a coloring book, creating brilliant wax-tinted works of art. For many people, coloring the pages of a coloring book was a popular childhood pastime. For others, maybe it was just yesterday.

Given the choice between an 8-color box of crayons and a 64-color box of crayons, which would you choose? Obviously, with 64 colors you would have ultimate flexibility in your creative designs. On the other hand, the 8-color box is much more portable and convenient if you want to carry it on a trip. The choice is dependent on how you plan to use it.

In the previous chapter, we saw how to use cards to add a visual complement to our skill responses. Working with cards is easy and straightforward, but they are quite limited, only allowing basic information and an optional image to be displayed. In this way, cards are like the 8-color box of crayons: portable and convenient, but limited in creative potential.

In this chapter, we're going to explore the Alexa Presentation Language (APL), a template language for screen-based Alexa devices. APL, much like the 64-color box of crayons, allows us complete freedom in designing any visual interface we can dream up.

Introducing the Alexa Presentation Language

In chapter Chapter 7, Mixing Audio, on page 161, we saw how to use the Alexa Presentation Language for Audio (APL-A) to mix sounds and voice to create rich audio experiences. But APL-A isn't the only form of the Alexa presentation language

Similar to APL-A that we learned about in chapter 7, APL is a JSON-based language for defining skill responses. But where APL-A produces rich audio responses, APL is for creating visual user-interfaces to complement voice user-interfaces on screen-enabled Alexa devices. It is for those devices what HTML is to a web-browser. Similar to HTML, APL allows for completely flexibility for designing any visual interface we can dream up.

APL comes with ten essential components that can be assembled into a user interface:

- Container—Contains one or more other components into a layout

- Frame—Displays a single child component and has a border and background color

- Image—Displays a bitmap image (for example, GIF, JPG, PNG)

- Pager—Displays a series of child components, one at a time, in a left-to-right order

- ScrollView—Displays a single child component with vertical scrolling if the child component is larger than the ScrollView component

- Sequence—Displays a set of components in a list that scrolls either vertically or horizontally

- Text—Displays textual content

- TouchWrapper—Wraps a single child component and responds to touch events

- VectorGraphic—Displays a scalable vector graphic image

- Video—Displays a video player

No visual user interface will need all of these components, but we'll use a few of them to create APL-based visual displays for the Star Port 75 Travel skill. We'll start with a simple APL template that employs two of the components—Container and Text—to create the obligatory "Hello World" APL example:

apl/starport-75/lambda/apl/hello.json
```
{
  "type": "APL",
  "version": "1.2",
  "theme": "dark",
  "mainTemplate": {
    "items": [
      {
        "type": "Container",
        "items": [
          {
            "type": "Text",
```

```
            "width": "100vw",
            "height": "100vh",
            "textAlign": "center",
            "textAlignVertical": "center",
            "fontSize": "80dp",
            "text": "Hello World"
        }
      ]
    }
  ]
 }
}
```

At the top level, the type and version properties specify that this is an APL version 1.2 document. Meanwhile, the theme property specifies a "dark" theme which imposes a dark background with light text.

APL Authoring Tools

It is possible to create APL documents using any text editor you like. But the same authoring tool we used in Chapter 7, Mixing Audio, on page 161 to edit APL-A also offers a similar editor for creating APL documents, including a what-you-see-is-roughly-what-you-get view of the template as you edit it.

Another great resource for APL development, which itself offers an APL editor is APL Ninja (https://apl.ninja). APL Ninja is a sort of social network where APL developer can share and learn from each other, including creating and sharing entire APL templates. Many of the APL templates shared on APL Ninja are quite impressive.

We're going to focus on APL itself in this chapter without concern for which editor you use to create it. But if you'd like to try the APL Authoring Tool, you can find it in the Alexa Developer Console, under the "Build" tab, near the bottom of the left-hand menu, labeled "Display".

All APL documents are rooted with a mainTemplate property. This property is roughly analogous to HTML's <body> element, being the top-level parent of the entire visual interface. The mainTemplate has an items property that includes its children, in this case, a Container component, as indicated by the child's type property.

The Container component's items property is populated by a single element, a Text element. It will display the "Hello World" message, as specified in the text property. The remaining properties of the Text component set the component's dimensions, alignment, and font details.

The width and height properties are set to "100vw" and "100vh", respectively. The "vw" and "vh" units indicate a percentage of the viewport's dimensions.

"100vw" is 100% of the viewport's width. Likewise, "100vh" is 100% of the viewport's height.

The textAlign and textAlignVertical properties are both set to "center" so that the text will appear in the middle of the component's space, both horizontally and vertically. Since this is the only component within the only Container, the text will be rendered in the dead center of the screen.

The fontSize property ensures that the text is large enough to not be overwhelmed by all of the empty space around it. The value is expressed in units of "dp", which is an abbreviation for display-independent pixels. Display-independent pixels are a relative size that allows the component size to be adapted relative to the resolution of the display it is rendered in.

Rendering the APL Document

Once the template has been created, we can now modify our skill's fulfillment code to return it in the response. Although we've not done much with it since the first chapter, we still have HelloWorldIntentHandler laying around. It's a perfect place to try out our "Hello World" APL document:

```
apl/starport-75/lambda/HelloWorldIntentHandler.js
const HelloWorldIntentHandler = {
  canHandle(handlerInput) {
     ...
  },
  handle(handlerInput) {
     ...
    if (Alexa.getSupportedInterfaces(handlerInput.requestEnvelope)
                            ['Alexa.Presentation.APL']) {
      handlerInput.responseBuilder
        .addDirective({
          type : 'Alexa.Presentation.APL.RenderDocument',
          document: require('./apl/hello.json')
        });
    }

    return handlerInput.responseBuilder
      .speak(speakOutput)
      .getResponse();
  }
};
```

Just before the response builder is given the text to speak and the handle() function ends, we step in and add the APL document to the response by calling the addDirective() function. The directive object passed to addDirective() is of type Alexa.Presentation.APL.RenderDocument. This tells the Alexa device to render the APL document given in the document property.

In this case, the document has been saved alongside the fulfillment code in a directory named apl and is pulled in using the require() function. But just as with APL-A, the template could be saved within the APL authoring tool and then be referenced as a "Link" document like this:

```
apl/starport-75/lambda/HelloWorldIntentHandler.js
handlerInput.responseBuilder
    .addDirective({
      type : 'Alexa.Presentation.APL.RenderDocument',
      document: {
        "type": "Link",
        "src": "doc://alexa/apl/documents/hello"
      },
    });
```

Not all Alexa devices have screens to render an APL document. Therefore, the call to addDirective() is wrapped in an if block so that the directive will only be included in the response if the device supports APL. As shown here, the Alexa.getSupportedInterfaces() helper function will return true if the requesting device supports the "Alexa.Presentation.APL" interface.

Enabling APL

We're almost ready to deploy our skill and try out our first APL user-interface. But first we must configure the skill manifest to support APL. In the interfaces property of skill.json, add an entry for the "ALEXA_PRESENTATION_APL" interface:

```
apl/starport-75/skill-package/skill.json
"apis": {
  "custom": {
    "endpoint": {
      ...
    },
    "interfaces": [
      {
        "type": "ALEXA_PRESENTATION_APL"
      }
    ]
  }
},
```

Now we're ready to see how the APL document is rendered in response to a "hello world" request.

Trying it Out

After deploying the skill, you can try it out using any Alexa device that has a screen, including the Echo Show or a Fire TV. Or you can just use the developer console, as shown in this screenshot:

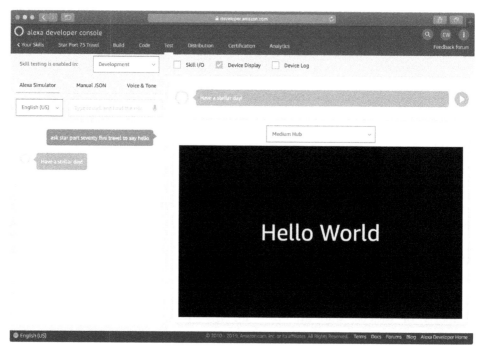

After asking the skill to say "hello", you can view the rendered APL document by scrolling past the request/response pane in the right-hand panel or by unchecking the "Skill I/O" checkbox to hide the request/response content. The result should be a black field (thanks to the "dark" theme) with the words "Hello World" in white.

Not bad for our first APL document. But most visual user-interfaces will require richer designs than just simple text. Fortunately, APL offers more than just text components. Let's step it up a bit with a more interesting APL document.

Creating a Rich APL Document

Let's put APL to work by creating an APL template that tells the user to enjoy their trip and includes some basic itinerary details.

APL affords us the opportunity to flex our creative muscles and come up with a visually interesting design. The following APL template employs a mix of

Container, Text, and Image components to wish the user an enjoyable trip and show some trip details, all in a outer-space landscape:

apl/starport-75/lambda/apl/tripComplete.json

```json
{
  "type": "APL",
  "version": "1.2",
  "theme": "dark",
  "mainTemplate": {
    "items": [
      {
        "type": "Container",
        "width": "100vw",
        "height": "100vh",
        "paddingLeft": "10dp",
        "paddingTop": "10dp",
        "paddingRight": "10dp",
        "paddingBottom": "10dp",
        "direction": "column",
        "items": [
          {
            "type": "Image",
            "width": "100vw",
            "height": "100vh",
            "source":
              "https://starport75.dev/images/planets/stars.jpg",
            "scale": "fill",
            "position": "absolute"
          },
          {
            "type": "Image",
            "position": "absolute",
            "bottom": "0",
            "width": "85vw",
            "height": "175dp",
            "source": "https://starport75.dev/images/planets/
                                             earth_cropped.png",
            "scale": "fill"
          },
          {
            "type": "Image",
            "position": "absolute",
            "bottom": "90dp",
            "left": "200dp",
            "width": "300dp",
            "height": "250dp",
            "source": "https://starport75.dev/images/planets/
                                             spaceship.png",
            "scale": "best-fill"
          },
```

```
        {
          "type": "Text",
          "color": "yellow",
          "fontSize": "42dp",
          "text": "Enjoy your trip to Jupiter"
        },
        {
          "type": "Container",
          "width": "100vw",
          "height": "100%",
          "direction": "row",
          "items": [
            {
              "type": "Container",
              "width": "60vw",
              "height": "100%",
              "direction": "column",
              "items": [
                {
                  "type": "Text",
                  "color": "lightblue",
                  "fontSize": "24dp",
                  "paddingTop": "12dp",
                  "text": "<b>Departing</b>: 2020-06-09"
                },
                {
                  "type": "Text",
                  "fontSize": "24dp",
                  "color": "lightblue",
                  "paddingTop": "12dp",
                  "text": "<b>Returning</b>: 2020-06-12"
                }
              ]
            },
            {
              "type": "Image",
              "width": "300dp",
              "height": "250dp",
              "source": "https://starport75.dev/images/
                                          planets/Jupiter.png"
            }
          ]
        }
      ]
    }
  ]
}
}
```

The top-level Container component exists primarily to create margins for most of the screen's contents so that text isn't bumped up right next to the edge. It's width and height properties are set to "100vw" and "100vh", respectively, so that it fills the entire screen. But its paddingTop, paddingBottom, paddingLeft, and paddingRight properties are all set to "10dp" to set the margins.

You'll also notice that the direction property is set to "column". This specifies that all of this Container component's children that are relatively positioned (which is the default) will flow from top to bottom.

That said, the first three children of the Container have their position property set to "absolute", which frees them from automatic relative positioning and gives us control over the positioning of the components. These Image components establish most of the space scenery that decorates the user-interface and we'll need to position them in places that relative positioning won't allow.

The first Image component displays a starfield image that stretches across the entire screen (per the width, height, and scale properties).

The next image represents an Earth landscape that will be spread across the bottom of the screen. The bottom property is set to "0" which, along with absolute positioning, pushes the image to the bottom of the screen (0 pixels from the bottom). The width property is set to "85vw" so that it only stretches across 85% of the screen, leaving a small empty space to its right.

The third image is that of a spaceship that is launching from Earth toward the user's selected destination. Its positioning and dimensions are a bit more precise to ensure that it appears exactly where we want it relative to the Earth landscape, near the center of the screen.

The remaining children of the top-level Container are relatively positioned, starting with a Text component that is the title of the screen. The Text component is configured to have yellow text and a font size of "40dp" to make it stand out at the top of the screen.

The title Text component is followed by another Container component with direction set to "row", indicating that its children will flow left-to-right. The left-most child is itself a Container with "column" direction that contains two Text components, one each for the trip's departure and return dates (hard-coded for now). The right-most child will be an image of the destination planet, currently hard-coded to Jupiter.

To put this template to work, edit the ScheduleTripIntentHandler and add the following before returning the response:

apl/starport-75/lambda/ScheduleTripIntentHandler.js
```
if (Alexa.getSupportedInterfaces(handlerInput.requestEnvelope)
                              ['Alexa.Presentation.APL']) {
  const locale = Alexa.getLocale(handlerInput.requestEnvelope);
  handlerInput.responseBuilder
    .addDirective({
      type : 'Alexa.Presentation.APL.RenderDocument',
      document: require('./apl/tripComplete.json')
  });
}
```

If APL is supported by the requesting device, then the Alexa.Presentation.APL.RenderDocument directive will be included in the response and the template will be rendered when the user finishes planning a trip. The result will look a little something like this:

That's an awesome start! But you may have noticed that there are several styling details such as font sizes and colors being set explicitly on the components. Let's see how to extract those properties into style definitions.

Applying Styles

While setting style properties directly on components certainly will work, there's no semantic connection between the style and the purpose of the component. What's more, if we decide later to change the style of the two Text components for the trip dates, we'll have to apply identical changes to both.

APL documents support separation of style from the components that styles apply to. This is analogous to how Cascading Style Sheets (CSS) are used to separate style from HTML components in a webpage design. Unlike CSS, which can be defined in a completely separate file from the HTML it is applied to, APL styles are defined in the same APL document, but in a separate styles property.

We'll apply styles in the "enjoy your trip" template by extracting properties that are explicitly set on the title and date Text components into a "titleText" style and a "datesText" style. These styles will be declared in the APL document under a styles property that is a peer of the mainTemplate property:

apl/starport-75/lambda/apl/tripComplete.json

```json
{
  "type": "APL",
  "version": "1.2",
  "theme": "dark",
  "mainTemplate": {
    ...
  },
  "styles": {
    "titleText": {
      "values": [
        {
          "fontWeight": "heavy",
          "fontSize": "48dp",
          "color": "yellow"
        }
      ]
    },
    "datesText": {
      "values": [
        {
          "color": "lightblue",
          "fontSize": "24dp"
        }
      ]
    }
  }
}
```

Now that the styles are defined, we just need to edit each component, removing the explicit properties and setting a style property that references one of the styles we've defined. The changes to the title and date Text components will look like this:

apl/starport-75/lambda/apl/tripComplete.json

```json
{
    "type": "Text",
    "style": "titleText",
    "text": "Enjoy your trip to Jupiter"
},
{
    "type": "Container",
    "width": "100vw",
    "height": "100%",
    "direction": "row",
```

```
    "items": [
        {
            "type": "Container",
            "width": "60vw",
            "height": "100%",
            "items": [
                {
                    "type": "Text",
                    "paddingTop": "12dp",
                    "style": "datesText",
                    "text": "<b>Departing</b>: 2020-06-09"
                },
                {
                    "type": "Text",
                    "paddingTop": "12dp",
                    "style": "datesText",
                    "text": "<b>Returning</b>: 2020-06-12"
                }
            ]
        },
        ...
    ]
}
```

The style property tells each of these components to adopt the properties defined by the corresponding entry we defined in styles. It's important to notice, however, that not all properties are considered style properties, which is why paddingTop is still explicitly specified on the two Text components for the trip's starting and ending dates.

Even so, it is unfortunate that we couldn't capture the paddingTop property in the styles. It would be nice if there were some way to collect the values for those places in one place, separate from the components themselves, so that they can be easily found and edited in the APL document. Let's have a look at how to define resources in an APL document to carry reusable values.

Defining Resource Values

A common and very useful technique when developing software is to stow often-used values in constants. This helps give semantic meaning to what would otherwise be simple values. And it provides for a single location where the value can be maintained and changed, regardless of how many places the value is used.

APL offers a similar means of declaring constants called *resources*. Resources let us declare constant values for dimensions, colors, or just arbitrary text in a single place and refer to them throughout the APL document.

For example, rather than hard-code "12dp" in the paddingTop property of the two Text components for the trip dates, we can declare it once, as a resource, giving it a semantically significant name like this:

```
"resources": [
  {
    "dimensions": {
      "dateSpacing": "12dp"
    }
  }
]
```

Here, the name dateSpacing describes exactly what the purpose of that resource value is used for: To define spacing between the two date components. Now we can use that resource name everywhere we previously hard-coded "12dp":

```
{
  "type": "Text",
  "paddingTop": "@dateSpacing",
  "style": "datesText",
  "text": "<b>Departing</b>: 2020-06-09"
},
{
  "type": "Text",
  "paddingTop": "@dateSpacing",
  "style": "datesText",
  "text": "<b>Returning</b>: 2020-06-12"
}
```

Here the paddingTop property is set to "@dateSpacing". The "@" prefix indicates that this is not a literal value of "dateSpacing", but a reference to the resource with that name. Later, if we decide to change the spacing to "50dp" or some other value, we won't need to change the value of paddingTop for every Text component. We only need to change the value once where it's defined as a resource.

Dimension resources are only one of three types of resources. We can also define color and string resource values. Using color resources and a few more dimension resources, we can capture the title and body text color as well as the font sizes for all text like this:

```
"resources": [
  {
    "dimensions": {
      "dateSpacing": "12dp",
      "titleFontSize": "48dp",
      "dateFontSize": "24dp"
    },
```

```
     "colors": {
       "titleTextColor": "yellow",
       "dateTextColor": "lightblue"
     }
   }
]
```

Then we can change styles for the Text components in the document to reference those resources:

```
{
  "titleText": {
    "values": [
      {
        "fontWeight": "heavy",
        "fontSize": "@titleFontSize",
        "color": "@titleTextColor"
      }
    ]
  },
  "datesText": {
    "values": [
      {
        "color": "@dateTextColor",
        "fontSize": "@dateFontSize"
      }
    ]
  }
}
```

Now, if we decide to change those values later or reuse them on new components, they're all defined in a single, easy to find location in the APL document.

A third type of resource, String resources, enables you to declare resources that hold any arbitrary textual values. For example, you could assign a couple of resources that hold the URLs for the starfield and logo images:

```
"resources": [
  {
    "dimensions": {
      "dateSpacing": "12dp",
      "titleFontSize": "48dp",
      "dateFontSize": "24dp"
    },
    "colors": {
      "titleTextColor": "yellow",
      "dateTextColor": "lightblue"
    },
    "strings": {
      "stars": "https://starport75.dev/images/planets/stars.jpg",
```

```
      "earth": "https://starport75.dev/images/planets/earth_cropped.png",
      "spaceship": "https://starport75.dev/images/planets/spaceship.png"
    }
  }
]
```

With those defined, you would change the source property of the Image components to reference the resource strings:

```
{
    "type": "Image",
    "width": "100vw",
    "height": "100vh",
    "source": "@stars",
    "scale": "fill",
    "position": "absolute"
},
{
    "type": "Image",
    "position": "absolute",
    "bottom": "0",
    "width": "85vw",
    "height": "175dp",
    "source": "@earth",
    "scale": "fill"
},
{
    "type": "Image",
    "position": "absolute",
    "bottom": "90dp",
    "left": "200dp",
    "width": "300dp",
    "height": "250dp",
    "source": "@spaceship",
    "scale": "best-fill"
},
```

You could also use string resources to hold the values for the title and date
components. But that would lock those text components into a specific set
of text in a given language. Rather than write those values in the template,
let's have a look at how they can be given to the template from the skill's fulfillment code as model data.

Injecting Model Data

Often it is useful to pass data from the fulfillment to a template to be rendered.
This keeps the display from being static and helps provide useful visual
information to the user. A skill that deals with weather forecasts, for example,
could display a five-day forecast while Alexa speaks the current weather

conditions. It would be less useful if the display only showed a fixed logo or text while Alexa speaks the weather.

You can pass data to an APL template using the datasources property of the Alexa.Presentation.APL.RenderDocument directive. For the "enjoy your trip" screen, we could pass along the trip details as well as some text from the intent handler to the APL template like this:

```
apl/starport-75/lambda/ScheduleTripIntentHandler.js
      const locale = Alexa.getLocale(handlerInput.requestEnvelope);
      handlerInput.responseBuilder
         .addDirective({
            type : 'Alexa.Presentation.APL.RenderDocument',
            document: require('./apl/tripComplete.json'),
            datasources: {
              "tripData": {
                "titleText": handlerInput.t('ENJOY_YOUR_TRIP_TITLE'),
                "destination": destination,
                "departureLabel": handlerInput.t('DEPARTURE_LABEL'),
                "departureDate": toFriendlyDate(departureDate, locale),
                "returnLabel": handlerInput.t('RETURNING_LABEL'),
                "returnDate": toFriendlyDate(returnDate, locale)
              }
            }
         });
```

For convenience, all of the properties are carried in a single object named tripData. The title text and date labels are pulled from the languageStrings.js module using handlerInput.t(), the same as the text that Alexa speaks in responses. This ensures that both the spoken text and the visual displays are presented in the user's chosen language.

The trip's destination and dates are also passed through the model data. Because the dates are going to be displayed, they are passed through a toFriendlyDate() function that is defined in a separate utility module:

```
apl/starport-75/lambda/dateUtils.js
const toFriendlyDate = function(dateString, locale) {
  var dateDate = new Date(dateString);
  return dateDate.toLocaleDateString(locale,
      {month:"long", day:"numeric", year: "numeric"});
};

module.exports = toFriendlyDate;
```

The toFriendlyDate() function takes the given date string and formats it in a locale-specific friendly date format. For example, if the locale is "en-US" and the date is 2021-10-25, then the friendly date will be "October 25, 2021". On the other hand, for the "es-US" locale, the friendly date will be "25 de octubre de 2021".

With the data being passed to the APL template, we can start changing some of the Text components to present the model data instead of hardcoded text. For instance, we can change the text property of the title Text component to render values from the model like this:

```
{
  "type": "Text",
  "width": "100vw",
  "height": "60dp",
  "color": "yellow",
  "fontSize": "42dp",
➤ "text": "${payload.tripData.titleText} ${payload.tripData.destination}"
},
```

The value of the text property uses ${} notation to reference the titleText and destination properties from the tripData object that is carried in payload.

In order for this to work, however, we'll need to declare the payload parameter in the template. Near the top of the mainTemplate, add a parameters property that declares payload like this:

```
"mainTemplate": {
    "parameters": [
        "payload"
    ],
    ...
}
```

As for the date Text components, their text properties reference model data in a very similar way:

```
{
  "type": "Text",
  "color": "lightblue",
  "fontSize": "24dp",
  "paddingTop": "12dp",
➤ "text": "<b>${payload.tripData.departureLabel}:</b>
➤           ${payload.tripData.departureDate}"
},
{
  "type": "Text",
  "fontSize": "24dp",
  "color": "lightblue",
  "paddingTop": "12dp",
➤ "text": "<b>${payload.tripData.returnLabel}:</b>
➤           ${payload.tripData.returnDate}"
}
```

There's one more thing we can use the model data for in this template. Rather than hard-code a URL for the planet image to always display Jupiter, we can

${payload.tripData.destination} to dynamically create that URL in the Image component like this:

```
{
    "type": "Image",
    "width": "300dp",
    "height": "250dp",
    "source": "https://starport75.dev/images/planets/
                     ${payload.tripData.destination}.png"
}
```

Now the template is fully dynamic with every part, except the background images, populated from model data. Redeploy the skill and give it a try. The resulting display should look like this:

Here, a trip was planned to Uranus between February 19th and 21st. What's more, the planet image is an image for the chosen planet.

So far, we've treated APL as a one-way form of communication where an APL template is sent from the server and rendered on the device's screen. Let's see how to turn things around by handling touch events.

Handling Touch Events

Most screen-enabled Alexa devices are actually touch screen devices. Echo Show devices, for example, are able to respond to touch gestures much like tablets. You can take advantage of this by handling touch events in your APL-enabled skill.

To add touch events to an APL template, you need to wrap one or more elements in your APL template with the TouchWrapper component. For example, suppose that the skill has a welcome APL template that is displayed when the user launches the skill. And suppose that in the welcome template, you have an Image component that renders the Star Port 75 logo. Before you add the TouchWrapper, that Image component might be defined like this:

```
{
    "type": "Image",
    "width": "340dp",
    "height": "100%",
    "source": "https://starport75.dev/images/SP75_lg.png",
    "align": "center"
}
```

Now, let's suppose that you want to add touch capability to the welcome screen such that when the user touches the logo, a marketing soundbyte about Star Port 75 is played. The first thing you'll need to do is wrap the Image component with TouchWrapper like this:

```
{
  "type": "TouchWrapper",
  "item": {
    "type": "Image",
    "width": "340dp",
    "height": "100%",
    "source": "https://starport75.dev/images/SP75_lg.png",
    "align": "center"
  },
  "onPress": {
    "type": "SendEvent",
    "arguments": [
      "starport75Logo"
    ]
  }
}
```

Here, the Image component we started with is now the value of the TouchWrapper components's item property. It will still be rendered the same as before, but now it will also react to touch. How it reacts is defined by the onPress property.

The onPress property is defined to send an event to the skill's fulfillment backend with a single argument of "starport75Logo". We'll use this argument in a handler's canHandle() function to handle touch events for this specific component.

A touch event handler is much like an intent request handler, in that it has both canHandle() and handle() functions. If canHandle() returns true, then handle() will handle the event. The key difference between a touch event handler and other kinds of handlers is in how the canHandle() evaluates the request type. Instead of looking for an IntentRequest, LaunchRequest, or some other kind of request we've seen already, a touch event handler checks for requests whose type is "Alexa.Presentation.APL.UserEvent".

For example, look at the canHandle() function in the following touch event handler:

apl/starport-75/lambda/TouchHandlers.js
```
const Alexa = require('ask-sdk-core');

const LogoTouchHandler = {
  canHandle(handlerInput) {
    return Alexa.getRequestType(
        handlerInput.requestEnvelope) === 'Alexa.Presentation.APL.UserEvent'
      && Alexa.getRequest(
        handlerInput.requestEnvelope).arguments.includes('starport75Logo');
  },
  handle(handlerInput) {
    return handlerInput.responseBuilder
      .speak(handlerInput.t('WELCOME_TOUCH'))
      .withShouldEndSession(false)
      .getResponse();
  }
};

module.exports={
  LogoTouchHandler:LogoTouchHandler
};
```

The canHandle() function checks for a request type of "Alexa.Presentation.APL. UserEvent", indicating that this is a touch event from the user. It also checks that the request arguments contain "starport75Logo". This ensures that this handler will only handle events from the TouchWrapper we created on the welcome screen and not any other touch events that may be defined elsewhere in our skill's visual user interface.

As for the handle() function, it's not much different from the handle() method of any of our request handlers we've already defined. It simply speaks the message defined in languageStrings.js with the key "WELCOME_TOUCH" and leaves the session open so that the skill will continue listening for utterances about planetary travel.

Speaking of the languageStrings.js module, here's the new "WELCOME_TOUCH" entry to support the touch event handler:

apl/starport-75/lambda/languageStrings.js
```
WELCOME_TOUCH:
  'Star Port 75 Travel, your source for ' +
  '<audio src="soundbank://soundlibrary/scifi/' +
            'amzn_sfx_scifi_small_zoom_flyby_01"/> ' +
  'out-of-this world adventures.',
```

Touch events provide another way that users can interact with your skill along with voice. But remember that Alexa skills are voice-first user interfaces. It's important that you design the visual interface of your skill to complement the voice interface, not replace it.

Wrapping Up

The Alexa Presentation Language is a JSON-based template language for skills to render visual user-interfaces to screen-enabled Alexa devices. APL offers complete flexibility in designing any visual user-interface you can imagine.

APL offers the option of extracting style details into stylesheets that are roughly analogous to how CSS is used to style HTML. This enables common styles to be defined in one place and reused for many components, and it creates a semantic link between the styles and the components that they are applied to.

Resource values offer a way to create named values, similar to how constants are created in many programming languages. The named values can represent dimensions, colors, or arbitrary strings. Those named values can then be referenced in component properties and styles, offering many of the same benefits of styles and be used for properties that aren't supported in styles.

A skill's request handlers can pass data they receive, lookup, or calculate in model data to be rendered in the APL templates. This makes for a dynamic experience in visual user-interfaces.

Touch events add another dimension to Alexa's visual user interface when a user interacts with a screen-enabled device. The TouchWrapper component can be placed around any other component in an APL template to fire events back to the skill's fulfillment code when the user physically touches the screen. In the fulfillment code, touch event handlers are written much the same as the handlers for other kinds of Alexa requests such as intent requests.

So far, all of the interaction between a user and our skill has been initiated by the user when speaking to Alexa. Coming up in the next chapter, we're going to flip that around and look at sending reminders and notifications—ways to have Alexa initiate communication without first being spoken to.

CHAPTER 11

Sending Events

Usually Alexa keeps to herself, waiting for you to call on her to answer a question, play some music, or interact with some skill. She doesn't interject in a conversation or randomly make observations. She'll remain silent unless you ask her for something.

But it doesn't have to be that way. It would be nice if Alexa would notify you when your favorite team scores or let you know when a book by your favorite author is released. You might be able to take it a little slower going to the airport if Alexa were to proactively tell you that your flight is delayed. And you won't forget to pack the night before if Alexa were to remind you of your trip the day before.

In this chapter, we're going to look at some ways to enable Alexa to chime in and speak up without it being in direct response to an intent. We'll see how to have Alexa speak up to remind users of some event at a specific time. But first, let's look at how an external application can cause Alexa to send notification to its users on demand.

Publishing Proactive Events

Proactive events give a skill the ability to notify users of significant information out-of-session, even though the user isn't actively using the skill. When the notification is received, all of the user's Alexa devices will chime and display a visual indication of pending notifications (a pulsing yellow ring on Echo and Echo Dot devices, for instance). The user can then ask Alexa to read the notifications by saying, "Alexa, read notifications."

A common example of proactive events is when an Amazon order has been delivered. If the user has notifications enabled, their Alexa devices will notify them of the delivery. But proactive events aren't limited to Amazon orders.

Any skill can take advantage of them to communicate updates and events to its users.

Proactive events come in eight predefined schemas:[1]

- *Media Content Alerts*—Alert users about upcoming book, television episode, album, music single, movie, or game release

- *Message Alerts*—Alert users about messages (e.g, text or voice message) they have received

- *Occasions*—Notifies user about upcoming reservations or appointments

- *Order Status*—Notifies user about order status changes

- *Social Game Invitations*—Invites a user to join another user in playing some game

- *Sports Events*—Updates users regarding a sporting event, such as scores from a soccer match

- *Trash Collection Alerts*—Alerts users regarding trash collection dates

- *Weather Alerts*—Alerts users regarding significant weather events

As you can see, each of these schemas targets a specific domain. Sending a user scores of a sporting event is very different than alerting a user when their trash will be collected. When using proactive events, it's important to select the schema that is most suitable for your skill's needs.

For the purposes of Star Port 75 Travel, the Occasions schema is most relevant and we'll use it to notify users regarding their trip's reservation. To get started, we'll enable proactive events in the skill's manifest.

Enabling Proactive Events

In order for a skill to send events to its users, the events must be declared in the skill's manifest, under the events property:

```
"events": {
  "publications": [
    { "eventName": "AMAZON.Occasion.Updated"}
  ],
  "endpoint": {
    "uri": "arn:aws:lambda:us-east-1:4944..."
  }
}
```

---

1.   https://developer.amazon.com/en-US/docs/alexa/smapi/schemas-for-proactive-events.html

Here, under the publications sub-property, we have declared that this skill will be able to send occasion events. Notice that publications is an array and can declare one or more entries where eventName is one of the following:

- AMAZON.MediaContent.Available
- AMAZON.MessageAlert.Activated
- AMAZON.Occasion.Updated
- AMAZON.OrderStatus.Updated
- AMAZON.SocialGameInvite.Available
- AMAZON.SportsEvent.Updated
- AMAZON.TrashCollectionAlert.Activated
- AMAZON.WeatherAlert.Activated

We also must declare the skill's endpoint URI. If you're not sure what the skill's endpoint URI is, you can easily look it up using the ASK CLI like this:

```
$ ask smapi get-skill-manifest \
    --skill-id amzn1.ask.skill.28e3f37-2b4-4b5-849-bcf4f2e081 \
{
  "manifest": {
    "apis": {
      "custom": {
        "endpoint": {
          "uri": "arn:aws:lambda:us-east-1:4944..."
        }
      }
    },
    ...
}
```

The ask smapi get-skill-manifest command requires that the skill ID be passed in via the --skill-id parameter. The skill's endpoint URI is found near the top of the response, under the manifest.apis.custom.endpoint.uri property. Just copy the value of the property into the events.endpoint.uri property in skill.json when declaring events.

Now the skill declares that it can send proactive events. But it must also be given permission to do so. Let's see how to configure the skill with permission to send events and how to ask the user for permission.

Asking for Permission to Send Events

We've had a little experience asking our skill users for permission. In Chapter 5, Integrating User Data, on page 105, we configured the skill's manifest with permissions for fetching the user's given name and email, then returned a permissions consent card for the user to grant those permissions.

Permissions for sending proactive events are established in exactly the same way. First, we need to add a new entry to the permissions section of skill.json:

```
events/starport-75-reminders/skill-package/skill.json
"permissions": [
  {
    "name": "alexa::profile:given_name:read"
  },
  {
    "name": "alexa::profile:email:read"
  },
  {
    "name": "alexa::devices:all:notifications:write"
  }
]
```

The newly created permission, alexa::devices:all:notifications:write, declares that our skill may ask the user for permission to write notifications to the user's Alexa devices.

Now all we must do is send a permissions consent card in the response of a request handler. Any of the skill's request handlers could work, but it makes the most sense to ask for permission to send a reservation notification in response to a successfully scheduled trip. The following change to how the response is built in ScheduleTripIntentHandler will do the trick:

```
events/starport-75-events/lambda/ScheduleTripIntentHandler.js
return handlerInput.responseBuilder
  .speak(speakOutput)
  .withAskForPermissionsConsentCard(
      ['alexa::devices:all:notifications:write'])
  .withShouldEndSession(true)
  .getResponse();
```

The call to withAskForPermissionsConsentCard() replaces a call to withStandardCard() we had originally added in Chapter 9, Complementing Responses with Cards, on page 213. Unfortunately, a response can only include one card and the permissions consent card is more important here than the informational standard card we were returning before.

The permissions consent card won't do any good if the user doesn't know to go to the Alexa companion application to grant permission. Therefore, we should also change the spoken text to tell the user to give notifications permission:

```
events/starport-75-events/lambda/languageStrings.js
SCHEDULED_MSG: "You're all set. Enjoy your trip to {{destination}}!" +
  "If you want, I can send you a notification when the reservation " +
  "is confirmed. I've sent a card to the Alexa application for you " +
  "to give permission for notifications.",
```

With these changes in place, deploy the skill and try it out. Plan a trip to any place you'd like and confirm the trip plans. It shouldn't behave much differently than before, although it should send a card to the Alexa companion application prompting you to grant permission for notifications:

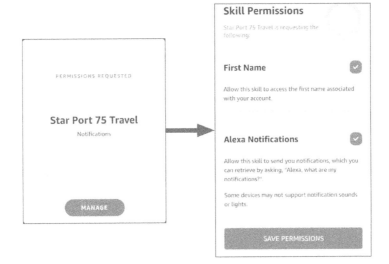

After clicking on the "Manage" button on the card, be sure that the "Alexa Notifications" checkbox is checked and click "Save Permissions". Then the skill can send you proactive events any time it needs. Let's see how to fire off an event to our skill's users.

Dispatching Events

Although proactive events are sent from a skill to a user's Alexa device(s), the events actually originate in an external system. This is typically some backend system for which the skill is a user interface.

We've not implemented an actual backend trip booking system for the Star Port 75 Travel skill. We used Google Calendar as a stand-in for a booking system in Chapter 5, Integrating User Data, on page 105. In this chapter, we will create a NodeJS script to act as a stand-in for the backend system to send events through the skill. Although it will be a standalone NodeJS script, the approach taken can apply to any real-world application, regardless of the language.

Sending events through a skill to the user involves two steps:

- Obtaining an access token
- Sending an HTTP POST request to the Alexa API

Not just any application should be allowed to post notifications through the skill. Therefore, the Alexa API is secured as an OAuth2 resource server. Our script will need to obtain an access token that will allow it to submit notifications. The following Javascript code sends a POST request to Amazon's authorization server's token endpoint [2] to obtain an access token:

```
events/starport-75-events/send-scripts/sendEvent.js
const request = require('request-promise-native');
const clientId = 'amzn1.application-oa2-client.9160db0...';
const clientSecret = '69fcab9...';
const eventPublisher = {
  async getAccessToken(clientId, clientSecret) {
    const requestPayload = require('./tokenRequest.json');
    requestPayload.client_id = clientId;
    requestPayload.client_secret = clientSecret;

    const token = await request({
      method: 'POST',
      uri: 'https://api.amazon.com/auth/o2/token',
      headers: {
        'Content-type': 'application/json'
      },
      body: JSON.stringify(requestPayload)
    });
    return JSON.parse(token).access_token;
  },
};
```

The payload of the request is pulled in with a require() call from an external file named tokenRequest.json, which looks like this:

```
events/starport-75-events/send-scripts/tokenRequest.json
{
  "grant_type": "client_credentials",
  "scope": "alexa::proactive_events",
  "client_id": "",
  "client_secret": ""
}
```

Once the token request payload is loaded, the script replaces the values of the client_id and client_secret properties with actual client ID and secret values for our skill. You'll need to replace the clientId and clientSecret properties in sendEvent.js with the actual client ID and secret from the skill. You can look them up using the ask smapi get-skill-credentials command:

```
$ ask smapi get-skill-credentials --skill-id=amzn1.ask.skill.28e36f37-...
{
  "skillMessagingCredentials": {
    "clientId": "amzn1.application-oa2-client.916...",
    "clientSecret": "69fcab9..."
  }
}
```

Once the POST request completes, the getAccessToken() function extracts the
access token from the response and returns it to the caller. Speaking of the caller,
the first thing that the sendOccasionEvent() function does is make a call to getAc-
cessToken():

events/starport-75-events/send-scripts/sendEvent.js

```javascript
const request = require('request-promise-native');
const crypto = require("crypto");

const clientId = 'amzn1.application-oa2-client.9160db0...';
const clientSecret = '69fcab9...';
const userId = 'amzn1.ask.account.AF3DEHA...';
const reservationTime = "2020-03-10T00:00:00Z";
const destination = "Jupiter";

Date.prototype.addHours = function(h) {
  this.setTime(this.getTime() + (h*60*60*1000));
  return this;
}

const eventPublisher = {
  ...

  async sendOccasionEvent(clientId, clientSecret, userId,
                          reservationTime, destination) {
    const accessToken =
        await eventPublisher.getAccessToken(clientId, clientSecret);

    const requestPayload = require('./eventRequest.json');
    requestPayload.referenceId = crypto.randomBytes(16).toString('hex');
    requestPayload.timestamp = new Date().toISOString();
    requestPayload.expiryTime = new Date().addHours(1).toISOString();
    requestPayload.event.payload.occasion.bookingTime = reservationTime;
    requestPayload.relevantAudience.payload.user = userId;
    requestPayload.localizedAttributes.push({
      locale: 'en-US',
      subject: `Trip to ${destination}`,
      providerName: "Star Port 75 Travel"
    });
    requestPayload.localizedAttributes.push({
      locale: 'es-ES',
      subject: `Viaje a ${destination}`,
      providerName: "Star Port 75 Travel"
    });
```

```javascript
    const eventsUri = 'https://api.amazonalexa.com/v1/proactiveEvents';
    await request({
      method: 'POST',
      uri: eventsUri + '/stages/development',
      headers: {
        'Content-type': 'application/json',
        'Authorization': `Bearer ${accessToken}`
      },
      body: JSON.stringify(requestPayload)
    });

    console.log('Notification sent');
  }
};

eventPublisher.sendOccasionEvent(
    clientId, clientSecret, userId, reservationTime, destination);
```

With the access token in hand, sendOccasionEvent() uses require() to load the event request payload template into a constant. The template itself looks like this:

events/starport-75-events/send-scripts/eventRequest.json

```json
{
  "referenceId": "TBD",
  "timestamp": "TBD",
  "expiryTime": "TBD",
  "event": {
    "name": "AMAZON.Occasion.Updated",
    "payload": {
      "state": {
        "confirmationStatus": "CONFIRMED"
      },
      "occasion": {
        "occasionType": "RESERVATION",
        "subject": "localizedattribute:subject",
        "provider": {
          "name": "localizedattribute:providerName"
        },
        "bookingTime": "TBD"
      }
    }
  },
  "localizedAttributes": [],
  "relevantAudience": {
    "type": "Unicast",
    "payload": {
      "user": "TBD"
    }
  }
}
```

As you can see, there are several properties that are set to a placeholder value of "TBD". Much of the request payload template is boilerplate, but a handful of the template's properties will need to be replaced with actual values. Those properties are:

- referenceId—A value that uniquely identifies the notification. This can contain any value and could be used to reference some entity in the backend system (such as an order ID or booking ID).

- timestamp—The timestamp of the notification, typically set to the current time

- expiryTime—When the notification will expire. Can be any time between 5 minutes from the current time and 24 hours from the current time. After the expiry time passes, the notification will be automatically deleted.

- bookingTime—The time of the reservation or appointment

- user—The skill user ID whose Alexa devices will receive the notification

Replacing the placeholder values on these properties is the very next thing that the sendOccasionEvent() function does once it has loaded the template. The referenceId property is generated randomly using the crypto module. The timestamp property is set to the current time. As for the expiryTime, it is set to the current time plus one hour (with help from the addHours() function added to the Date class).

The user and bookingTime properties are set from constants defined earlier in the script. You'll need to set the reservationTime property to some date in the future. If this were an actual backend booking system, this would be the time of departure date of the schedule trip.

The userId property will need to be set to the skill user's ID. Each skill user is assigned an ID that is unique to that user and to the skill. If this script were an actual backend system, this ID would need to be extracted from the requests's session.user.userId property and sent to the backend when the trip is scheduled. When sending the notification, the user ID will be sent in the request. For demonstration purposes, the easiest way to get the user ID is to find it in the request JSON in the developer console's JSON input box.

Looking back at the request template, notice that there are two properties whose values start with "localizedattribute:": subject and provider.name:

```
"occasion": {
  "occasionType": "RESERVATION",
  "subject": "localizedattribute:subject",
  "provider": {
    "name": "localizedattribute:providerName"
  },
  "bookingTime": "TBD"
}
```

The subject property describes the subject of the notification, while the provider.name property describes who is responsible for creating the reservation. We could hard-code those values with "Trip to Jupiter" and "Star Port 75 Travel", but then those values would be language specific. Instead, the values localizedattribute:subject and localizedattribute:providerName reference localized values in the template under the localizedAttributes property.

For example, suppose that the localizedAttributes property were set like this:

```
"localizedAttributes": [
  {
    "locale": "en-US",
    "subject": "Trip to Jupiter",
    "providerName": "Star Port 75 Travel"
  },
  {
    "locale": "es-ES",
    "subject": "Viaje a Jupiter",
    "providerName": "Star Port 75 Travel"
  }
],
```

As shown here, if the notification were sent to a user whose device is configured for English, the subject would be "Trip to Jupiter". But if the device is configured with Spanish as the chosen language, it would be "Viaje a Jupiter". Even though the providerName won't be different regardless of language, it is a required property in localized attribute entries.

But rather than hard-code either of those in the request template, the sendOccasionEvent() function adds them to the template so that the subject can contain the destination from the reservation. For our stand-in booking system, the sendOccasionEvent() function pushes English and Spanish entries into the localizedAttributes property like this:

events/starport-75-events/send-scripts/sendEvent.js
```
requestPayload.localizedAttributes.push({
  locale: 'en-US',
  subject: `Trip to ${destination}`,
  providerName: "Star Port 75 Travel"
});
```

```
requestPayload.localizedAttributes.push({
  locale: 'es-ES',
  subject: `Viaje a ${destination}`,
  providerName: "Star Port 75 Travel"
});
```

Finally, the sendOccasionEvent() sends the payload in a POST request with the access token in the Authorization header. The request is sent to https://api.amazonalexa.com/v1/proactiveEvents/stages/development, which is the URI of the proactive events staging API for North America. There are two more staging URLs for Europe and the Far East:

- *Europe*—https://api.eu.amazonalexa.com/v1/proactiveEvents/stages/development
- *Far East*—https://api.fe.amazonalexa.com/v1/proactiveEvents/stages/development

Staging URLs ensure that no actual users will receive notifications while we test our skill. But once the skill is published to production, we'll need to post notification requests to production URLs instead:

- *North America*—https://api.amazonalexa.com/v1/proactiveEvents
- *Europe*—https://api.eu.amazonalexa.com/v1/proactiveEvents
- *Far East*—https://api.fe.amazonalexa.com/v1/proactiveEvents

Once you've filled in values for the clientId, clientSecret, userId, reservationTime, and destination properties, you can run the script like this:

```
$ node sendEvent.js
Notification sent
```

If all goes well, then all of the Alexa devices connected to your developer account will chime to indicate that you have a new notification. Say, "Alexa, what are my notifications?" and Alexa will read the notification to you. Otherwise, after one hour the notification will automatically be deleted.

Sending Multicast Events

In the relevantAudience.payload.user property, our script sends a reservation notification that targets a specific user by their skill user ID. That's because the relevantAudience.type property is sent to "Unicast".

But not all notifications are user-specific. For instance, if your skill is sending updates regarding the score of a basketball game, it would be very tedious to send the same notification to all of your skill's users. Instead, you can broadcast the same event to all users of your skill by setting relevantAudience.type to "Multicast":

```
"relevantAudience": {
  "type": "Multicast",
  "payload": {}
}
```

Since a multicast event isn't user-specific, there's no need to set the relevantAudience.payload.userId property. The relevantAudience.payload property, however, is still required and may be left empty.

Proactive events are great ways to inform a skill's users of an event as it happens, such as the change of an order status or the confirmation of a reservation. On the other hand, sometimes it's helpful for Alexa to remind users of an upcoming event. Let's see how to use reminders to give users a heads-up on something that is about to happen.

Sending Reminders

Similar to proactive events, reminders are activated out-of-session when the user isn't actively using the skill. Unlike proactive events, reminders don't involve a backend system. Instead, reminders are kind of like alarm clocks, triggered at a specified date and time.

In the Star Port 75 skill, we can set a reminder to remind the user that their trip is about to happen. After the user has scheduled a trip, the skill can ask them if they want to set a reminder for one day before their trip begins. We'll start by creating a new module responsible for scheduling reminders.

Creating a Reminder

When scheduling a trip, our skill walks the user through a dialog to make sure that it has captured the destination, departure date, and return date from the user. It then confirms that the information gathered meets the user's expectations. And, if so, it finishes by scheduling the trip and sending the trip details to the backend booking system (which is Google Calendar for our purposes).

It's at the end of that flow, after the trip has been scheduled, that the skill could offer to set a reminder. We could write the code that sets reminders in the handle() function of ScheduleTripIntentHandler, which is at the tail end of the trip planning flow. But that function is already rather lengthy, so to keep it from getting any longer and to afford us some flexibility in how reminders are set, let's create a separate module that is solely responsible for the creation of reminders:

events/starport-75-reminders/lambda/reminderSender.js

```javascript
const Alexa = require('ask-sdk-core');

module.exports = {
  async setReminder(handlerInput, destination, departureDate) {
    const { serviceClientFactory, responseBuilder } = handlerInput;

    const reminderRequest = require('./reminderRequest.json');
    reminderRequest.requestTime = new Date().toISOString();
    const reminderText =
        handlerInput.t('REMINDER_MSG', { destination: destination });
    reminderRequest.alertInfo.spokenInfo.content.push({
        'locale': Alexa.getLocale(handlerInput.requestEnvelope),
        'text': reminderText,
        'ssml': `<speak>${reminderText}</speak>`
      });

    try {
      const reminderClient =
          serviceClientFactory.getReminderManagementServiceClient();
      await reminderClient.createReminder(reminderRequest);

    } catch (error) {
      if (error.name === 'ServiceError' &&
          (error.statusCode == 403 || error.statusCode == 401)) {
        responseBuilder.withAskForPermissionsConsentCard(
            ['alexa::alerts:reminders:skill:readwrite']);
        throw new Error(handlerInput.t('REMINDER_PERMISSION'));
      } else {
        throw new Error(handlerInput.t('REMINDER_ERROR'));
      }
    }

  }
};
```

As you can see, this module has a single function called setReminder(). The setReminder() function logically has three main sections. The first thing it does is load a reminder request object from a JSON-based template file named reminderRequest.json and populate a few of its properties. The template looks like this:

events/starport-75-reminders/lambda/reminderRequest.json

```json
{
  "requestTime" : "TBD",
  "trigger": {
    "type" : "SCHEDULED_RELATIVE",
    "offsetInSeconds" : "30"
  },
  "alertInfo": {
    "spokenInfo": {
      "content": []
    }
  },
```

```
  "pushNotification" : {
    "status" : "ENABLED"
  }
}
```

The first thing to notice about this template is the trigger property. Its type is set to "SCHEDULED_RELATIVE" with offsetInSeconds set to "30" to indicate that the reminder should be triggered exactly 30 seconds after it is created. Ultimately, we'll want to set a "SCHEDULED_ABSOLUTE" trigger so that the reminder can be set to a time one day before the trip begins. But absolute triggers can be difficult to test because we'll need to potentially wait several days to see if they work. For now, we'll use a relative trigger so we can test our skill and get quick feedback.

As you can see, the requestTime property is set to "TBD" as a placeholder value. The setReminder() function overwrites this value with the current time. Also, notice that the alertInfo.spokenInfo.content property is an empty list. setReminder() populates this by pushing a locale-specific object with the text that is to be spoken when the reminder triggers.

The second thing that the setReminder() function does is create the reminder. It does this by passing the reminder request object to the createReminder() function on the reminder client (which was obtained by calling getReminderManagementServiceClient() on the service client factory). If the reminder is created successfully, then the setReminder() function is done. But if anything goes wrong, then that brings us to the third part of the function: the catch block.

The catch block considers the error name and status code to determine if the error occurred because the user hasn't granted the skill permission to create reminders. If that's the case, it adds a permissions consent card to the response builder to ask for alexa::alerts:reminders:skill:readwrite permission. It then throws a new error with a localized message telling the user to grant permission in the Alexa application.

In the unlikely event that the createReminder() function fails for any other reason, the setReminder() function ends by throwing an error with a more generic message saying that it couldn't create the reminder.

The three localized messages referenced in setReminder() will need to be defined in languageStrings.js for each of the supported languages. For English and Spanish, they might look like this:

events/starport-75-reminders/lambda/languageStrings.js
```
module.exports = {
  en: {
    translation: {
      ...
      REMINDER_MSG: 'A reminder from Star Port 75 Travel: ' +
                    'Your trip to {{destination}} is tomorrow!',
      REMINDER_PERMISSION: 'I was unable to set a reminder. Please grant ' +
        'me permission to set a reminder in the Alexa app.',
      REMINDER_ERROR: 'There was an error creating the reminder.',
      ...
    }
  },
  es: {
    translation: {
      ...
      REMINDER_MSG: 'Un recordatorio de  Star Port 75 Travel: ' +
        '¡Tu viaje a {{destination}} es mañana!',
      REMINDER_PERMISSION: 'No pude establecer un recordatorio. ' +
        'Por favor, concédame permiso para configurar un recordatorio en ' +
        'la aplicación Alexa.',
      REMINDER_ERROR: 'Se produjo un error al crear el recordatorio.',
      ...
    }
  }
}
```

Since setReminder() may need to ask for alexa::alerts:reminders:skill:readwrite permission, we'll also need to declare that permission in skill.json, as we've done for other permissions before:

events/starport-75-reminders/skill-package/skill.json
```
"permissions": [
  {
    "name": "alexa::profile:given_name:read"
  },
  {
    "name": "alexa::profile:email:read"
  },
  {
    "name": "alexa::devices:all:notifications:write"
  },
  {
    "name": "alexa::alerts:reminders:skill:readwrite"
  }
],
```

Having created setReminder() and declaring alexa::alerts:reminders:skill:readwrite per-missions in the skill manifest, the only thing remaining is to find a place to call setReminder(). You might be thinking that we should add it to ScheduleTripIn-tentHandler to set the reminder at the same time that the trip is scheduled. Instead, let's ask the user if they even want a reminder.

Making Reminders Optional

It would certainly be possible to set a reminder at the end of the trip planning flow. But doing so would be presumptuous without first asking if the user even wants a reminder. Our skill should ask the user if that's what they want.

There's a difference between the user granting permission to set reminders and allowing the skill to set a specific reminder. If the user plans several trips through Star Port 75 Travel, they may want to set reminders for some and not for others. The user would need to grant permission once for the skill to set reminders, but the skill shouldn't assume it should set reminders for every trip and instead should ask each time whether that's what they want.

In its current form, the handle() function of ScheduleTripIntentHandler concludes by telling the user to enjoy their trip and then closes the session. We'll need to change it so that it asks if the user wants to set a reminder:

events/starport-75-reminders/lambda/ScheduleTripIntentHandler.js
```
return handlerInput.responseBuilder
  .speak(speakOutput)
  .reprompt(speakOutput)
  .withAskForPermissionsConsentCard(
      ['alexa::devices:all:notifications:write'])
  .getResponse();
```

Notice how in addition to calling speak() on the response builder, we now also call reprompt() with the same text to be spoken. By calling reprompt(), we're telling Alexa to keep the session open and the microphone on to wait for another utterance. If the user doesn't say anything, then Alexa will reprompt them after a few moments.

More specifically, we're going to ask the user if they want the skill to set a reminder. To do that, we'll need to make a small addition to the text that's spoken. The following change in languageStrings.js asks the question at the end of the existing text:

events/starport-75-reminders/lambda/languageStrings.js
```
SCHEDULED_MSG: "You're all set. Enjoy your trip to {{destination}}!" +
  "If you want, I can send you a notification when the reservation " +
  "is confirmed. I've sent a card to the Alexa application for you " +
  "to give permission for notifications. " +
  "Would you like me to send you a reminder about this trip?",
```

Now our skill will ask the user whether or not they want to set a reminder and then leaves the microphone on to wait for a "Yes" or a "No" in response. The built-in AMAZON.YesIntent and AMAZON.NoIntent intents are perfect for this kind of response. To use these intents, we'll need to declare them in the interaction model, as we've done for our other intents:

```
{
    "name": "AMAZON.YesIntent",
    "samples": []
},
{
  "name": "AMAZON.NoIntent",
  "samples": []
},
```

Be sure to declare them in all of the interaction models for all locales or else they may not work in certain locales.

We'll also need to create a request handler for each of these intents:

```
events/starport-75-reminders/lambda/YesNoIntentHandlers.js
const Alexa = require('ask-sdk-core');
const reminderSender = require ('./reminderSender');

const YesIntentHandler = {
  canHandle(handlerInput) {
    const requestEnvelope = handlerInput.requestEnvelope;
    const sessionAttributes =
        handlerInput.attributesManager.getSessionAttributes();

    return Alexa.getRequestType(requestEnvelope) === 'IntentRequest'
        && Alexa.getIntentName(requestEnvelope) === 'AMAZON.YesIntent'
        && sessionAttributes.questionAsked === 'SetAReminder';
  },
  async handle(handlerInput) {
    const sessionAttributes =
        handlerInput.attributesManager.getSessionAttributes();
    sessionAttributes.questionAsked = null;
    const destination = sessionAttributes.destination;
    const departureDate = sessionAttributes.departureDate;
    handlerInput.attributesManager.setSessionAttributes(sessionAttributes);

    var speakOutput = handlerInput.t('YES_REMINDER');

    try {
      await reminderSender.setReminder(
                handlerInput, destination, departureDate);
    } catch (error) {
      speakOutput = error.message;
    }
```

```
      return handlerInput.responseBuilder
        .speak(speakOutput)
        .withShouldEndSession(true)
        .getResponse();
  }
};
const NoIntentHandler = {
  canHandle(handlerInput) {
    const requestEnvelope = handlerInput.requestEnvelope;
    const sessionAttributes =
        handlerInput.attributesManager.getSessionAttributes();

    return Alexa.getRequestType(requestEnvelope) === 'IntentRequest'
        && Alexa.getIntentName(requestEnvelope) === 'AMAZON.NoIntent'
        && sessionAttributes.questionAsked === 'SetAReminder';
  },
  handle(handlerInput) {
    const sessionAttributes =
        handlerInput.attributesManager.getSessionAttributes();
    sessionAttributes.questionAsked = null;
    handlerInput.attributesManager.setSessionAttributes(sessionAttributes);

    const speakOutput = handlerInput.t('NO_REMINDER');

    return handlerInput.responseBuilder
        .speak(speakOutput)
        .withShouldEndSession(true)
        .getResponse();
  }
};
module.exports = {
  YesIntentHandler: YesIntentHandler,
  NoIntentHandler: NoIntentHandler
};
```

The canHandle() function of both request handlers look pretty much like any of our other request handlers, except for one thing. Like other intent request handlers, they check to see the request is an intent request and the intent name is either AMAZON.YesIntent or AMAZON.NoIntent. But they also check a session attribute to understand exactly what the user is saying "Yes" or "No" to.

The problem with AMAZON.YesIntent and AMAZON.NoIntent is that on their own there's no obvious way to correlate the intent with a question that it is in answer to. If a skill asks multiple yes/no questions, then it is important for the skill to know which question the "Yes" and "No" utterances are for. Even in our skill, where there's only one yes/no question, we don't want to handle those intents if the user utters "Yes" or "No" randomly, without being asked a question.

Therefore, the canHandle() of both of these intent handlers inspects a session attribute named questionAsked to see if the "Yes" or "No" is in response to a question identified as "SetAReminder". That session attribute is set in ScheduleTripIntentHandler, just before returning the response that asks the question:

events/starport-75-reminders/lambda/ScheduleTripIntentHandler.js
```
const sessionAttributes =
    handlerInput.attributesManager.getSessionAttributes();
sessionAttributes.questionAsked = 'SetAReminder';
handlerInput.attributesManager.setSessionAttributes(sessionAttributes);
```

If either request handler matches, the first thing that their respective handle() functions does is clear the questionAsked attribute. Clearing the attribute ensures that the user won't be able to trigger these intents at any time after the first response to the question.

After clearing the response, both request handlers end by speaking their respective messages to the user, as defined in languageStrings.js:

events/starport-75-reminders/lambda/languageStrings.js
```
YES_REMINDER: "Okay, I'll send you a reminder a day before your trip.",
NO_REMINDER: "Okay, I won't send you a reminder."
```

The main difference between the two request handlers is that the handler for AMAZON.YesIntent calls the setReminder() function from the module we created earlier to set the reminder. The call is wrapped in a try/catch block so that if there is an error while setting the reminder, the error's message will be spoken to the user instead of the localized "YES_REMINDER" message.

Don't forget to use require to load these two request handlers and register them with the skill builder:

events/starport-75-reminders/lambda/index.js
```
const YesNoIntentHandlers = require('./YesNoIntentHandlers');
  ...
exports.handler = Alexa.SkillBuilders.custom()
    .addRequestHandlers(
        HelloWorldIntentHandler,
        ScheduleTripIntentHandler_Link,
        ScheduleTripIntentHandler,
        ScheduleTripIntentHandler_InProgress,
        YesNoIntentHandlers.YesIntentHandler,
        YesNoIntentHandlers.NoIntentHandler,
        StandardHandlers.LaunchRequestHandler,
        StandardHandlers.HelpIntentHandler,
        StandardHandlers.CancelAndStopIntentHandler,
        StandardHandlers.FallbackIntentHandler,
```

```
        StandardHandlers.SessionEndedRequestHandler,
        StandardHandlers.IntentReflectorHandler
        )
    .addErrorHandlers(
        StandardHandlers.ErrorHandler)
    .withApiClient(new Alexa.DefaultApiClient())
    .addRequestInterceptors(
        LocalisationRequestInterceptor)
    .lambda();
```

Now we're ready to deploy the skill and try it out. Unfortunately, you won't be able to fully test reminders using the test facility in the developer console, because it is incapable of triggering a reminder. The skill will still work for the most part, but you'll get an error in the intent handler for AMAZON.YesIntent when it tries to set a reminder.

Instead, you'll need to use an actual Alexa device, such as an Echo, Echo Dot, or Echo Show. Or you can also use the Alexa companion application on your phone to test the skill. Launch the skill and plan a trip just as we've been doing for the past several chapters. But at the end, when Alexa asks if you want to set a reminder, answer "Yes". Wait about 30 seconds and Alexa should chime and then immediately speak the reminder text. She'll repeat the reminder a second time, but you can cancel the timer by saying, "Alexa, cancel timer."

Setting an Absolutely Timed Reminder

Setting a reminder for 30 seconds after booking a trip gives us immediate satisfaction of hearing the results of our work. But ultimately we want Alexa to speak the reminder one day before the trip starts. To do that, we'll need to change the reminder request template to use an absolute trigger:

events/starport-75-reminders/lambda/reminderRequest.json
```
{
  "requestTime" : "TBD",
  "trigger": {
➤    "type" : "SCHEDULED_ABSOLUTE",
➤    "scheduledTime": "TBD"
  },
  "alertInfo": {
    "spokenInfo": {
      "content": []
    }
  },
  "pushNotification" : {
    "status" : "ENABLED"
  }
}
```

In addition to changing the type property to "SCHEDULED_ABSOLUTE", we've replaced the offsetInSeconds property with a scheduledTime property that will be set to a time that is 24 hours in advance of the departure date of the planned trip. In the setReminder() function we'll set that time like this:

events/starport-75-reminders/lambda/reminderSender.js

```
const Alexa = require('ask-sdk-core');

const subtractDay = function(orig, d) {
  orig.setTime(orig.getTime() - (d*24*60*60*1000));
  return orig;
}

module.exports = {

    ...

    if (reminderRequest.trigger.type === 'SCHEDULED_ABSOLUTE') {
      reminderRequest.trigger.scheduledTime =
            subtractDay(new Date(departureDate), 1).toISOString();
    }

    ...

  }
};
```

If the template's trigger type is "SCHEDULED_ABSOLUTE", then the subtractDay() utility function will be used to subtract one day from the trip's departure date and the result will be set to the template's reminderRequest.trigger.scheduledTime property.

Now if you try the skill and agree to set a reminder, it will set the reminder to trigger 24 hours before the trip's departure date. As you can imagine, if the trip's departure date is several days in the future, you will have to wait a while to know if this works.

Although both proactive events and reminders offer ways to communicate with a user outside of an interactive session, they each serve different purposes. Proactive events are best used when triggered by some event. For example, proactive events could be used to alert the user when seats to a sold-out concert become available. Reminders, on the other hand, are best used to remind a user of something that is soon to occur. Using the concert scenario, a reminder could be set to remind the user about the show 24 hours in advance.

Wrapping Up

Not all interactions with Alexa begin with the user invoking a skill. Employing proactive events and reminders in a skill enables Alexa to chime in and speak up at any time, even when the user isn't actively using a skill.

Proactive events are designed around eight domain-specific use cases, including sending updates regarding order status, sporting events, weather, and reservations. These events are published to a user's Alexa devices through the skill by a backend system using a REST endpoint, and are delivered to all of the devices connected to the user's Amazon account. Proactive events can also be multicast to all users of an event.

Reminders enable a skill to speak up and remind a user about some occasion at a specific time. Unlike proactive events, reminders are freeform, allowing for any message to be sent at the reminder time. Also, reminders are only delivered to the device from which they were created.

Coming up in the next chapter, we're going to switch gears a little by looking at how to monetize voice applications by enabling in-skill purchasing.

CHAPTER 12

Selling Stuff

It has been said that if you have a job you love, you'll never work a day in your life. And certainly developing skills for Alexa is so incredibly fun that it doesn't seem like work. Even so, it never hurts if you can make a little money while having fun developing Alexa skills.

Many skills are completely free to use, no string attached. But some skills offer their initial experience for free, then offer additional content or features for a small up-charge. Because these add-ons can be offered, purchased, and used, all within the course of using the skill, they are called In-Skill Purchases or ISPs for short.

Believe it or not, the money you can potentially make from ISPs can range from a little extra spending money up to an incredibly lucrative side income.[1] The good news is that no matter how you decide to monetize your skills, defining and offering ISPs is rather straightforward, which you'll see in this chapter as we offer an upgrade to the Star Port 75 Travel skill as an ISP. We'll start by defining the product.

Creating Products

In-skill purchases enable users to add additional content and functionality to a skill while they are using the skill. For example, a skill that teaches a foreign language might provide some essential language lessons for free, but may offer upgrade packs for additional languages or advanced language usage for 99 cents each.

There are three kinds of ISPs that a skill may offer:

---

1. https://www.cnn.com/2019/05/06/tech/amazon-alexa-skills-blueprints/index.html

- Entitlements—One-time purchases that add a feature or content to the skill that will be available to the user from the time of purchase going forward

- Consumables—Purchases that enable a feature or content that will be taken away once used and must be purchased again

- Subscriptions—Purchases that enable a feature or content for a specified period of time, after which it must be renewed

All customers of Star Port 75 Travel are able to plan travel to any of the planets in our solar system. But we're going to add a new "Magnificent Moons" option which will afford them the option of planning trips to a few of our solar system's most notable moons, including Jupiter's four largest moons (Io, Callisto, Ganymede, and Europa), Saturn's moon (Titan), and of course Earth's moon (Luna).

Defining a Product

Before we can offer the Magnificent Moons package to our users, we need to define it as a product. We could design this option around any of Alexa's ISP types. We'll choose to define it as an entitlement; the choice made here makes little difference in how the skill is implemented. As an entitlement, travelers may pay a one-time fee for the product and book as many trips to moons as they want.

To create a product, we must define the product in a JSON file and use the ASK CLI to associate it with our skill. The following JSON file describes the Magnificent Moons product:

sell/starport-75/isps/entitlement/Magnificent_Moons.json

```
{
  "vendorId": "M1FYKCCJ8MU4MO",
  "inSkillProductDefinition": {
    "version": "1.0",
    "type": "ENTITLEMENT",
    "referenceName": "MAGNIFICENT_MOONS",
    "publishingInformation": {
      "locales": {
        "en-US": {
          "name": "Magnificent Moons",
          "summary": "Enables travel to some of our solar system's moons.",
          "description":
              "Enables travel to some of our solar system's moons.",
          "smallIconUri":
              "https://starport75.s3.amazonaws.com/planets/Moon_sm.png",
          "largeIconUri":
              "https://starport75.s3.amazonaws.com/planets/Moon_lg.png",
```

```
            "examplePhrases": [
              "buy magnificent moons",
              "add magnificent moons",
              "enable magnificent moons"
            ],
            "keywords": [
              "moons"
            ],
            "customProductPrompts": {
              "purchasePromptDescription": "Add the Magnificent Moons package
                  and plan travel to several of the moons in our solar system!",
              "boughtCardDescription": "You now have Magnificent Moons enabled."
            }
          }
        },
        "distributionCountries": [
          "US"
        ],
        "pricing": {
          "amazon.com": {
            "releaseDate": "2020-03-12T00:00Z",
            "defaultPriceListing": {
              "price": 9.99,
              "currency": "USD"
            }
          }
        },
        "taxInformation": {
          "category": "SOFTWARE"
        }
      },
      "privacyAndCompliance": {
        "locales": {
          "en-US": {
            "privacyPolicyUrl": "https://starport75.dev/privacy.html"
          }
        }
      },
      "testingInstructions": "TBD",
      "purchasableState": "PURCHASABLE"
    }
}
```

There are several properties to be set in the ISP JSON definition:

- *vendorId*—Your vendor ID

- *type*—The product type. For our product, we set it to "ENTITLEMENT", but it can also be "SUBSCRIPTION" or "CONSUMABLE".

- *name*—The name of the product

- *smallIconUri*—A URI to a 108x108px PNG file that will be the small icon for the product

- *largeIconUri*—A URI to a 512x512px PNG file that will be the large icon for the product

- *summary*—A summary explaining why the user may want to buy this product

- *description*—A longer description of the product

- *examplePhrases*—A list of sample utterances that the user may speak to buy this product (for example, "buy Magnificent Moons package")

- *keywords*—A list of keywords to be used for search indexing the product

- *purchasePromptDescription*—How Alexa will describe the project in the purchase prompt

- *boughtCardDescription*—The text to display in a card in the companion application when the product has already been purchased

- *releaseDate*—The date that the product will first be available, in "yyyy-MM-dd'T'HH:mm'Z'" or "yyyy-MM-dd" format

- *privacyPolicyUrl*—A URL to a webpage describing the privacy policy for the product

- *testingInstructions*—Instructions for the certification team to know how to purchase this product when you publish the skill and product

- *pricing*—Pricing information for the product. Our product will cost $9.99 in U.S. dollars.

You'll need to know your vendor ID in order to fill out the vendorId property. If you aren't sure what your vendor ID is, the easiest way to find it is to inspect the contents of your ASK CLI configuration:

```
$ more ~/.ask/cli_config| grep "vendor_id"
    "vendor_id": "M1YFKCC8JMU5NO",
```

Some of the properties, such as testingInstructions and privacyPolicyUrl aren't important until you're ready to publish the skill (which we'll talk about in the next chapter). For now, we'll just put temporary values in those properties.

If this were a subscription product, the subscriptionInformation property would require additional information describing how often the subscription is renewed (either monthly or yearly) and how long a trial period should last in days. Had we created a subscription instead of an entitlement, the subscription-Information property might have looked something like this:

```
"subscriptionInformation": {
  "subscriptionPaymentFrequency": "MONTHLY",
  "subscriptionTrialPeriodDays": 10
},
```

This defines a subscription that has a trial period of 10 days and renews monthly. Optionally, the subscriptionPaymentFrequency property could be set to "YEARLY" for an annual renewal period.

Adding Products to the Model

So that users can plan travel to the various moons, we must add the moon destinations to our interaction model. Way back in Chapter 3, Parameterizing Intents with Slots, on page 57 we created a custom PLANETS slot type in our skill's interaction model. It included all of the planets in our solar system (including Pluto) as well as several synonyms for those destinations. Although the destinations in the "Magnificent Moons" package aren't technically planets, we now need to add them to the PLANETS type so that they are candidates for a trip's destination:

sell/starport-75/skill-package/interactionModels/custom/en-US.json
```
{
  "name": "PLANETS",
  "values": [
  ...
  {
    "id": "LUNA",
    "name": {
      "value": "Luna",
      "synonyms": [
        "the moon",
        "the earth's moon"
      ]
    }
  },
  {
    "id": "IO",
    "name": {
      "value": "Io",
      "synonyms": []
    }
  },
  {
    "id": "EUROPA",
```

```
      "name": {
        "value": "Europa",
        "synonyms": []
      }
    },
    {
      "id": "CALLISTO",
      "name": {
        "value": "Callisto",
        "synonyms": []
      }
    },
    {
      "id": "GANYMEDE",
      "name": {
        "value": "Ganymede",
        "synonyms": []
      }
    },
    {
      "id": "TITAN",
      "name": {
        "value": "Titan",
        "synonyms": []
      }
    }
  }
]
```

When the interaction model is deployed with these changes, users of our skill will be able to plan travel to any of the previously declared planets or these six moons. Later, we'll prevent users from booking trips to the moons in the skill fulfillment code. But first, let's deploy the product definition.

Deploying Products

Now that we've defined our product definition JSON file, we're ready to use it to create the product. The ask smapi create-isp-for-vendor command will do that for us:

```
$ ask smapi create-isp-for-vendor \
  --create-in-skill-product-request \
    file:isps/entitlement/Magnificent_Moons.json
{
  "productId": "amzn1.adg.product.0791a588-c7a8-411a-8f3d-36d38cfc01b2"
}
```

The ask smapi create-isp-for-vendor command requires that you specify the product definition JSON via the --create-in-skill-product-request parameter. This parameter can accept an entire JSON definition as a string, but it's much easier to use the file: prefix to reference a file containing the product definition JSON.

The JSON returned in response from creating the product will contain the new product's "productId". You'll need the product ID, as well as the skill ID in the next step, as you associate the product with your skill. To create the association, you'll use the ask smapi associate-isp-with-skill command:

```
$ ask smapi associate-isp-with-skill \
    --product-id amzn1.adg.product.0791a588-c7a8-411a-8f3d-36d38cfc01b2 \
    --skill-id amzn1.ask.skill.28e3f37-2b4-4b5-849-bcf4f2e081
Command executed successfully!
```

The product ID is specified with the --product-id parameter and the skill ID is given through the --skill-id parameter. Once this command completes, the product is linked to the skill. You can confirm this by using the ask smapi get-isp-list-for-skill-id command:

```
$ ask smapi get-isp-list-for-skill-id \
    --skill-id=amzn1.ask.skill.28e3f37-2b4-4b5-849-bcf4f2e081
{
  "_links": {
    "next": {
      "href": "/v1/skills/amzn1.ask.skill.28e3f37-2b4-4b5-849-bcf4f2e081
                                      /stages/development/inSkillProducts"
    },
    "self": {
      "href": "/v1/skills/amzn1.ask.skill.28e3f37-2b4-4b5-849-bcf4f2e081
                                      /stages/development/inSkillProducts"
    }
  },
  "inSkillProductSummaryList": [
    {
      "editableState": "EDITABLE",
      "lastUpdated": "2020-05-08T03:36:21.554Z",
      "nameByLocale": {
        "en-US": "Magnificent Moons"
      },
      "pricing": {
        "amazon.com": {
          "defaultPriceListing": {
            "currency": "USD",
            "price": 9.99,
            "primeMemberPrice": 8
          },
          "releaseDate": "2020-03-12T00:00:00Z"
        }
      },
      "productId": "amzn1.adg.product.0791a588-c7a8-411a-8f3d-36d38cfc01b2",
      "purchasableState": "PURCHASABLE",
      "referenceName": "MAGNIFICENT_MOONS",
      "stage": "development",
      "status": "COMPLETE",
```

```
        "type": "ENTITLEMENT"
      }
  ],
  "isTruncated": false
}
```

The response to the ask smapi get-isp-list-for-skill-id command includes a list of product definitions in the inSkillProductSummaryList property, showing you which products are associated with the skill. In this case, the inSkillProductSummaryList contains our "Magnificent Moons" product.

Now that the product is created and linked to our skill, we can start selling it to our users. Let's add a new intent and intent handler for users to purchase the Magnificent Moons package.

Handling Purchases

There're two paths through which a user may buy the Magnificent Moons package. They can either buy it directly by saying, "Buy the Magnificent Moons pack" or as a side effect of attempting to plan a trip to one of the moons. We'll start by defining an intent to handle the direct approach. Later we'll see how to create an upsell directive to offer the package if the user tries to plan a trip to a premium destination.

Defining a Buy Intent

A user of our skill could potentially decide to purchase the Magnificent Moons package at any time after launching the skill. To enable them to do so, we should define an intent that is triggered whenever they say something like, "buy the Magnificent Moons pack." The following definition of BuyIntent shows such an intent:

sell/starport-75/skill-package/interactionModels/custom/en-US.json
```
{
  "name": "BuyIntent",
  "samples": [
    "buy the {productName} pack",
    "buy the {productName} package",
    "buy the {productName} extension"
  ],
  "slots": [
    {
      "name": "productName",
      "type": "ADDON_PRODUCTS"
    }
  ]
},
```

The first thing to notice is that the intent isn't specific to the Magnificent Moons product. Although we could have defined an intent specifically for the Magnificent Moons package, this one intent is able to handle a multitude of products and will prevent unnecessary duplication should we decide to add another product later.

The "productName" slot is where we'll capture the desired product. The slot type is a custom type called ADDON_PRODUCTS. For now, the ADDON_PRODUCTS type will only include a single product, the Magnificent Moons package:

```
sell/starport-75/skill-package/interactionModels/custom/en-US.json
"types": [
  ...
  {
    "name": "ADDON_PRODUCTS",
    "values": [
      {
        "id": "MAGNIFICENT_MOONS",
        "name": {
          "value": "Magnificent Moons",
          "synonyms": [
            "Moons",
            "Massive Moons"
          ]
        }
      }
    ]
  }
]
```

Because some users might misspeak or forget the name of the package, we've also declared a couple of synonyms to make it more flexible. Also notice that the id property is set to "MAGNIFICENT_MOONS", which is not-so-coincidentally the same as the value we gave in referenceName property when creating the product definition. We'll take advantage of that in the intent handler to lookup the product.

Should Star Port 75 Travel later decide to start offering trips to asteroids or destinations outside of our solar system as add-on products, then we'd only need to define the new products as values under ADDON_PRODUCTS.

Handling Buy Intent Requests

Just as we've done for all of our skill's other intents, we'll need to create a request handler that handles the intent whose name is BuyIntent. The following handler does that:

```
sell/starport-75/lambda/PurchaseHandlers.js
const Alexa = require('ask-sdk-core');
const ProductUtils = require('./productUtils');
const StandardHandlers = require('./StandardHandlers');

const BuyIntentHandler = {
  canHandle(handlerInput) {
    const requestEnvelope = handlerInput.requestEnvelope;
    return Alexa.getRequestType(requestEnvelope) === 'IntentRequest'
      && Alexa.getIntentName(requestEnvelope) === 'BuyIntent';
  },
  async handle(handlerInput) {
    const slot = Alexa.getSlot(handlerInput.requestEnvelope, 'productName');
    const referenceName =
      slot.resolutions.resolutionsPerAuthority[0].values[0].value.id;
    const productId =
      (await ProductUtils.getProduct(handlerInput, referenceName))
      .productId;

    const rsp = handlerInput.responseBuilder
      .addDirective({
        type: "Connections.SendRequest",
        name: "Buy",
        payload: {
          InSkillProduct: {
            productId: productId
          }
        },
        token: "correlationToken"
      })
      .getResponse();
    return rsp;
  }
};
```

Much like the intent handlers we've created before, the canHandle() function checks that this is an intent request and that the intent name matches the intent to be handled (BuyIntent in this case). If it matches, then the handle() function retrieves the "productName" slot from the request and extracts the id property from the resolved entity. Since we only have one possible value for the slot at this point, "MAGNIFICENT_MOONS" should be assigned to the referenceName property.

Ultimately, we'll need the product's ID to be able to complete the purchase. Rather than hard-code the product ID in the handler code, we'll use reference-Name to lookup the product and extract the product's ID. To achieve that, let's create a separate utility module that looks up a product using Alexa's monetization service:

sell/starport-75/lambda/productUtils.js

```
module.exports = {
  async getProduct(handlerInput, referenceName) {
    const ispService = handlerInput
                  .serviceClientFactory
                  .getMonetizationServiceClient();
    const locale = handlerInput.requestEnvelope.request.locale;
    return ispService.getInSkillProducts(locale).then(
      function(result) {
        const matches = result.inSkillProducts.filter(
                        product => product.referenceName === referenceName);
        return (matches.length > 0) ? matches[0] : null;
      }
    );
  }
};
```

This module starts by retrieving the monetization service by calling getMonetizationServiceClient() on the service client factory (similar to how we obtained a UpsServiceClient in Chapter 5, Integrating User Data, on page 105). Using the monetization service client, the getProduct() function calls getInSkillProducts() which returns a promise with the response. From the response, it filters the results down to a single product that matches the given product reference name. Assuming such a product can be found, it is returned. Otherwise, the getProduct() function returns null.

Back in the handler's handle() function, the only thing we really need from the product is the product ID. Therefore, the productId property is extracted from the product and assigned to productId. With the product ID in hand, the handle() function finishes up by creating and returning a response that includes a Connections.SendRequest directive. The name property is set to "Buy", which indicates the user is buying the product whose ID is specified under the payload property.

The token property can be set to any value you want. Alexa does nothing with this value but will send it back in a purchase response request so you can correlate the purchase request with the response. For that reason, the value should typically be unique to the transaction. We're not going to use it in our skill, so setting it to a placeholder value of "correlationToken" will be fine.

What Happens to Purchases if the User Disables the Skill?

If the user has purchased one or more products, those products are associated with the user's ID. If the user disables the skill and then re-enables the skill, the user's purchases aren't lost. Since the user's ID will not change, the purchases will be retained and made available again when the user re-enables the skill.

Although the handler returns a buy directive, the purchase flow is not yet complete. Behind the scenes, Alexa will process the order, charge the user's account, and send them an email receipt. After all of that, Alexa will send a request to our skill indicating that the transaction has completed. Let's see how to write response request handlers.

Handling Purchase Responses

After Alexa handles a purchase as specified in a Connections.SendRequest directive, she will send a request to the skill with the slightly confusing request type of Connections.Response. This is essentially a callback to let our skill know that the purchase has been handled. From that point, our skill may transition right into the trip planning dialog flow or may simply thank the user for their purchase.

Assuming the purchase completes successfully, the request's payload will have a purchaseResult property set to "ACCEPTED". This indicates that the user accepted the purchase and there were no errors in processing it. But the transaction could fail for a handful of reasons as well. In that case, the purchaseResult property could be any one of the following values:

- *DECLINED*—The user declined the purchase.

- *ALREADY_PURCHASED*—The user has previously purchased the product. (Only applies to entitlements.)

- *ERROR*—There was some error in processing the transaction.

The following request handler covers all of these cases:

```
sell/starport-75/lambda/PurchaseHandlers.js
const ContinueAfterPurchaseHandler = {
  canHandle(handlerInput) {
    const requestEnvelope = handlerInput.requestEnvelope;
    return Alexa.getRequestType(requestEnvelope) === 'Connections.Response';
  },
  handle(handlerInput) {
    const requestEnvelope = handlerInput.requestEnvelope;
    const purchaseResult = requestEnvelope.request.payload.purchaseResult;
    return handlerInput.responseBuilder
      .speak(handlerInput.t('PURCHASE_RESPONSE_' + purchaseResult))
      .getResponse();
  }
};
```

The canHandle() function checks for a request type of Connections.Response. If it matches, then the handle() function simply looks up the localized text to speak, where the lookup key is the value of the purchaseResult property prefixed with

"PURCHASE_RESPONSE_". In the languageStrings.js module, those localized strings look like this (for English):

```
sell/starport-75/lambda/languageStrings.js
PURCHASE_RESPONSE_ACCEPTED: 'Thanks for purchasing the Magnificent ' +
    'Moons extension! You may now book travel to several of the ' +
    'most prominent moons in our solar system.',
PURCHASE_RESPONSE_DECLINED: "That's too bad. If you change your " +
    'mind let me know by saying "Buy the Magnificent Moons pack".',
PURCHASE_RESPONSE_ALREADY_PURCHASED: 'You have already purchased the ' +
    'Magnificent Moons package.',
PURCHASE_RESPONSE_ERROR: 'There was an error processing your ' +
    'purchase. Try again later.'
```

With the request handlers defined, don't forget to export them from the PurchaseHandlers.js module:

```
sell/starport-75/lambda/PurchaseHandlers.js
module.exports = {
  BuyIntentHandler: BuyIntentHandler,
  ContinueAfterPurchaseHandler: ContinueAfterPurchaseHandler
};
```

And then import them and register them with the skill builder:

```
sell/starport-75/lambda/index.js
const PurchaseIntentHandlers = require('./PurchaseHandlers');

exports.handler = Alexa.SkillBuilders.custom()
    .addRequestHandlers(
        ...
        PurchaseIntentHandlers.BuyIntentHandler,
        PurchaseIntentHandlers.ContinueAfterPurchaseHandler,
        ...
    )
    .addErrorHandlers(
        StandardHandlers.ErrorHandler)
    .withApiClient(new Alexa.DefaultApiClient())
    .addRequestInterceptors(
        LocalisationRequestInterceptor)
    .lambda();
```

Now you can deploy the skill and try it out. Assuming that you haven't previously purchased the Magnificent Moons package, the conversation with Alexa might look like the screenshot on page 280.

Notice that Alexa injects some of her own content into the response when she says, "Great! Your order is complete and I've emailed you a receipt." This is just a generic response from Alexa in-skill purchasing, letting the user know to expect a receipt in their email. Just as payment processing is automatically

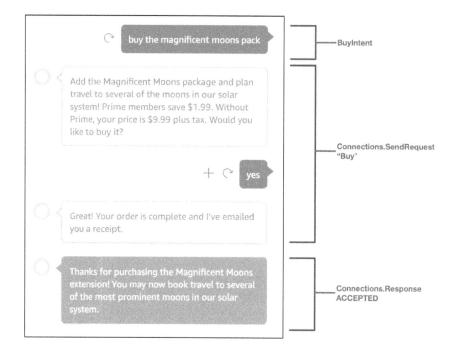

handled by the platform, so is sending of receipts and this message regarding receipt emails.

Then, if you were to try to buy the Magnificent Moons package again, Alexa would stop you and tell you that you've already bought it:

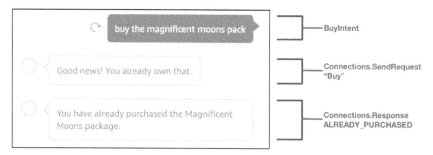

Once again, Alexa has injected a generic phrase into the response: "Good news! You already own that." But the response message we provided follows the generic message.

The "ALREADY_PURCHASED" response only applies to entitlements. You'll never get it for subscription or consumable products. But while testing entitlements, you may want to reset your purchase so that you can try it again. To do that, the ask smapi reset-entitlement-for-product command can be very handy:

```
$ ask smapi reset-entitlement-for-product \
    --product-id amzn1.adg.product.0791a588-c7a8-411a-8f3d-36d38cfc01b2
```

The ask smapi reset-entitlement-for-product command requires the product ID, specified with the --product-id parameter.

You'll be happy to know that as the author of the skill, you won't be actually charged for any purchases you make while testing. So, feel free to buy the Magnificent Moons package as many times as you like!

Our skill now lets users buy the Magnificent Moons package. But there's nothing stopping them from planning a trip to one of the package's destinations if they don't buy it. Let's make a change to the trip scheduling flow to only allow trips to moons if the user has purchased the Magnificent Moons package. And, in doing so, we'll offer the package as an upsell.

Upselling Products

You may recall from Chapter 4, Creating Multi-Turn Dialogs, on page 83 that ScheduleTripIntent doesn't complete until the user has specified the destination, departure date, and return date and those slots are validated. Until then the dialog is considered "in progress", enabling us to step into the dialog to do custom validation.

In fact, we took advantage of this to validate that the return date is after the departure date in the ScheduleTripIntentHandler_InProgress.js module. We'll apply a similar technique to verify that the user has purchased the Magnificent Moons package before allowing them to plan a trip to one of those premium destinations.

To start, let's create a local helper function that checks to see if the user is requesting a trip to a moon and, if so, that they have bought the "Magnificent Moons" package:

```
sell/starport-75/lambda/ScheduleTripIntentHandler_InProgress.js
const ProductUtils = require('./productUtils');
async function validateMoonsDestination(handlerInput) {
  const destinationSlot =
      Alexa.getSlot(handlerInput.requestEnvelope, 'destination');
  if (destinationSlot.resolutions) {
    const resolution =
        destinationSlot.resolutions.resolutionsPerAuthority[0];
    const destination = resolution.status.code === 'ER_SUCCESS_MATCH' ?
        resolution.values[0].value.id :
        destinationSlot.value;
    const destinationName = resolution.status.code === 'ER_SUCCESS_MATCH' ?
        resolution.values[0].value.name :
        destinationSlot.value;
```

```
      if (destination && ['LUNA','IO','EUROPA','CALLISTO','GANYMEDE','TITAN']
                          .includes(destination)) {
        const product =
            await ProductUtils.getProduct(handlerInput, 'MAGNIFICENT_MOONS');
        if (!product || product.entitled !== 'ENTITLED') {
          throw {
            message: handlerInput.t('UPSELL_MOONS_PACK',
                      { destination: destinationName }),
            productId: product.productId
          };
        }
      }
    }
  }
}
```

The first thing that validateMoonsDestination() does is fetch the resolved entity value from the "destination" slot and then compare it with a set of destination IDs known to be part of the add-on package. If the "destination" slot's value is one of those premium destinations, then the function checks whether the product has been purchased by the user.

To check whether the product has been purchased or not, the validateMoonsDestination() calls getProduct() to fetch the product whose reference name is "MAGNIFICENT_MOONS". Then, it'll inspect the product's entitled property. If the user has purchased the package, then entitled will be set to "ENTITLED". Otherwise, the user hasn't purchased the product and the function will throw an error containing the localized "UPSELL_MOONS_PACK" message and the product ID. The error's localized message is in languageStrings.js, like this:

```
sell/starport-75/lambda/languageStrings.js
UPSELL_MOONS_PACK: 'Travel to {{destination}} is only available ' +
    'with the "Magnificent Moons" add-on. Do you want to learn more ' +
    'about this option?',
```

Within the intent handler's handle() function, we'll call the validateMoonsDestination() function, passing in the handlerInput:

```
sell/starport-75/lambda/ScheduleTripIntentHandler_InProgress.js
try {
  await validateMoonsDestination(handlerInput);
} catch (error) {
  console.error(error);
  return handlerInput.responseBuilder
      .addDirective({
          type: "Connections.SendRequest",
          name: "Upsell",
```

```
        payload: {
            InSkillProduct: {
              productId: error.productId,
            },
            upsellMessage: error.message,
        },
        token: "correlationToken",
    })
    .getResponse();
}
```

If validateMoonsDestination() returns successfully, then either the destination is not a moon or the user must have purchased the Magnificent Moons package. In that case, the request handler's handle() method moves on, validating the dates and continuing through the dialog.

But if validateMoonsDestination() throws an error, then the handle() message ends by returning a Connections.SendRequest directive, much like how the handler for BuyIntent works. What's different, however, is that the name property is set to "Upsell" instead of "Buy". This causes Alexa to pause the dialog flow and enter into an upsell sub-flow.

In the upsell sub-flow, Alexa will first ask if the user wants to learn more about the product and, if the user replies "yes," then it will describe the product and ask if they want buy it. If the user chooses to buy the product, Alexa will handle the transaction automatically. The flow then resumes with a special Connections.Response request.

Assuming the user hasn't already purchased the Magnificent Moons package, the conversation flow with the upsell sub-flow looks like the screenshot on page 284.

If you were to deploy the skill at this point, the skill should work as it always has. But if the user were to try to plan a trip to Titan, Callisto, or any other moons in the "Magnificent Moons" package, the flow will be redirected through the upsell sub-flow, offering the user the option of buying the package. And, if the user chooses to do so, the flow will automatically handle the purchase.

Now that we've enabled our skill to offer and sell in-skill products, let's see how to reverse the purchase to allow a refund.

Refunding a Purchase

Hopefully our users will never second guess their decision to buy the Magnificent Moons package. But in the event that they have buyer's remorse, we should offer them a means to return their purchase for a refund.

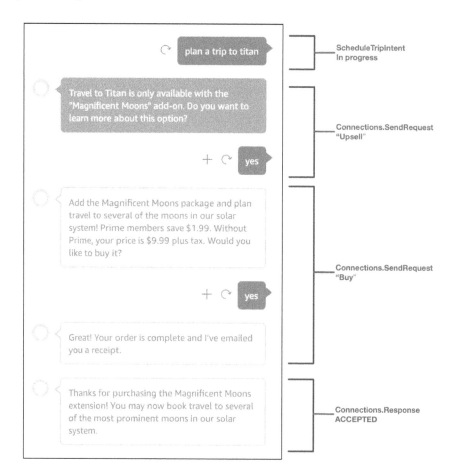

To do that, we'll add a new intent through which a user can ask for a refund. In the interaction model, the intent is defined like this:

```
sell/starport-75/skill-package/interactionModels/custom/en-US.json
{
  "name": "RefundIntent",
  "samples": [
    "refund the {productName} pack",
    "return the {productName} package",
    "return the {productName} extension"
  ],
  "slots": [
    {
      "name": "productName",
      "type": "ADDON_PRODUCTS"
    }
  ]
},
```

As defined here, when the user wants a refund, they can say, "refund the Magnificent Moons pack," "return the Magnificent Moons package," or "return the Magnificent Moons extension." Just as with BuyIntent, the "productName" slot is used here to allow flexibility in what products this intent works with, should we decide to offer more products later.

Now we need a request handler for this new intent. Here's a handler implementation that should do the job:

```
sell/starport-75/lambda/PurchaseHandlers.js
const RefundIntentHandler = {
  canHandle(handlerInput) {
    const requestEnvelope = handlerInput.requestEnvelope;
    return Alexa.getRequestType(requestEnvelope) === 'IntentRequest'
        && Alexa.getIntentName(requestEnvelope) === 'RefundIntent';
  },
  async handle(handlerInput) {
    const slot = Alexa.getSlot(handlerInput.requestEnvelope, 'productName');
    const referenceName =
        slot.resolutions.resolutionsPerAuthority[0].values[0].value.id;
    const productId =
        (await ProductUtils.getProduct(handlerInput, referenceName))
        .productId;

    return handlerInput.responseBuilder
        .addDirective({
            type: "Connections.SendRequest",
            name: "Cancel",
            payload: {
                InSkillProduct: {
                    productId: productId
                }
            },
            token: "correlationToken"
        })
        .getResponse();
  }
};
```

You might be feeling a bit of deja vu looking at the implementation of RefundIntentHandler. Indeed, it looks an awful lot like how we implemented BuyIntentHandler. Aside from the fact that it checks for an intent name of RefundIntent in the canHandle() function (instead of BuyIntent), the only difference is the value of the name property in the Connections.SendRequest directive. Since this is a refund, we set name to "Cancel" instead of "Buy".

Finally, we need to handle the response request. Just like the other times we've sent a Connections.SendRequest directive for buying and upselling, Alexa will send us a Connections.Response request as a callback after handling the refund. If we do nothing, our existing ContinueAfterPurchaseHandler handler will handle the request and thank the user for their purchase—which is a little weird considering that they just asked for a refund.

So, let's write a new handler specific to a refund callback request. As it turns out the name property we send in the Connections.SendRequest directive is sent back in the Connections.Response request. So we can write a canHandle() function in our handler that checks to see if the incoming request's name property is equal to "Cancel". If so, we know that the request follows a refund directive.

In the case of a refund, the handler can return anything you want to be spoken, but should end the session. The following request handler does that:

```
sell/starport-75/lambda/PurchaseHandlers.js
const ContinueAfterRefundHandler = {
  canHandle(handlerInput) {
    const requestEnvelope = handlerInput.requestEnvelope;
    return Alexa.getRequestType(requestEnvelope) === 'Connections.Response'
        && requestEnvelope.request.payload.purchaseResult === 'ACCEPTED'
        && requestEnvelope.request.name === 'Cancel';
  },
  handle(handlerInput) {
    return StandardHandlers.CancelAndStopIntentHandler.handle(handlerInput);
  }
};
```

Notice that the canHandle() function checks that the request's name property is "Cancel", and additionally that the request type is Connections.Response and the purchase result is "ACCEPTED". If so, then the handle() function simply hands off the handlerInput object to the handle() function of the CancelAndStopIntentHandler request handler, telling the user goodbye and ending the session.

For both of these new request handlers, don't forget to export them from the module:

```
sell/starport-75/lambda/PurchaseHandlers.js
  ...
module.exports = {
  BuyIntentHandler: BuyIntentHandler,
➤ ContinueAfterRefundHandler: ContinueAfterRefundHandler,
➤ RefundIntentHandler: RefundIntentHandler,
  ContinueAfterPurchaseHandler: ContinueAfterPurchaseHandler
};
```

And then be sure to register them with the skill builder:

```
sell/starport-75/lambda/index.js
exports.handler = Alexa.SkillBuilders.custom()
    .addRequestHandlers(
```

```
          . . .
➤         PurchaseIntentHandlers.RefundIntentHandler,
➤         PurchaseIntentHandlers.ContinueAfterRefundHandler,
          . . .
    )
```

After deploying these changes, you should be able to request a refund for the Magnificent Moons package. The flow will look something like this:

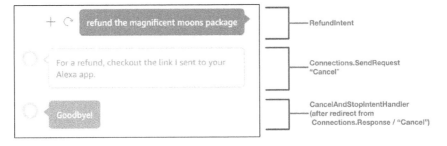

Notice that the refund isn't handled directly in the flow of the skill. Instead, a card is sent to the user and they are instructed to contact Amazon customer service for the refund. The card, as it appears in the companion application, looks like this:

Refund an in-skill
purchase

Contact Customer Service for help with in-skill
purchases.

HELP & CUSTOMER SERVICE

More ⌄

Finally, after the card is sent, the session ends and Alexa says "Goodbye" when the handler for the Connections.Response request forwards the handlerInput to the CancelAndStopIntentHandler.

Wrapping Up

Alexa skills can be fun to develop, but they can also be a source of income. In-Skill Purchasing enables a skill to offer additional functionality or content via add-ons that can be bought during a user's session with the skill.

The three types of in-skill products—entitlements, consumables, and subscriptions—enable a range of products, from one-time purchases to buy-per-use to periodic renewal. Which you choose depends on how you've designed your merchandising goals for your skill. Even so, the way you define and offer those products are very similar in ASK.

Products are defined in JSON and deployed using the ASK CLI. Upsells, purchases, and refunds are handled through request handlers that include a Connections.SendRequest directive in the response. These directives take the user on a subflow that is entirely handled by Alexa, requiring no work on the skill developer's part to deal with payment or any other details of the transaction. Finally, upon completion of the transaction, Alexa makes a Connections.Response request to the skill for post-purchase handling.

Whether you hope to make money with your Alexa skill or not, nobody will be able to use it if you don't make it available outside of your Amazon developer account. In the next chapter, we're going to take steps to prepare our skill for production use, publishing it so that all Alexa users can plan trips through our solar system.

CHAPTER 13

Publishing Your Skill

After several iterations of work, our skill is quite feature-filled. We can use it to book a trip to any location in our solar system, including several of the most popular moons as a premium add-on. It can add that trip as an entry on the user's Google Calendar. And it can remind the user of their trip when the time for travel gets close.

At this point, the skill is still in the development stage. We can only use the skill on devices that are associated with the Amazon account under which we developed the skill. That's perfectly fine if you are the only audience for the skill. But if you want to offer the skill for others to use, then it must be published.

In this chapter, we're going to submit the skill for review and certification by Amazon, publish it, and then see how to monitor post-publication analytics to understand how well the skill is working in production. But first, we need to tie up a few loose ends to ready the skill for certification.

Tying Up Loose Ends

Before we can publish our skill, there are a few to-do items we should address. Specifically, there's an intent and its associated handler that we no longer need and that should be removed. We should also review and fine-tune a few of the responses returned from a few of the built-in intent handlers. We'll start by saying goodbye to the HelloWorldIntent.

Removing Unused Intents

When we first began working on our skill, we based it on the "Hello World" template. With the "Hello World" template came the HelloWorldIntent and its associated intent handler. That helped us get started with a working skill right away and provided a convenient and simple intent to play around with until we could add more intents. Although we could publish the skill with this intent intact, it's really just extra baggage and needs to go.

To get rid of the HelloWorldIntent, we'll start by deleting the HelloWorldIntent definition from the interaction model for all locales. Specifically, remove the intent definition that looks like this in all of the JSON files in skill-package/interactionModels/custom:

```
{
    "name": "HelloWorldIntent",
    "slots": [],
    "samples": [
        ...
    ]
},
```

With the intent definition gone, Alexa will no longer handle requests for utterances like "hello" or "say hello". Since those requests will no longer be dispatched to the HelloWorldIntentHandler, we can delete that intent handler. That's easy because it's defined in its own JavaScript file at lambda/HelloWorldIntentHandler.js. So just delete that file:

```
$ rm lambda/HelloWorldIntentHandler.js
```

The HelloWorldIntentHandler is referenced in lambda/index.js in a couple of places that will also need to be removed. Near the top of index.js is the line where the HelloWorldIntentHandler module is imported with require():

```
const HelloWorldIntentHandler = require('./HelloWorldIntentHandler');
```

Remove that line as well as the line in which the HelloWorldIntentHandler constant is registered with the skill builder:

```
exports.handler = Alexa.SkillBuilders.custom()
    .addRequestHandlers(
        HelloWorldIntentHandler,
    )
```

With no intent handler for the HelloWorldIntent, we no longer need the HELLO_MSG entries in lambda/languageStrings.js, so they can also be removed. There should be two such entries, one for English...

```
HELLO_MSG: 'Have a stellar day!',
```

...and another one for Spanish:

```
HELLO_MSG: '¡Que tengas un día estelar!',
```

Now all traces of the HelloWorldIntent are gone from the skill's fulfillment code and interaction model. All that's left is to remove the tests that trigger that intent:

```
$ rm test/unit/hello.test.yml
$ rm test/unity/hello-given-name.test.yml
```

With that extra baggage gone, let's have a look at a few of the built-in intents and see how to improve the responses.

Fine-Tuning Response Messages

As we've added new intent handlers to our skill, we've made sure that the textual responses are well-written and fitting to their respective intents. But there are a few intents given by the "Hello World" template that we've not paid much attention to. The AMAZON.CancelIntent, AMAZON.StopIntent, and AMAZON.Fallback-Intent still respond with the same text as when we first created the skill. Let's have a quick look at them to see if there's any opportunity for improvement.

Fortunately, all of those intents are handled by simply having Alexa speak a fixed message defined in languageStrings.js. If we want to tweak those messages, all of the work can be done by editing that file. The English values for those localized strings are defined like this:

```
GOODBYE_MSG: 'Goodbye!',
FALLBACK_MSG: 'Sorry, I don\'t know about that. Please try again.',
```

The GOODBYE_MSG string is used for both AMAZON.StopIntent and AMAZON.CancelIntent while FALLBACK_MSG is used for AMAZON.FallbackIntent. We can customize them for our skill like this:

```
publish/starport-75/lambda/languageStrings.js
GOODBYE_MSG: 'Goodbye and thanks for traveling with ' +
  'Star Port 75 Travel!',
FALLBACK_MSG: 'I\'m not sure that I can help with that. ' +
  'Please ask again.',
```

Likewise, the Spanish messages can be changed to match:

```
publish/starport-75/lambda/languageStrings.js
GOODBYE_MSG: '¡Adiós y gracias por viajar con Star Port 75 Travel!',
FALLBACK_MSG: 'No estoy seguro de poder ayudar con eso. ' +
  'Por favor pregunte nuevamente.',
```

With the new messages defined, the tests that trigger those intents will also need to be updated:

```
publish/starport-75/test/unit/standard-handlers.test.yml
---
configuration:
  description: Tests for standard request handlers

---
- test: Cancel request
- AMAZON.CancelIntent:
  - prompt:  Goodbye and thanks for traveling with Star Port 75 Travel!

---
- test: Stop request
- AMAZON.StopIntent:
  - prompt:  Goodbye and thanks for traveling with Star Port 75 Travel!

---
- test: Fallback Intent
- AMAZON.FallbackIntent:
  - prompt: I'm not sure that I can help with that. Please ask again.

---
- test: Session ended request
- SessionEndedRequest:
```

These changes may seem insignificant, but it's important that our skill has its own personality and that the messages are set apart from the "Hello World" template that we started with.

Another way to give a skill its own identity is in how we define the skill manifest. Let's crack open the skill.json file and make sure it's ready for publication.

Completing the Skill Manifest

So far, we've barely touched the skill manifest, only tweaking it slightly to enable permissions for accessing a user's given name, send reminders, and trigger notifications. While developing a skill, the values in the skill manifest aren't that important. But before we can publish our skill, we need to ensure that the skill manifest completely and accurately describes our skill.

Specifying Publishing Information

The skill-package/skill.json file contains a section under the publishingInformation property that we'll need to edit to be ready for publication. That section, unchanged from when we first initialized our skill from the "Hello World" template, looks like this:

```
publish/starport-75/skill-package/skill.json
"publishingInformation": {
  "locales": {
    "en-US": {
```

```
      "summary": "Sample Short Description",
      "examplePhrases": [
        "Alexa open hello world",
        "hello",
        "help"
      ],
      "name": "starport-75",
      "description": "Sample Full Description"
    }
  },
  "isAvailableWorldwide": true,
  "distributionCountries": [],
  "testingInstructions": "Sample Testing Instructions.",
  "category": "KNOWLEDGE_AND_TRIVIA"
},
```

This section of the manifest describes the skill details as they'll appear in the Alexa application. Obviously most of what's there now is just placeholder information (as evidenced by the use of the word "sample"). We'll want to edit this section to accurately describe our skill so that potential users may discover it, and so actual users may recognize it when it appears in the Alexa application.

The first thing we'll need to do is flesh out the locales property. Currently, it only contains an entry for U.S. English, although our skill supports all English and Spanish-speaking locales. Even for the "en-US" locale, the information given is just placeholder information.

After updating the locales property to cover both English and Spanish locales, it will look like this:

publish/starport-75/skill-package/skill.json
```
"locales": {
  "en-US": {
    "summary":
        "Star Port 75 Travel - Your source for out-of-this-world adventure!",
    "examplePhrases": [
      "Alexa open star port seventy five travel",
      "schedule a trip to Mars",
      "plan a trip to Jupiter"
    ],
    "name": "Star Port 75 Travel",
    "description": "Star Port 75 Travel helps you schedule trips to the most
                    popular destinations in our solar system."
  },

  ...
```

```
"es-ES": {
  "summary":
      "Star Port 75 Travel - Tu fuente de aventura fuera de este mundo!",
  "examplePhrases": [
    "Alexa abre star port seventy five travel",
    "programar un viaje a Mars",
    "planear un viaje a Júpiter"
  ],
  "name": "Star Port 75 Travel",
  "description": "Star Port 75 Travel lo ayuda a programar viajes a los
                  destinos más populares de nuestro sistema solar."
},

  ...
}
```

This is, of course, abridged to only show one locale for each language. The
"en-US" entry will be duplicated for "en-AU", "en-CA", "en-GB", and "en-IN".
Likewise, the "es-ES" entry will be duplicated for "es-MX" and "es-US".

One thing to keep in mind is that the first locale listed will be the first offered
in the developer console's testing tool. Therefore, it's a good idea to list your
default locale first in the locales property so that you won't have to explicitly
select it while testing your skills.

After locales, the next two properties are isAvailableWorldwide and distributionCountries.
When isAvailableWorldwide is set to true, it indicates that the skill should be
available to all Alexa users in all countries. While it's easy to leave it as true,
if your skill is only intended for specific countries, you can set it to false and
then list the supported countries in the distributionCountries property like this:

```
"isAvailableWorldwide": false,
"distributionCountries": [ "US", "AU", "CA", "GB", "IN", "ES", "MX" ],
```

Each country listed in distributionCountries should be a two-letter country code
in ISO 3166-1 alpha-2 format.[1]

Next is the testingInstructions property. This property should supply any special
instructions to the Amazon certification team that will test the skill, including
any prerequisites. In the case of the Star Port 75 Skill, we should tell the
testers to have a Google Calendar account:

```
"testingInstructions":
      "To complete booking you will need a Google Calendar account",
```

---

1.   https://en.wikipedia.org/wiki/ISO_3166-1_alpha-2

Finally, the category property specifies how the skill will be categorized. This helps potential users find our skill, when browsing skills in the Alexa companion application, and understand what purpose it serves. There are several categories to choose from[2] but the "NAVIGATION_AND_TRIP_PLANNER" category seems to suit our skill best:

```
"category":"NAVIGATION_AND_TRIP_PLANNER",
```

Now that our skill manifest seems to be more fleshed out, we can deploy it and see how it appears in the companion applications. After deployment, it looks a little like this in the browser-based Alexa application:

As you can see, much of what will added in the manifest now appears in the skill's page in the companion application. We must be ready to publish now, right?

Hold on. Although we're a lot closer to publishing than before, there's a little more work to do. If you take a closer look at the skill's page, you might notice that to the left of the skill name is an empty speech balloon. That empty space is supposed to contain an icon to uniquely brand the skill. We won't be able to publish the skill without supplying the icon.

2. https://developer.amazon.com/en-US/docs/alexa/smapi/skill-manifest.html#category-enum

Adding an icon to the skill is as easy as providing two URIs—one for a large icon image and one for a small icon image—in the smallIconUri and largeIconUri properties of each locale entry in the skill manifest. For example, for the "en-US" locale, those two properties might be defined like this:

```
"en-US": {
  "summary":
        "Star Port 75 Travel - Your source for out-of-this-world adventure!",
  "examplePhrases": [
    "Alexa open star port seventy five travel",
    "schedule a trip to Mars",
    "plan a trip to Jupiter"
  ],
  "name": "Star Port 75 Travel",
  "description": "Star Port 75 Travel helps you schedule trips...",
  "smallIconUri": "https://starport75.dev/images/SP75_sm.png",
  "largeIconUri": "https://starport75.dev/images/SP75_lg.png"
}
```

Often, you'll just use the same icon for all locales, duplicating those properties for each locale entry. But if you wish to define locale-specific icons, you can give different URIs for each locale.

The smallIconUri and largeIconUri properties are required for each locale before publication. But this presents an interesting question: If the "Hello World" template didn't specify those properties and yet they are required, what other properties are required in the skill manifest prior to publication?

Validating the Skill Manifest

Fortunately, the ASK CLI can help us figure out what's missing by performing validation on the manifest. Using the ask smapi submit-skill-validation, we can submit our skill for validation like this:

```
$ ask smapi submit-skill-validation \
  --skill-id amzn1.ask.skill.28e3f37-2b4-4b5-849-bcf4f2e081 \
  --locales en-US
{
  "id": "c74e8444-0ae4-453c-89d1-4d372208e21a",
  "status": "IN_PROGRESS"
}
```

The --skill-id, and --locales parameters are required. In this case, we're only submitting for validation of the "en-US" locale, but we can submit multiple locales by listing them with comma separation.

The result from ask smapi submit-skill-validation is a JSON response that includes the ID of the validation report and the status of the validation. Validation may

take several minutes, so the status will likely always be "IN_PROGRESS" in
the response.

```
$ ask smapi get-skill-validations \
  --skill-id amzn1.ask.skill.28e3f37-2b4-4b5-849-bcf4f2e081 \
  --validation-id c74e8444-0ae4-453c-89d1-4d372208e21a
{
  "id": "c74e8444-0ae4-453c-89d1-4d372208e21a",
  "status": "FAILED",
  "result": {
    "validations": [
      {
        "title": "Eligibility to update your live skill instantly",
        "description": "Your skill contains changes that make it ineligible
            to update your live skill instantly. For more information see
            https://developer.amazon.com/en-US/docs/alexa/devconsole
            /about-the-developer-console.html#update-live-skill",
        "status": "FAILED",
        "importance": "RECOMMENDED"
      },
      {
        "title": "A selection is missing for the question 'Does this skill
            contain advertising?'. In the Distribution tab, go to the
            Privacy &amp; Compliance section to provide an answer.",
        "status": "FAILED",
        "importance": "REQUIRED"
      },
      {
        "title": "Confirmation for 'Export compliance' is missing. In the
            Distribution tab, please go to the Privacy &amp; Compliance
            section to resolve the issue.",
        "status": "FAILED",
        "importance": "REQUIRED"
      },
      {
        "locale": "en-US",
        "title": "A Large Skill Icon is missing for the en-US locale. In
            the Distribution tab, go to Skill Preview for en-US to add a
            large skill icon.",
        "status": "FAILED",
        "importance": "REQUIRED"
      },
      {
        "title": "A selection is missing for the question 'Does this skill
            allow users to make purchases or spend real money?'. In the
            Distribution tab, go to the Privacy &amp; Compliance section to
            provide an answer.",
        "status": "FAILED",
        "importance": "REQUIRED"
      },
```

```
        {
          "locale": "en-US",
          "title": "A Small Skill Icon is missing for the en-US locale. In
              the Distribution tab, go to Skill Preview for en-US to add a
              small skill icon.",
          "status": "FAILED",
          "importance": "REQUIRED"
        },
        {
          "title": "A selection is missing for the question 'Does this Alexa
              skill collect users' personal information?'. In the Distribution
              tab, go to the Privacy &amp; Compliance section to provide an
              answer.",
          "status": "FAILED",
          "importance": "REQUIRED"
        },
        {
          "locale": "en-US",
          "title": "The privacy policy URL is missing for the en-US locale.
              The privacy policy URL is required for skills that collect user
              information (e.g. account linking). In the Distribution tab, go
              to Skill Preview for en-US to add the privacy policy URL.",
          "status": "FAILED",
          "importance": "REQUIRED"
        },
        {
          "title": "A selection is missing for the question 'Is this skill
              directed to or does it target children under the age of 13?'.
              In the Distribution tab, go to the Privacy &amp; Compliance
              section to provide an answer.",
          "status": "FAILED",
          "importance": "REQUIRED"
        }
      ]
    }
}
```

As with ask smapi submit-skill-validation, the ask smapi get-skill-validations command requires the --skill-id parameter. It doesn't require the --locales parameter, but does require the --validation-id parameter, which will be the ID given in response to ask smapi submit-skill-validation.

The response to ask smapi get-skill-validations will be a potentially lengthy JSON document that includes the validation status (in this case, "FAILED") and a list of validation problems to be addressed. If the status in the response shows "IN_PROGRESS" wait a few moments and try ask smapi get-skill-validations again. When the validation is complete, the status will change to either "FAILED" or "SUCCESSFUL" and the list can be used as a checklist to help you complete the missing pieces of the skill manifest.

There are two kinds of entries in the validations list: locale-specific validations and privacy and compliance validations. Locale-specific validations will have a locale property to tell you which locale needs properties set or changed. Most privacy and compliance validations do not have a locale property unless it is a locale-specific privacy and compliance detail that needs to be addressed. Privacy and compliance validations are addressed by adding or editing sub-properties under a privacyAndCompliance property in the manifest (which we haven't yet added).

You'll also notice that the title of each validation includes instructions on how to address the problem by filling in fields via the development console. You're welcome to address these problems in the development console if you wish. But for our purposes, we'll edit the skill manifest directly by adding properties in skill.json.

The first failed validation is neither a locale validation problem nor a privacy and compliance validation problem. It is a recommendation that you enable the skill for instant updates. Since we've not even published the skill yet, there's no way we can update it. It is not required that we address this at this time, so for now we'll ignore this recommendation.

Next, let's address the locale-specific validations. Two of them are asking us to provide smallIconUri and largeIconUri properties for the "en-US" locale, which we've already discussed before.

The other is asking us to specify a URL to a privacy policy page for the skill. This validation is actually a locale-specific privacy and compliance validation. To fix it, we'll need to add the following privacyAndCompliance property in the skill manifest, as a peer to the publishingInformation property:

```
"privacyAndCompliance": {
  "locales": {
    "en-US": {
      "privacyPolicyUrl": "https://starport75.dev/privacy.html"
    },
    "en-AU": {
      "privacyPolicyUrl": "https://starport75.dev/privacy.html"
    },
    ...
    "es-ES": {
      "privacyPolicyUrl": "https://starport75.dev/privacy_es.html"
    },
    ...
  }
}
```

The locales sub-property specifies privacy and compliance information for each locale. Here we're only specifying the location of a privacy policy with the privacyPolicyUrl property. But you may also specify a terms of use document for each locale by setting a termsOfUseUrl property, although that's not required.

Now let's look at the remaining privacy and compliance validations:

- "A selection is missing for the question 'Does this skill contain advertising?'"—This indicates whether or not the skill advertises any products or services. You can fix this validation by adding a containsAds property under privacyAndCompliance and setting it to either true or false.

- "Confirmation for 'Export compliance' is missing."—This indicates that the skill meets the requirements to be exported to any country or region. You can fix this validation by adding a isExportCompliant property under privacyAndCompliance and setting it to either true or false.

- "A selection is missing for the question 'Does this skill allow users to make purchases or spend real money?'"—This indicates whether or not purchases are allowed through the skill. To fix this validation, add an allowsPurchases property under privacyAndCompliance and set its value to either true or false.

- "A selection is missing for the question 'Does this Alexa skill collect users' personal information?'"—This indicates whether or not the skill collects any personal information from the user. This validation can be fixed by setting a usesPersonalInfo property under privacyAndCompliance to either true or false.

- "A selection is missing for the question 'Is this skill directed to or does it target children under the age of 13?'"—This indicated whether or not the skill's audience includes children under the age of 13. This validation can be addressed by setting an isChildDirected property under privacyAndCompliance to either true or false.

In the case of Star Port 75 Travel, our skill does not have any advertising and does not target children. It is, however, export compliant, allows purchases, and collects user information. Therefore, the completed privacyAndCompliance section of the skill manifest should look like this:

```
"privacyAndCompliance": {
  "containsAds": false,
  "isExportCompliant": true,
  "allowsPurchases": true,
  "usesPersonalInfo": true,
  "isChildDirected": false,
  "locales": {
```

```
      "en-US": {
        "privacyPolicyUrl": "https://starport75.dev/privacy.html"
      },
      "en-AU": {
        "privacyPolicyUrl": "https://starport75.dev/privacy.html"
      },
      ...
      "es-ES": {
        "privacyPolicyUrl": "https://starport75.dev/privacy_es.html"
      },
      ...
    }
  },
```

Now we can redeploy our skill and run the validation check again. If you get any errors in deploying the skill, double-check that the icon URIs and the privacy policy URL point to an actual resource and don't return an HTTP 404 or any other error response.

Once redeployed, we can run ask smapi submit-skill-validation and ask smapi get-skill-validations again. This time there are several successful validations, along with a few new failures. One of those failures requires attention:

```
{
  "locale": "en-US",
  "title": "Example phrases should contain the sample utterances that you
          have provided.",
  "description": "The skill's example phrases should contain the sample
        utterances that you have provided. For example: \"Alexa, ask {your
        invocation name} to {sample utterance present in your intent}.\" The
        example phrases (s) that do not contain your sample utterances are
        provided below.schedule a trip to Marsplan a trip to Jupiter...",
  "status": "FAILED",
  "importance": "REQUIRED"
},
```

The formatting of the failure's description may be missing some whitespace that would make it easier to ready, but it seems that the example phrases "schedule a trip to Mars" and "plan a trip to Jupiter" don't match any of the sample utterances in the interaction model. A quick look at the en-US.json file confirms that we never defined that utterance. So, let's add a few sample utterances to the interaction model in en-US.json as well as for the other English interaction model JSON files:

```
{
  "name": "ScheduleTripIntent",
  "samples": [
➤    "schedule a trip to {destination}",
➤    "plan a trip to {destination}",
```

```
    "schedule a trip to {destination} leaving {departureDate} and
        returning {returnDate}",
    "plan a trip to {destination} leaving {departureDate} and
        returning {returnDate}",
    "plan a trip between {departureDate} and {returnDate} to
        visit {destination}"
  ],
  ...
}
```

Similarly, we'll need to add the Spanish equivalents to the three Spanish interaction models:

```
{
  "name": "ScheduleTripIntent",
  "samples": [
➤    "programar un viaje a {destination}",
➤    "planifique un viaje a {destination}",
    "programar un viaje a {destination} dejando {departureDate} y
        regresando {returnDate}",
    "planifique un viaje entre {departureDate} y {returnDate} para
        visitar {destination}",
    "planear un viaje entre {departureDate} y {returnDate}"
  ],
  ...
}
```

Now, let's deploy and run validation checks one more time. This time, the results are still lengthy, but all required validations are successful. Most importantly, the overall status is "SUCCESSFUL":

```
$ ask smapi submit-skill-validation \
  --skill-id amzn1.ask.skill.28e3f37-2b4-4b5-849-bcf4f2e081 \
  --locales en-US,en-AU,en-CA,en-GB,en-IN,es-ES,es-MX,es-US
{
  "id": "70e0c86e-07f2-425c-ab94-1c6044621d95",
  "status": "IN_PROGRESS"
}
$ ask smapi get-skill-validations \
  --skill-id amzn1.ask.skill.28e3f37-2b4-4b5-849-bcf4f2e081 \
  --validation-id 70e0c86e-07f2-425c-ab94-1c6044621d95
{
  "id": "70e0c86e-07f2-425c-ab94-1c6044621d95",
➤  "status": "SUCCESSFUL",
  "result": {
    "validations": [
      ...
    ]
  }
}
```

At this point, we've written the code, we've run the tests, and we've performed pre-publication validation. We've done almost everything that can be done to prepare the skill for publication. With no further delay, let's submit our skill for certification.

Submitting for Certification and Publication

You can use the ASK CLI to submit a skill for certification using the ask smapi submit-skill-for-certification command. This command only requires that the skill ID be given via the --skill-id parameter. For example:

```
$ ask smapi submit-skill-for-certification \
  --skill-id amzn1.ask.skill.28e3f37-2b4-4b5-849-bcf4f2e081
Command executed successfully!
```

This submits the skill. If it passes certification, then it will automatically be published and made available in all locales specified in the skill's manifest. You may, however, specify that it should only be certified without publication by specifying the --publication-method parameter:

```
$ ask smapi submit-skill-for-certification \
  --skill-id amzn1.ask.skill.28e3f37-2b4-4b5-849-bcf4f2e081 \
  --publication-method MANUAL_PUBLISHING
Command executed successfully!
```

By setting --publication-method to "MANUAL_PUBLISHING", it puts you in control of precisely when the skill is made available. This is useful if, for example, you want to sync up a skill's availability with some marketing campaign or special event. In this case, once the skill passes certification, you can publish the skill on demand or schedule it to be published on a specific date and time through the developer console.

Shortly after submitting the skill for certification, you should receive an email informing you the skill has been submitted. Keep an eye out for an email from the Alexa Skills Team with a subject of "Your skill Star Port 75 Travel has been submitted for certification" (where "Star Port 75 Travel" will be the name of your submitted skill). The email will include a link to the submission checklist in the developer console to track certification status.

You can also track the certification status using the ASK CLI with the ask smapi get-certifications-list command:

```
$ ask smapi get-certifications-list \
  --skill-id amzn1.ask.skill.28e3f37-2b4-4b5-849-bcf4f2e081
```

If you try this command immediately after submitting the skill for certification, you'll probably get an HTTP 404 response with a JSON payload indicating that no certifications are found for the given skill ID. But after about a half hour or so, it will return the submission status:

```
$ ask smapi get-certifications-list \
  --skill-id amzn1.ask.skill.28e3f37-2b4-4b5-849-bcf4f2e081
{
  "_links": {
    "self": {
      "href": "/v1/skills/amzn1.ask.skill.28e3f37-.../certifications"
    }
  },
  "isTruncated": false,
  "items": [
    {
      "id": "dKAuRIdN",
      "reviewTrackingInfo": {
        "estimatedCompletionTimestamp": "2020-06-11T04:18:33.616Z",
        "lastUpdated": "2020-06-08T04:57:22.028Z"
      },
      "skillSubmissionTimestamp": "2020-06-20T22:10:12.088Z",
      "status": "IN_PROGRESS"
    }
  ],
  "totalCount": 1
}
```

The submission status includes several timestamps related to the certification submission, but three properties are of particular interest:

- estimatedCompletionTimestamp—This gives you some insight into when the certification should be complete, although in practice certification typically completes well before the given date.

- status—This provides the current certification status. As shown here, the status is "IN_PROGRESS".

- lastUpdated—This shows the time that the status was last changed.

At this point, a little patience is required. A skill may take anywhere from a few hours up to a few weeks before it completes certification. The time to complete certification seems to depend on the complexity of the skill. A simple skill that doesn't involve account linking, user information, or in-skill processing may only take a few hours to certify. On the other hand, you may be waiting several days or weeks for certification of a skill that requires those things.

Also, while your skill is in certification, you won't be able to make any modifications. If you want to change anything, you'll need to wait until certification has completed.

Eventually, however, you'll receive another email that will let you know if your skill has passed certification or not. If you receive an email with a subject line saying, "Certification feedback for your Alexa skill Star Port 75 Travel", it means that your skill has failed certification and cannot be published without some changes. While it may seem disheartening to receive such an email, the text of the email will tell you what needs to be fixed and offer guidance in correcting the certification problems.

At about the same time you receive that email, your skill's status will have changed to "FAILED" in the response to the ask smapi get-certifications-list:

```
$ ask smapi get-certifications-list \
  --skill-id amzn1.ask.skill.28e3f37-2b4-4b5-849-bcf4f2e081
{
  "_links": {
    "self": {
      "href": "/v1/skills/amzn1.ask.skill.
                        28e3f37-2b4-4b5-849-bcf4f2e081/certifications"
    }
  },
  "isTruncated": false,
  "items": [
    {
      "id": "dKAuRIdN",
      "reviewTrackingInfo": {
        "actualCompletionTimestamp": "2020-06-22T12:07:22.799Z",
        "estimatedCompletionTimestamp": "2020-07-10T22:10:12.088Z",
        "lastUpdated": "2020-06-22T12:07:22.799Z"
      },
      "skillSubmissionTimestamp": "2020-06-20T22:10:12.088Z",
      "status": "FAILED"
    }
  ],
  "totalCount": 1
}
```

You may also note that the response now contains a new actualCompletionTimestamp property indicating precisely when the skill's certification changed status. More often than not, the timestamp of the actual completion is well in advance of the estimated completion time. That means that after you address the certification problems and resubmit, you should have hope of getting a quick turnaround.

Even so, it will still take awhile for the certification's status to change. But assuming you addressed the issues to Amazon's satisfaction, you'll receive an email with a subject like "Your Alexa skill Star Port 75 Travel is now live!" (where "Star Port 75 Travel" will be the name of your skill). At this point, if you were to query the certification list again, you'd get a "SUCCEEDED" response:

```
$ ask smapi get-certifications-list \
  --skill-id amzn1.ask.skill.28e3f37-2b4-4b5-849-bcf4f2e081
{
  "_links": {
    "self": {
      "href": "/v1/skills/amzn1.ask.skill.28e3f37-.../certifications"
    }
  },
  "isTruncated": false,
  "items": [
    {
      "id": "dKAuRIdN",
      "reviewTrackingInfo": {
        "actualCompletionTimestamp": "2020-06-08T04:57:22.028Z",
        "estimatedCompletionTimestamp": "2020-06-11T04:18:33.616Z",
        "lastUpdated": "2020-06-08T04:57:22.028Z"
      },
      "skillSubmissionTimestamp": "2020-06-08T04:18:33.616Z",
      "status": "SUCCEEDED"
    }
  ],
  "totalCount": 1
}
```

The skill is now certified and, assuming you didn't request manual publishing, is available for everyone in the skill's configured locales to use. If you chose to publish your skill manually, then you'll find a new entry for your skill in the developer console, as shown in this screenshot:

The entry whose status is "Certified" represents the certified, but not yet published skill. If you click on the "Publish" link in the Actions column, you will be taken to a screen from which you can either publish the skill immediately or schedule it for publication at a later date.

Congratulations! You've just published an Alexa skill! Feel free to treat yourself to a release party and take a victory lap. You deserve it!

Promoting Your Skill with Quick Links

Now that the skill is live, you'll want to tell the world about it. The easiest way to do that it to publish a quick link to your skill.

Quick links are URLs that can be published on a web site or blog, an email, on Twitter, or anywhere else you can share an HTTP URL. When someone clicks on a quick link for a skill, they'll be prompted to login to their Amazon account (if they are not already logged in) and select one of their Alexa devices to launch the skill from. Then, the skill will be automatically launched on the selected device.

All you need to create a quick link is the published skill's ID to plug into the following URL template: https://alexa-skills.amazon.{domain}/apis/custom/skills/{skill-id}/launch

You'll need to replace "{skill-id}" with skill ID. And you'll need to replace "{domain}" with the top-level domain of the country that the quick link is for. The following table shows what the top-level domain should be for each country supported in the Alexa marketplace:

Country Code	Top-Level Domain
AU	.com.au
BR	.com.br
CA	.ca
DE	.de
ES	.es
FR	.fr
GB	.co.uk
IN	.in
IT	.it
JP	.co.jp
MX	.com.mx
US	.com

For example, if the Star Port 75 Travel skill has a skill ID of "amzn1.ask .skill.28e3f37-2b4-4b5-849-bcf4f2e081", then the quick link for the United States will be https://alexa-skills.amazon.com/apis/custom/skills/amzn1.ask.skill.28e3f37-2b4-4b5-849-bcf4f2e081/launch. Similarly, the quick link for Spain would be https://alexa-skills.amazon.es/apis/custom/skills/amzn1.ask.skill.28e3f37-2b4-4b5-849-bcf4f2e081/launch.

With the quick link URL in hand, share it anywhere and with anyone you want. Although it's not necessary, it's usually a good idea to include instructions for how to launch the skill vocally with the invocation name. For example, you might include a link to the skill's quick link on a webpage along side some text that says "...or say Alexa, open Star Port 75 Travel." This offers the user two ways to launch the skill—vocally and by clicking the link.

The skill has been published and you've told everyone about it with a quick link. But, we're far from finished. After celebrating, come back and settle in for what happens after publication: tracking skill analytics.

Gathering Usage Metrics

Now that your skill is live, you may already be thinking about changes you want to make for a new release. You might have an all new feature in mind. Or you may have some ideas on improving the interaction model to make it handle user requests more accurately. And, it's possible you've found some bugs that need to be sorted out in the next version.

Before diving into the code to address these concerns, it can be very informative to review some of the metrics around your skill's usage. Amazon automatically tracks several helpful metrics about a skill, requiring no additional coding or configuration. You can use these metrics to learn how many customers are using your skill and how they are using it. With these insights, you can better plan how to prioritize changes to your skill.

Skill metrics are available both from the developer console and via the ASK CLI. Let's have a look at the how metrics are presented in a graphical form in the developer console first.

Viewing Analytics in the Developer Console

If you visit the developer console after your skill has been published, you'll notice that there are two entries for the skill in the list of skills. The first screenshot on page 309 shows what you might see.

The first entry represents the published skill, while the second entry represents your skill in the development stage. As you continue to develop your skill for future versions, it's the second entry that you'll be working with. The first entry, however, is where you'll go to view the analytic data for your skill. You can either click on the "Analytics" link in the Actions column or click the skill name and then click on the "Analytics" tab. The second screenshot on page 309 shows the analytics summary page.

As shown here, the summary page includes some basic information such as the number of sessions, unique customers, and utterances handled by our skill over the past week. This screenshot was taken only a couple of weeks after the skill was submitted for certification, so the only data available was created by the certification process and isn't sufficient for some metrics to be shown. For example, the user enablements and account linking completion rate metrics require a significant amount of data before they're shown.

As you dig into the analytics pages, you'll find more information, including historical metrics presented as graphs. For example, clicking the "Sessions" item in the left-hand menu will show several graphs pertaining to session count, as shown in this screenshot:

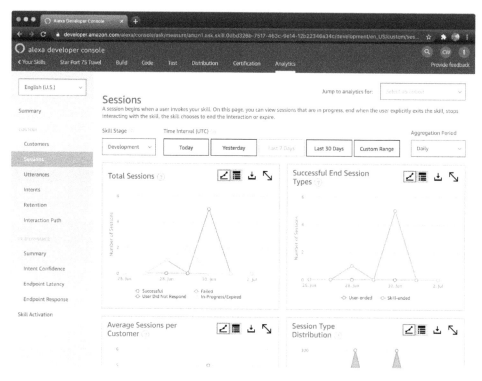

Feel free to explore the various graphs and metrics offered under the "Analytics" tab on your own. As you do, be sure to have a look at the "Interaction Path" graph. This graph shows the various paths users have taken through the skill, going from one intent to the next until their session ends. An example of what this graph looks like is shown in the screenshot on page 311.

The interaction path graph requires a lot of data before it can be displayed; this screenshot was taken from the analytics page of a skill that was published some time ago. But once it is available, the interaction graph gives a great visualization of how your skill's users are using the skill. You can use this information to improve the skill. For example, if you find that a lot of users are following lengthy paths through several intents to get to a piece of information, you might optimize your skill to make the same information available with a single intent.

Accessing Skill Metrics with the ASK CLI

While the graphs provided in the "Analytics" tab are generally useful and interesting, you might find a need to crunch the numbers yourself or create your own custom visualizations of the metrics. If so, then the ask smapi get-skill-metrics command is what you'll need.

To give the get-skill-metrics a try, let's use it to find the total sessions per day for a specific week in June 2020:

```
$ ask smapi get-skill-metrics \
  --skill-id amzn1.ask.skill.28e3f37-2b4-4b5-849-bcf4f2e081 \
  --start-time 2020-06-07T00:00:00Z \
  --end-time 2020-06-14T00:00:00Z \
  --period P1D \
  --metric totalSessions \
  --stage live \
  --skill-type custom
{
  "metric": "totalSessions",
  "timestamps": [
    "2020-06-07T00:00:00Z",
```

```
      "2020-06-08T00:00:00Z",
      "2020-06-09T00:00:00Z",
      "2020-06-10T00:00:00Z",
      "2020-06-11T00:00:00Z",
      "2020-06-12T00:00:00Z",
      "2020-06-13T00:00:00Z"
    ],
    "values": [
      1,
      0,
      1,
      8,
      11,
      1,
      85
    ]
  }
}
```

The get-skill-metrics command requires several parameters, including:

- skill-id—The ID of the skill to fetch metrics for

- start-time and end-time—The range of time for which metrics should be fetched

- period—The granularity of the metrics. Can be "SINGLE" (a single count for the entire range), "P1D" (per day), "PT1H" (hourly), or "PT15M" (every 15 minutes)

- metric—The specific metric you are interested in. Can be "uniqueCustomers", "totalEnablements", "totalUtterances", "successfulUtterances", "failedUtterances", "totalSessions", "successfulSessions", "incompleteSessions", "userEndedSessions", or "skillEndedSessions"

- stage—The stage of the skill, either "live" or "development". This defaults to "development", but in this case we're more interested in the metrics for our "live" skill.

- skill-type—The type of skill. Often "custom", but can also be "smartHome" or "flashBriefing"

As you can see, the response includes timestamps and values properties. The timestamps property is an array of timestamps for each point that data is recorded. Each entry in timestamps corresponds to an entry in values which is the value of the metric at that timestamp. In this case, there are seven dates with one value for each date falling within the specified date range.

Wrapping Up

There are few things more rewarding than publishing software into production. An application will only be able to fulfill its purpose once it is in front of a wider audience. In this chapter, that's what we've done for the Alexa skill we have created.

We started by fleshing out some of the missing details of the skill manifest, using the ASK CLI's ask smapi submit-skill-validation command to help find missing or incorrect manifest entries. Then we submitted the skill for certification so that Amazon can verify that our skill meets certain guidelines and expectations. After fixing any certification concerns, we published the skill. Then we saw how to explore the metrics that are automatically collected for our skill to learn how it's being used and plan for follow-up releases.

Now that our skill has been published, it would seem that we're at the end of our journey. But before we close the book (literally) on developing Alexa skills, there's one more thing you will want to learn. In the next and final chapter, we're going to look at a relatively new technique available to Alexa skill developers that mixes a bit of artificial intelligence with dialogs to create even more natural conversations between Alexa and a user.

CHAPTER 14

Defining Conversational Flows

Have you ever wished that you could get a do-over on a conversation? Maybe you said something that you regret. Or perhaps you feel that you could've expressed your thoughts more clearly or more effectively than you did. If only you could have a second chance to say the things you could have said.

Alexa dialogs, which we learned about and employed in Chapter 4, Creating Multi-Turn Dialogs, on page 83, are a mighty powerful feature that enable multi-turn conversations in the skills we create. As it turns out, though, dialogs aren't perfect. If only we had another chance at creating multi-turn conversations, we might be able to do even better.

In this chapter, we're going to look at a relatively new Alexa feature called *Alexa Conversations* which will provide that second chance at creating multi-turn conversations in our skills. And, as you'll see, Alexa Conversations will enable us to improve greatly upon the original dialogs we created before.

Introducing Alexa Conversations

Alexa Conversations is a relatively new feature of the Alexa platform that enables richer and more flexible multi-turn conversations than what the original dialog model could ever achieve. At this time, Alexa Conversations is generally available in the "en_US" locale and in beta for "en-AU", "en-CA", "en-IN", "en-GB", "de-DE", "ja-JP", "es-ES", and "es-US".

Alexa Conversations, much like the dialogs we created in Chapter 4, Creating Multi-Turn Dialogs, on page 83, work toward the goal of achieving some sort of task, such as planning a interplanetary vacation. Along the way, there is a back and forth exchange between Alexa and the user in which questions asked by Alexa are answered by the user, ultimately arriving at the completion of the task.

Where Alexa Conversations differs from dialogs is that Alexa Conversations are backed by an artificial intelligence engine that expands a conversation model defined by the Alexa developer, to cover conversations that the developer may have never imagined.

Creating a Better Dialog

To illustrate the power of Alexa Conversations, consider the following trip-planning dialog:

> User: Let's plan a trip
>
> Alexa: Where do you want to go?
>
> User: Mars
>
> Alexa: When will your trip start?
>
> User: June 9th
>
> Alexa: When will your trip end?
>
> User: June 16th
>
> Alexa: I've got you down for a trip to Mars between June 9th and June 16th. Is that correct?
>
> User: Yes
>
> Alexa: Great! Enjoy your trip to Mars!

This kind of dialog is what we created in Chapter 4, Creating Multi-Turn Dialogs, on page 83 using Alexa dialogs. It handles the essential case where the user wishes to plan a trip and Alexa interviews the user to find out details of the trip. It works well, as long as the user doesn't go off-script.

For example, what might happen if instead of sticking to the designed dialog, the user were to take a slight tangent along the way, asking about the weather:

> User: Let's plan a trip
>
> Alexa: Where do you want to go?
>
> User: What's the weather like on Jupiter?
>
> Alexa: Star Port 75 Travel doesn't offer travel to the weather like on Jupiter. Where else would you like to go?

Oops! Alexa didn't understand the question. Alexa asked the user where they want to go, but then the user asked a question about the weather on Jupiter. At this point, Alexa expects the user to specify a destination, but instead heard "What's the weather like on Jupiter?" This fails validation with the destination slot (because the phrase "weather like on Jupiter" isn't one of the entries in the PLANETS slot type) and results in a confusing response from Alexa.

Or what if the user changes their mind on a previously given answer? Consider the following dialog:

> User: Let's plan a trip
>
> Alexa: Where do you want to go?
>
> User: Mars
>
> Alexa: When will your trip start?
>
> User: June 9th
>
> Alexa: When will your trip end?
>
> User: June 16th
>
> Alexa: I've got you down for a trip to Mars between June 9th and June 16th. Is that correct?
>
> User: I want to visit Saturn instead
>
> Alexa: Okay, let's start over. How can I help you?

Once all of the slots have been filled, Alexa just needs confirmation of the trip details. The user decides on a different destination, which Alexa incorrectly interprets as a negative response, and sends an intent request for the ScheduleTripIntent intent with a confirmation status of "DENIED".

As you can see, standard Alexa dialogs have a few shortcomings. But Alexa Conversations can do better. Alexa Conversations is an alternative approach to designing multi-turn conversations. With Alexa Conversations, you define a conversation model that includes handful of sample dialog—each representing a possible exchange between a user and Alexa. Then you feed the conversation model to Alexa's AI engine which expands the conversation model to include many more dialogs that could happen.

Before we start on our Alexa Conversations skill, let's cover a few basic concepts that you'll encounter as you define a conversation model.

Understanding the Conversation Models

These are the most important Alexa Conversations concepts to grasp:

- Dialogs
- Events and Utterance Sets
- Actions

- Acts (Request and Response)
- Types

Dialogs are the fundamental element of a conversation. They describe the back and forth exchange between Alexa and the user to ultimately achieve some task. As you define a conversation model for your skills, you will create a dialog that itself will contain one or many sample dialogs describing different paths that the discussion can take toward achieving the task.

Events are triggers that are external to a skill, most often something that the user says. Events are defined around *utterance sets* which list several possible things a user may say to trigger the event.

An *action* is something that represents some aspect of the skill's behavior. Some examples of actions include when Alexa says something to the user, when the skill expects an event, or the confirmation of some other action. You can also define your own custom actions for your skill, most commonly as a means of transferring data to your skill's fulfillment code.

There are two kinds of *acts*: request and response acts. Request acts provide semantic meaning to an event. Events themselves are only triggered in response to an utterance spoken by a user. But a request act applies meaning to what was spoken. For example, if the user says, "I want to visit Pluto," then an event will be triggered and an *inform* request act will be associated with the event, enabling Alexa to understand that the user is providing information to the conversation.

Response acts, on the other hand, apply semantic meaning to a response action. For example, if the response has Alexa saying, "Are you sure you want to visit Pluto?" a human may understand that as Alexa asking for confirmation, but it requires that the response be associated with a confirmation act for the conversation model to understand the response's role in the dialog.

Finally, *types* represent some information or concept within the context of a dialog. Both request and response acts themselves are defined as types in Alexa Conversations. But more commonly, you'll think of types as some custom type that you'll use to carry data around in the course of a conversation. Custom types like the PLANETS type we defined in Chapter 3, Parameterizing Intents with Slots, on page 57 can be used in Alexa Conversations, but you can also define record types as part of the conversation model that act as holders for a conversation's context. For example, you might define a custom type that holds trip details that are given by the user in the course of planning a trip.

Those basic concepts will become more apparent as you build your Alexa Conversations skill. Speaking of which, let's get started on that right now.

Starting a New Alexa Conversations Project

There is not (yet) a way to add Alexa Conversations to an existing Alexa skill project. Therefore, we are unable to retrofit the Star Port 75 skill to make use of Alexa Conversations. Instead, we'll start an all new skill project, using Alexa Conversations to recreate the multi-turn dialog we defined in Chapter 4, *Creating Multi-Turn Dialogs*, on page 83.

Two Ways to Create a Conversational Skill

There are actually two ways to create and develop Alexa Conversations projects: within the Alexa developer console or at the command line using the ASK CLI. Currently, these are mutually exclusive options and the means by which conversation models are defined are vastly different. Either is a valid choice, but developing Alexa Conversations skills using the ASK CLI has one distinct advantage over using the developer console: it allows for our conversation model to be stored and managed in version control (such as Git), the same as the interaction model and fulfillment code. In contrast, conversation models created in the developer console can't be versioned. If you make a mistake as your conversation model evolves, there's no way to roll back to a previously working version. You'll have to resolve the mistake without the benefit of rollback. Because of that advantage, we'll use the ASK CLI to create a Conversations-based skill in this chapter.

Support for Alexa Conversations in the ASK CLI is relatively new and (at least for now) is only available in a beta version of the ASK CLI. To install the ASK CLI beta, use npm to install "ask-cli-x" as a global model like this:

```
$ npm install -g ask-cli-x
```

The beta version can be installed alongside the non-beta ASK CLI installation, so you don't need to worry about one stepping on the other. When using the non-beta ASK CLI, you'll use the ask command as we've done throughout this book. But when using the beta version, you'll use the askx command instead.

The askx new command creates a new Alexa Conversations project, the same as ask new. The following session shows how you might use the ASK CLI to create a new Alexa Conversations skill:

```
$ askx new
Please follow the wizard to start your Alexa skill project ->
? Choose the programming language you will use to code your skill:  NodeJS
? Choose a method to host your skill's backend resources:  AWS Lambda
  Host your skill code on AWS Lambda (requires AWS account).
```

```
? Choose a template to start with:  Weather Bot (Beta)
  Quick sample weather bot skill using Alexa Conversations ACDL.
? Please type in your skill name:  starport-75-conversations
? Please type in your folder name for the skill project (alphanumeric):
      starport-75-conversations
Executing git custom command..
remote: Counting objects: 104, done.
Receiving objects: 100% (104/104), 24.88 KiB | 772.00 KiB/s, done.
Resolving deltas: 100% (11/11), done.
Project for skill "starport-75-conversations" is successfully created at
    /Users/habuma/Projects/starport-75-conversations

Project initialized with deploy delegate "@ask-cli/lambda-deployer" successfully.
```

As you can see, after invoking askx new, you'll be asked some very familiar questions. For purposes of developing an Alexa Conversations skill, you'll need to be sure to answer some of the questions with very specific answers. To start with, Alexa Conversations are only supported in NodeJS. Also, when developing Alexa Conversations using the ASK CLI, Alexa-hosted skills are not an option; Only AWS Lambda-hosting is supported.

For the starting template, you'll be presented with a handful of choices, three of which are specific to Alexa Conversations: Empty, Weather Bot, and Pizza Bot. The Empty template will give you a bare-bones Alexa Conversations project to start from, but it is perhaps a bit too empty; you'll need to add the lambda directory and initialize the NodeJS project before you can write the fulfillment code. At the other extreme is the Pizza Bot example which is a great example of a complex Alexa Conversations skill, but is far too complicated to serve as a starting point for a new skill project.

Therefore, we'll start with the Weather Bot skill. You will probably want to delete some weather-specific artifacts from it before you publish your skill. But for a starter project, it gives you everything you need to create a custom Alexa Skill.

Now that the new project has been created, we're almost ready to define the skill's conversation model. But first, let's get acquainted with the Alexa Conversations Definition Language (ACDL), a language dedicated to defining conversation models.

Getting to know ACDL

ACDL is a language created specifically to make easy work of defining conversation models for Alexa skills. If you're familiar with languages like Java and C#, ACDL will be syntactically familiar, but is more declarative in nature than those other languages.

Clearing Out Weather-Specific Artifacts

The Weather Bot project is designed as a simple example of an Alexa Conversations project, but includes some components dedicated to providing a weather forecast. These components probably won't get in your way, but at some point you'll probably want to remove them.

These are the files you'll want to remove from a project based on the Weather Bot template:

- lambda/weather.json
- lambda/WeatherClient.js
- skill-package/response/prompts/weather_apla
- skill-package/conversations/Weather.acdl

You'll also want to remove GetWeatherApiHandler from lambda/index.js, as well as the require() line that imports the ./WeatherClient module.

Because ACDL is a rich and expressive language for defining conversation models, there's no space to go over it in detail in this chapter. Instead, we'll cover a few ACDL basics and then focus on the aspects of ACDL necessary to define a conversation model suitable for scheduling trips to planetary destinations. For a thorough understanding of ACDL, check out the ACDL Reference.[1]

ACDL source files are created in a skill project's skill-package/conversations directory and have a .acdl file extension. You can use as few or as many ACDL source files as you'd like to define a conversation model, but it's typically best for the sake of organization to split the model across multiple ACDL files.

ACDL files are declared as being in a namespace using the namespace keyword at the beginning of the file. For example:

```
namespace com.starport75
```

This is quite similar to the namespace keyword in C# or the package keyword in Java, allowing related resources to be conceptually collected in a given namespace. Resources from different namespaces can be imported into an ACDL file using the import keyword. For example, the following two lines import several components commonly used from the com.amazon.alexa.ask.conversations namespace, as well as the Nothing type from the com.amazon.alexa.schema namespace:

```
import com.amazon.alexa.ask.conversations.*
import com.amazon.alexa.schema.Nothing
```

---

1. https://developer.amazon.com/en-US/docs/alexa/conversations/acdl-reference.html

One thing you might have already noticed about ACDL that is different from Java or C# is that the lines do not end with a semi-colon. In fact, semi-colons aren't necessary (or even allowed) in ACDL to designate the end of a line.

The remainder of an ACDL file, following the namespace and import lines, is where you'll define one or more conversational components such as events, actions, custom types, and dialogs.

Now that we have established a few ACDL basics, let's put it to work defining the conversation model for the Star Port 75 Travel skill.

Defining the Conversation Model

The core component of all conversation models is the dialog. Dialogs capture one or more sample conversations that will take place between Alexa and a user.

In ACDL, dialogs are declared with the dialog keyword, followed by the dialog's type and name. The beginnings of a dialog declaration will look like this:

```
dialog Nothing ScheduleTripDialog {
  // dialog body goes here
}
```

As shown here, the name of the dialog is ScheduleTripDialog and the type is Nothing. At this time, Nothing is the only valid type for dialogs, although that could change in the future as Alexa Conversations and ACDL evolve.

Within the body of the dialog, you'll define one or more sample conversations using the sample keyword:

```
dialog Nothing ScheduleTripDialog {
  sample {
    // dialog sample 1
  }
  sample {
    // dialog sample 2
  }
}
```

Each sample models a possible conversation between Alexa and the user. For example, consider the following conversation about planning a trip to Jupiter:

> User: Let's plan a trip
>
> Alexa: Where do you want to go?
>
> User: Jupiter
>
> Alexa: When will your trip start?

User: June 9th

Alexa: When will your trip end?

User: June 16th

Alexa: I've got you down for a trip to Jupiter between June 9th and June 16th. Is that correct?

User: Yes

Alexa: Great! Enjoy your trip to Jupiter!

As you can infer from this example, a conversation always starts with the user saying something that initiates the conversation and ends with Alexa having the final words. With that in mind, let's write some ACDL that defines a sample dialog that models this kind of conversation.

Initiating the Conversation

The first element of any dialog is an expectation of an Invoke request. Invoke is one of a handful of request acts that may take place in a dialog. The following snippet shows how a trip-scheduling conversation might get started.

conv/starport-75/skill-package/conversations/ScheduleTripDialog.acdl
```
  sample {
    scheduleTripRequest = expect(Invoke, ScheduleTripEvent)
    ...
}
```

Here, the sample dialog begins when the user speaks an utterance from the set of utterances defined in the event named ScheduleTripEvent. ScheduleTripEvent is defined in ACDL like this:

conv/starport-75/skill-package/conversations/events/ScheduleTripEvent.acdl
```
namespace com.starport75.events

import com.amazon.alexa.ask.conversations.*
import com.starport75.types.TripDetails

ScheduleTripEvent = utterances<TripDetails>(
  [
    "plan a trip",
    "schedule a trip to {destination}",
    "book a trip to {destination}",
    "i want to go to {destination}",
    "schedule a trip to {destination} starting {departureDate}",
    "plan a trip to {destination} between {departureDate} and {returnDate}",
    "schedule a trip for {departureDate} to {returnDate}"
  ]
)
```

ScheduleTripEvent is essentially a set of utterances that, when spoken by the user in the context of the skill, trigger the event, thus kicking off a conversation. The utterance set is parameterized with <TripDetails>, indicating that slots in the utterances can contribute to the custom record type named TripDetails, which is defined as follows:

conv/starport-75/skill-package/conversations/types/TripDetails.acdl

```
namespace com.starport75.types

import com.amazon.ask.types.builtins.AMAZON.DATE
import slotTypes.PLANETS

type TripDetails {
  PLANETS destination
  DATE departureDate
  DATE returnDate
}
```

Notice the properties of TripDetails are of types DATE and PLANETS. The DATE type is one of Alexa's built-in types and is imported from the com.amazon.ask .types.builtins namespace. The PLANETS type, however, is specific to our skill and defined in the interaction model (the same as we did in Chapter 3, Parameterizing Intents with Slots, on page 57). Whenever you need to import a custom slot type in ACDL, it should be imported from the slotTypes namespace.

Going back to the expect() action which begins the sample dialog, it is the TripDetails object that is being returned and assigned to a variable named scheduleTripRequest. A little later, we'll pass scheduleTripRequest to the backend fulfillment code to perform the business logic behind the conversation.

If the user were to initiate the conversation by saying, "Plan a trip to Neptune," then the destination property of TripDetails would be assigned the value "Neptune", while the date properties would be empty. On the other hand, if the user simply says, "Plan a trip," then all the properties of TripDetails will remain empty.

It is Alexa's job to fill in all empty properties in order to complete the dialog. To do that, she'll need to ask the user some questions and the user will need to provide some answers. Next, we'll define this back and forth discussion in the sample dialog.

Gathering Dialog Data

In order to schedule a trip, we need Alexa to request the trip's destination, departure date, and return date from the user. And, naturally, the user will need to provide those details. This means that the dialog should next have three question and answer pairs, each asking for and collecting the three properties of the TripDetails object.

In ACDL, these question and answer pairs are defined by a response(), in which Alexa prompts the user for some information, and a Inform act, in which the user provides that information. For example, the snippet of ACDL that requests and captures that destination looks like this:

conv/starport-75/skill-package/conversations/ScheduleTripDialog.acdl
```
response(
  response=request_destination_apla,
  act=Request{ arguments = [
    scheduleTrip.arguments.destination]}
)
destination = expect(Inform, InformDestinationEvent)
```

The response() action, as its name suggests, sends a response to the user. The response is either an APL or APL-A document. In this case, the response parameter is set to request_destination_apla which references an APL-A document that prompts the user for the trip's destination. We'll see how the APL-A document is defined in section Defining Response Templates, on page 333.

The act parameter defines the dialog act that this response() is performing. In this case, we are requesting information from the user, so act is set to Request{...}. Moreover, the Request{...} act is requesting the trip's destination, so arguments is set to [scheduleTrip.arguments.destination].

Next, we see the expect() action again. At the beginning of the sample dialog, we used expect() to initiate the conversation with the Invoke act. But this time, the user is informing the skill of some missing data, which means we need to use the Inform act.

Just as with the Invoke act, we need to specify an utterance-based event that's associated with the expect() action. In this case, it's InformDestinationEvent, which is defined as follows:

conv/starport-75/skill-package/conversations/events/InformDestinationEvent.acdl
```
namespace com.starport75.events

import com.amazon.alexa.ask.conversations.*
import com.starport75.types.TripDestination

InformDestinationEvent = utterances<TripDestination>([
  "{destination}",
  "I want to go to {destination}",
  "{destination} sounds nice",
  "I want to visit {destination}"
])
```

Here, the event is defined as utterances<TripDestination>, indicating that it contributes to the custom TripDestination type. All of the utterances have a {destination} placeholder, so the TripDestination type should have a destination property, as shown here:

conv/starport-75/skill-package/conversations/types/TripDestination.acdl
```
namespace com.starport75.types

import slotTypes.PLANETS

type TripDestination {
  PLANETS destination
}
```

Now we've defined how to have Alexa prompt the user for the trip's destination and accept the answer, we can apply the same constructs to ask for the departure and return dates:

conv/starport-75/skill-package/conversations/ScheduleTripDialog.acdl
```
response(
  response=request_departureDate_apla,
  act=Request{ arguments=[
    scheduleTrip.arguments.departureDate]}
)
departureDate = expect(Inform, InformDepartureDateEvent)

response(
  response=request_returnDate_apla,
  act=Request{ arguments=[
    scheduleTrip.arguments.returnDate]}
)
returnDate = expect(Inform, InformReturnDateEvent)
```

As you can see, the only significant differences are the APL-A document being used in each response and the event applied to each Inform act. Speaking of the events, the InformDepartureDateEvent and InformReturnDateEvent events are defined as follows:

conv/starport-75/skill-package/conversations/events/InformDateEvents.acdl
```
namespace com.starport75.events

import com.amazon.alexa.ask.conversations.*
import com.starport75.types.TripDepartureDate
import com.starport75.types.TripReturnDate

InformDepartureDateEvent = utterances<TripDepartureDate>([
  "{departureDate}",
  "I want my trip to start {departureDate}",
  "I want to depart {departureDate}"
])
```

```
InformReturnDateEvent = utterances<TripReturnDate>([
  "{returnDate}",
  "I want my trip to end {returnDate}",
  "I want to return {returnDate}"
])
```

And their corresponding types, TripDepartureDate and TripReturnDate, are defined here:

conv/starport-75/skill-package/conversations/types/TripDates.acdl

```
namespace com.starport75.types

import com.amazon.ask.types.builtins.AMAZON.DATE

type TripDepartureDate {
  DATE departureDate
}

type TripReturnDate {
  DATE returnDate
}
```

Once the user has supplied all of the trip details, we're ready to send them to the fulfillment backend for processing. Let's see how to define a custom action in the sample dialog.

Sending Dialog Data to Fulfillment

Up to this point, we've used a few of ACDL's built-in actions to define our sample dialog, including expect(), response(), and utterances(). But ACDL also supports the creation of custom actions, which come in very handy for sending the data gathered in a conversation to the backend fulfillment code for processing.

Custom actions are defined in ACDL using the action type. For example, our dialog will need to send the destination and trip dates to the backend. The following scheduleTrip() definition declares such an action:

conv/starport-75/skill-package/conversations/actions/ScheduleTripAction.acdl

```
namespace com.starport75.actions

import com.starport75.types.ScheduleTripResult
import com.amazon.ask.types.builtins.AMAZON.*
import slotTypes.PLANETS

action ScheduleTripResult scheduleTrip(PLANETS destination,
    DATE departureDate, DATE returnDate)
```

As you can see, the definition for scheduleTrip() doesn't provide any implementation details, but rather just declares the interface through which the dialog will interact with the fulfillment code. We'll define the fulfillment code that backs this declaration in section Handling the Action Request, on page 336.

The scheduleTrip() action accepts three parameters: one PLANETS parameter for the destination and two DATE parameters for each of the two trip dates. It returns a ScheduleTripResult, which is a custom type that just echoes back the destination:

conv/starport-75/skill-package/conversations/types/ScheduleTripResult.acdl

```
namespace com.starport75.types

import com.amazon.ask.types.builtins.AMAZON.DATE
import com.amazon.ask.types.builtins.AMAZON.NUMBER
import slotTypes.PLANETS

type ScheduleTripResult {
  PLANETS destination
}
```

Applying a custom action in ACDL appears very similar to calling a function in JavaScript. For example, here's the snippet of ACDL to add to the end of our dialog sample to send trip data to the action:

conv/starport-75/skill-package/conversations/ScheduleTripDialog.acdl

```
scheduleTripResult = scheduleTrip(
  scheduleTripRequest.destination,
  scheduleTripRequest.departureDate,
  scheduleTripRequest.returnDate)
```

Here, the destination and dates that have been collected into properties of scheduleTripRequest in the course of the dialog are being passed as parameters to scheduleTrip(), and the result is assigned to scheduleTripResult. Now we can wrap up the conversation by passing scheduleTripResult to the final response:

conv/starport-75/skill-package/conversations/ScheduleTripDialog.acdl

```
response(
  scheduleTrip_apla,
  Notify { actionName = scheduleTrip },
  payload = ResponsePayload
    { scheduleTripResult = scheduleTripResult }
)
```

This response() is slightly different from previous response() actions we have used. Since it is not asking the user for any information and is simply notifying them of a result, the Notify response act is used. The payload parameter is set to a ResultPayload object used to carry the value of scheduleTripResult on to the APL-A document. We will see in section Defining Response Templates, on page 333 how the APL-A document makes use of this property. Meanwhile, here's how ResponsePayload is defined:

conv/starport-75/skill-package/conversations/types/ResponsePayload.acdl

```
namespace com.starport75.types

type ResponsePayload {
  ScheduleTripResult scheduleTripResult
}
```

At this point, our sample dialog is mostly complete. It starts after the user speaks an utterance that triggers ScheduleTripEvent, gathers trip details, and then passes the data on to the scheduleTrip() action before ending the conversation. But there's one other thing that we should probably add. Let's take a step back and have Alexa confirm the trip details before invoking the scheduleTrip() action.

Confirming the Dialog Data

Conceptually, dialog confirmation isn't much different than the information-gathering parts of the dialog. Alexa asks a question (for example, "Is this right?") and the user responds with a yes or no answer. And, as it turns out, adding confirmation to the sample dialog in ACDL isn't much different than the ACDL we added in the previous section.

For example, here's a snippet of ACDL that shows how to add dialog confirmation to a sample dialog:

conv/starport-75/skill-package/conversations/ScheduleTripDialog.acdl

```
response(
  confirmTrip_apla,
  ConfirmAction { actionName = scheduleTrip },
  payload = TripDetails { destination = scheduleTripRequest.destination,
    departureDate = scheduleTripRequest.departureDate,
    returnDate = scheduleTripRequest.returnDate
  }
)
expect(Affirm, AffirmEvent)
```

Once again, the response() and expect() actions come into play. This time, however, the act parameter to response() references the ConfirmAction act, specifically establishing that before we can invoke the scheduleTrip() action, this confirmation should take place.

Meanwhile, the expect() here is assuming that the user replies in the affirmative by taking Affirm as the first argument. The affirmative utterances that the user could speak are listed in AffirmEvent as shown here:

conv/starport-75/skill-package/conversations/events/AffirmEvent.acdl
```
namespace com.starport75.events

import com.amazon.alexa.ask.conversations.utterances

AffirmEvent = utterances([
  "exactly",
  "yeah I'd like that",
  "you got it",
  "yup",
  "correct",
  "that's right",
  "yeah",
  "yep",
  "yes"
])
```

Notice that AffirmEvent isn't parameterized with any specific type as was the case with other event utterance sets. When there are no slots to gather variable input in an utterance set, then it's unnecessary to specify a type. Optionally, you could still specify the type as <Nothing> like this:

```
AffirmEvent = utterances<Nothing>([
  ...
])
```

Nothing is a special built-in type that, as its name suggests, has no value. It's similar to void in languages like Java and C#.

This particular dialog sample deals with the path where the user affirms the action. But you can also define a sample in which the user denies the action. For that, the expect() action would be defined like this:

```
expect(Deny, DenyEvent)
```

The Deny request act indicates that the user has denied the action and therefore the action being confirmed should not be called. Just like AffirmEvent, the DenyEvent can be a simple untyped utterance set:

```
DenyEvent = utterances<Nothing>([
  "no",
  "nope",
  "no way"
])
```

To be clear, you shouldn't include both Affirm and Deny request acts in the same dialog sample. We've defined a dialog sample that ends with an affirmation and call to the scheduleTrip() action. Another dialog sample would define the path where the user denies the confirmation.

Putting it All Together

We've written several components of ScheduleTripDialog, but it helps to see the dialog in its entirety. The following ACDL file pulls all of the individual expect(), response(), and scheduleTrip() actions together into the complete ScheduleTripDialog definition:

conv/starport-75/skill-package/conversations/ScheduleTripDialog.acdl
```
namespace com.starport75

import com.starport75.actions.*
import com.starport75.events.*
import com.starport75.types.*

import com.amazon.alexa.ask.conversations.*
import com.amazon.alexa.schema.Nothing

import prompts.request_destination_apla
import prompts.request_departureDate_apla
import prompts.request_returnDate_apla
import prompts.scheduleTrip_apla
import prompts.confirmTrip_apla
```

Reading it from top-to-bottom, the sample dialog aligns directly with the textual conversation outlined at the beginning of this section. The response() actions map to the "Alexa:"-prefixed lines, while the expect() actions match up with the lines that started with "User:".

But this sample dialog only shows one possible path through the conversation. What if the user initiates the conversation with some of the trip details by saying, "Plan a trip to Jupiter"? Or what if they provide all of the details up-front by saying, "Schedule a trip to Neptune leaving June 9th and returning June 16th"? Our sample dialog doesn't cover that path.

To help the AI engine cover as many conversation variations as possible, you should include several sample dialogs. You should also define variant samples where the user provides some or all trip parameters up front and Alexa prompts for the missing information. This could add up to over a half-dozen or more sample dialogs just to handle trip-scheduling.

But ACDL offers a way to make sample dialogs even easier and more powerful with a single sample. Let's take a look at one of the most magical of ACDL's built-in actions: ensure().

Simplifying the Conversation Model

The ensure() action behaves like a combination of response() with a Request act and an expect() all in one. Even better, a single ensure() call can achieve the same thing as several response()/expect() pairs.

In order to appreciate the full power of ensure(), consider the three response()/expect() pairs we defined to ask for and receive the trip destination and dates:

conv/starport-75/skill-package/conversations/ScheduleTripDialog.acdl
```
response(
  response=request_destination_apla,
  act=Request{ arguments = [
    scheduleTrip.arguments.destination]}
)
destination = expect(Inform, InformDestinationEvent)

response(
  response=request_departureDate_apla,
  act=Request{ arguments=[
    scheduleTrip.arguments.departureDate]}
)
departureDate = expect(Inform, InformDepartureDateEvent)

response(
  response=request_returnDate_apla,
  act=Request{ arguments=[
    scheduleTrip.arguments.returnDate]}
)
returnDate = expect(Inform, InformReturnDateEvent)
```

Although each response() clearly maps to a question that Alexa is asking and each expect() lines up perfectly with the user's response to those questions, it is a bit verbose. Compare it with the following ensure() action that can be dropped into the sample dialog in place of the response()/expect() pairs:

conv/starport-75/skill-package/conversations/ScheduleTripDialog.acdl
```
ensure(
  RequestArguments { arguments = [
    scheduleTrip.arguments.destination],
    response = request_destination_apla },
  RequestArguments { arguments = [
    scheduleTrip.arguments.departureDate],
    response = request_departureDate_apla },
  RequestArguments { arguments = [
    scheduleTrip.arguments.returnDate],
    response = request_returnDate_apla }
)
```

That's almost half as many lines of code! But what does it do?

The ensure() action takes a variable list of RequestArguments, each one declaring that a given conversation argument (destination, departure date, and return date) should be required and that the conversation should ensure that they are provided. The response parameter specifies the APL-A document that is used by Alexa to ask the user for the attribute, the same as the parameter used with the response() action.

What's more is that unlike response()/expect() pairs, you do not need to define multiple dialog samples when using ensure(). When the conversation model is processed in the AI engine, a single ensure() will be expanded into multiple variations of the dialog. So, in fact, ensure() achieves much more than response() and expect().

The one advantage that response()/expect() pairs have over ensure(), however, is that they are more clearly aligned with the structure of the actual conversation. ensure(), on the other hand, is a bit more obscure and magical. But if you can trust that ensure() will do the right thing, it will save you a lot of coding in defining your conversation model.

Our conversation model is now complete. But there are a few loose threads we need to tie up before we can deploy it and try it out. Specifically, we need to define a few APL-A templates that were referenced in various response() actions as well as create the backend fulfillment code that sits behind our scheduleTrip() action. Let's tackle those APL-A response templates next.

Defining Response Templates

When defining our sample dialog, we referenced a handful of APL-A documents that serve as a response to the user. Three of them ask the user for trip information, one asks the user to confirm the dialog, and one other ends the conversation with a final response. While we referenced them in our sample dialogs, we haven't yet defined them. Now it's time to create the APL-A documents that our conversation will use to communicate with the user.

Response templates can be either APL or APL-A documents. For simplicity, our skill will only use APL-A documents, but feel free to experiment and alter the skill to send graphical content with APL documents.

Regardless of whether you use APL-A or APL responses, you'll need to put your documents under the project's skill-package/response/prompts directory. Each response will need to be in a subdirectory named the same as the response, with a single document.json file inside that is the APL or APL-A document.

For example, our sample dialog references a response named request_destination_apla. To define such an APL-A template, we need to create a file named document.json in skill-package/response/prompts/request_destination_apla. Such a template might look like this:

conv/starport-75/skill-package/response/prompts/request_destination_apla/document.json

```
{
  "type": "APLA",
  "version": "0.9",
  "mainTemplate": {
    "parameters": [
      "payload"
    ],
    "item": {
      "type": "Speech",
      "contentType": "text",
      "content": "Where do you want to go?"
    }
  }
}
```

Here, there's a single APL-A "Speech" component that asks the user where they want to go. To mix things up a little, feel free to expand this to use a "Selector" component with "randomItem" strategy to phrase the question differently each time it is asked and to make Alexa seem less robotic and scripted.

The response APL-A documents for the trip dates and dialog confirmation are very similar, just with different questions being asked. For example, here's the APL-A document used to ask the user to specify a departure date:

conv/starport-75/skill-package/response/prompts/request_departureDate_apla/document.json

```
{
  "type": "APLA",
  "version": "0.9",
  "mainTemplate": {
    "parameters": [
      "payload"
    ],
    "item": {
      "type": "Speech",
      "contentType": "text",
      "content": "When will your trip start?"
    }
  }
}
```

And here's one that asks for a return date:

```
conv/starport-75/skill-package/response/prompts/request_returnDate_apla/document.json
{
  "type": "APLA",
  "version": "0.9",
  "mainTemplate": {
    "parameters": [
      "payload"
    ],
    "item": {
      "type": "Speech",
      "contentType": "text",
      "content": "When will your trip end?"
    }
  }
}
```

By now, you've likely observed a pattern in the structure of these APL-A documents. Ultimately only the content of the Speech element is different. However, even though these APL-A documents are very similar, you are welcome to use any valid APL-A document, including more complex documents that mix sounds and music if you'd like.

But, for the sake of completeness, here's another APL-A document that the dialog uses to ask for confirmation:

```
conv/starport-75/skill-package/response/prompts/confirmTrip_apla/document.json
{
  "type": "APLA",
  "version": "0.9",
  "mainTemplate": {
    "parameters": [
      "payload"
    ],
    "item": {
      "type": "Speech",
      "contentType": "text",
      "content":
    "I've got you down for a trip to ${payload.destination}. Is that right?"
    }
  }
}
```

The APL-A document that defines the final response is slightly different in that it accepts model data and uses it to fill in a placeholder in the Speech element's content:

```
conv/starport-75/skill-package/response/prompts/scheduleTrip_apla/document.json
{
  "type": "APLA",
  "version": "0.9",
```

```
  "mainTemplate": {
    "parameters": [
      "payload"
    ],
    "item": {
      "type": "Speech",
      "contentType": "text",
      "content":
        "Enjoy your trip to ${payload.scheduleTripResult.destination}!"
    }
  }
}
```

The scheduleTripResult parameter passed into the response by the dialog is used here to tell the user to enjoy their trip to whatever planetary destination that they have chosen. For example, if the user has asked for a trip to Venus, then scheduleTripResult will be set to "Venus" and the response from Alexa will be "Enjoy your trip to Venus!"

One important thing to understand about these response documents is how they are imported into ACDL. All of them will be placed in a prompts namespace and will have a name that is the same as the directory that holds the document.json file. For the templates we've defined, the import lines in ACDL will look like this:

```
import prompts.request_destination_apla
import prompts.request_departureDate_apla
import prompts.request_returnDate_apla
import prompts.scheduleTrip_apla
import prompts.confirmTrip_apla
```

Now we have created our conversation model and defined a handful of APL-A documents that serve as responses from Alexa in the course of a dialog. The one thing we've not done yet, though, is write the fulfillment code that sits behind the scheduleTrip action. Let's do that now.

Handling the Action Request

Once Alexa has gathered all of the information required for the dialog, the scheduleTrip() action is invoked, sending the trip data to fulfillment code for processing. The good news is that writing fulfillment code to handle action processing is very much the same as fulfillment code we've written before to handle intent requests. But rather than checking for a request type of IntentRequest in the handler's canHandle() function, we need to check for a request type of Dialog.API.Invoked, like this:

```
canHandle(handlerInput) {
  Alexa.getRequestType(handlerInput.requestEnvelope) === 'Dialog.API.Invoked'
      && handlerInput.requestEnvelope.request.apiRequest.name ===
          'com.starport75.scheduleTrip'
},
```

As you can see, the structure of this canHandle() function is very much like that of other canHandle() functions we've written, except that it returns true if the request type is Dialog.API.Invoked and if the request's apiRequest.name property is "com.starport75.scheduleTrip"—the fully-qualified name of the action in our conversation model.

Although this approach to writing a canHandle() function for an action request is pretty straightforward, if you created your Alexa skill from scratch using the "Weather Bot" template, you can instead take advantage of a helper function that comes in the project's util.js module. A slightly simpler form of canHandle() will look like this, using the isApiRequest() function:

conv/starport-75/lambda/index.js
```
canHandle(handlerInput) {
    return util.isApiRequest(
        handlerInput, 'com.starport75.actions.scheduleTrip');
},
```

Now, assuming that the canHandle() returns true, then it means that our fulfillment code has received an action request for the scheduleTrip action. We'll need to handle that action request in the handle() function:

conv/starport-75/lambda/index.js
```
handle(handlerInput) {
    const destination = util.getApiArguments(handlerInput).destination;

    const apiSlots = util.getApiSlots(handlerInput);

    const departureDate = util.getApiArguments(handlerInput).departureDate;
    const returnDate = util.getApiArguments(handlerInput).returnDate;

    const reservationNumber =
        scheduleTrip(destination, departureDate, returnDate);

    const response = {
        apiResponse: {
            reservationNumber: reservationNumber,
            destination: destination,
            departureDate: departureDate,
            returnDate: returnDate
        }
    };

    return response;
}
```

As you can see, this handle() function pulls the destination and trip dates out of the request. But it does it a little bit differently than we've seen before. All action arguments are available in the request as API arguments and can be obtained using the getApiArguments() function from the util.js module. That's precisely what this handle() function does for the departure and return dates.

The same would work for the destination, too. But since the destination is a custom list type, the destination API argument will contain the unresolved entity value and not the fully resolved value. If the user planned a trip to "the red planet", then the destination argument would contain the text "the red planet". It's the "Mars" value we need, so it's better to fetch the value as a slot instead of as an API argument.

After the trip is scheduled by calling the scheduleTrip() function, the handle() function returns the action response. Unlike intent handlers, API request handlers do not return a response created with the response builder. Instead, they simply return an object containing data to be given to the APL-A template associated with the action (scheduleTrip_apla/document.json in this case).

Just like any other request handler in an Alexa skill, you'll need to be sure to register the API request handler with the skill builder:

```
conv/starport-75/lambda/index.js
exports.handler = Alexa.SkillBuilders.custom()
    .addRequestHandlers(
        LaunchRequestHandler,
        ScheduleTripApiHandler,
        SessionEndedRequestHandler,
        IntentReflectorHandler,
    )
    .addErrorHandlers(
        ErrorHandler,
    )
    .lambda();
```

Now we're ready to deploy and try out this new Conversations-based skill.

Deploying and Testing the Conversation

At this point, for any other skill, all we'd need to do is use the ASK CLI to deploy our skill and then try it out, either with ask dialog, through the developer console, or with an actual device. But skills built with Alexa Conversations require an extra step to prepare the conversation model for upload. So before we can deploy and test our skill, we'll need to compile the conversation model.

Compiling the Conversation Model

ACDL is designed to be easily understood by developers, making it easy to define a conversation model. But ACDL isn't so easily understood by Alexa's AI engine. So, before we can deploy the skill, we need to compile the conversation model, transforming it from ACDL to a JSON format known as Alexa Conversations Intermediate Representation (ACIR).

To compile a project's ACDL files to ACIR, use the `askx compile` command:

```
$ askx compile
```

ACDL compilation only takes a few seconds and usually catches most common errors before the skill is deployed. Even if you're still working on the Conversation model and aren't ready to deploy the skill yet, it can be helpful to run the compiler every so often to make sure you haven't made any syntactic mistakes in your ACDL files. If there is an error, it'll be clearly displayed in the response from the compiler.

Once compilation is complete, you can find the ACIR files in the project's /skill-package/build directory. There will be one ACIR file (each with a .json file extension) for each ACDL file in the conversation model. Feel free to explore the ACIR files, but there's no need to change, understand, or edit them. But what you will no doubt notice is that ACIR files are significantly longer and more cryptic than the ACDL source that they were created from. Aren't you glad that you didn't have to define the conversation model in ACIR?

Once the compilation is complete and all other elements of your skill are ready, it's time to deploy the skill.

Deploy the Skill

Deploying a skill built with Alexa Conversations is the same as with any other AWS Lambda-hosted skill—using the `deploy` command with the ASK CLI. But since Alexa Conversations is (at this time) only supported by the beta version of the ASK CLI, only the beta version is aware of the ACIR files and knows to deploy them along with other skill artifacts. Therefore, you'll want to be sure to use `askx deploy` instead of `ask deploy` when deploying the skill.

```
$ askx deploy
```

Eventually, when Alexa Conversations support in the ASK CLI moves out of beta, you'll be able to use the standard ASK CLI to deploy your skill.

At this point, you may be asked "Skills with ACDL are not yet compatible with the https://developer.amazon.com, hence this skill will be disabled on the

Developer Console. Would you like to proceed?" All that this is saying is that, at this time, you won't be able to change anything about your skill from the developer console and must make and deploy all edits locally. Just agree and the skill will be deployed. Despite this warning and limitation, you can still test your skill in the developer console.

After initiating deployment, it's probably a good idea to step away for a bite to eat, mow the lawn, or some other task to kill the time. That's because deployment of an Alexa Conversations-based skill can take anywhere from 20-60 minutes while the conversation model is run through the AI engine. If your changes only involve the fulfillment code, then it is much faster. But if you've made any changes to the conversation model, then be prepared to wait awhile.

Although the compile step catches most common mistakes, it is still possible that you'll encounter an error when deploying the skill. So even if you step away for awhile, be sure to check in on it every so often in case there's a problem that needs to be corrected.

Testing the Skill

Once the skill has been successfully deployed, you're ready to test it. As with any Alexa skill, you have several options for testing. Unfortunately, automated testing tools like BST and the Alexa Skills Testing Framework have not yet caught up to Alexa Conversations. But you can still do manual testing with the ASK CLI, the developer console, or an actual device.

If you are planning to test with the ASK CLI, be sure to use the `askx dialog` command instead of the `ask dialog` command. The non-beta version of the ASK CLI isn't Alexa Conversations-aware and won't behave as you'd expect when interacting with a skill built with Alexa Conversations.

Using the ASK CLI as the testing tool, here's an example of how to test an Alexa Conversations skill:

```
$ askx dialog --locale=en-US
User  > open star port seven five travel
Alexa > Welcome to the Star Port 75 Travel.
        I can schedule an out-of-this-world trip for you.
        Just say "Plan a trip."
User  > plan a trip
Alexa > where do you want to go?
User  > Jupiter
Alexa > When will your trip start?
User  > June 9th
Alexa > When will your trip end?
User  > June 21st
```

```
Alexa > I've got you down for a trip to Jupiter. Is that right?
User  > yes
Alexa > Enjoy your trip to jupiter!
User  >
```

As you can see, the conversation plays out in the ASK CLI almost identical to how it was described at the beginning of this chapter. Well done!

Now, let's see how well our conversation model handles detours in the dialog path. Let's test it with a case where the user changes their mind about where they want to go:

$ askx dialog --locale=en-US

```
User  > open star port seven five travel
Alexa > Welcome to the Star Port 75 Travel.
        I can schedule an out-of-this-world trip for you.
        Just say "Plan a trip."
User  > plan a trip
Alexa > where do you want to go?
User  > Jupiter
Alexa > When will your trip start?
User  > June 9th
Alexa > When will your trip end?
User  > June 21st
Alexa > I've got you down for a trip to Jupiter. Is that right?
User  > Make that Neptune
Alexa > I've got you down for a trip to Neptune. Is that right?
User  > yes
Alexa > Enjoy your trip to Neptune!
User  >
```

Even though Alexa had already gathered all of the trip details and only needed confirmation, the user was able to specify a different destination. Alexa accepted the new destination, applied it to the conversational context, and then asked for confirmation of the new destination. This demonstrates one of the benefits of Alexa Conversations as compared to standard dialogs.

Wrapping Up

Alexa Conversations brings an exciting new way to build multi-turn conversations in a skill. By leveraging AI to expand on a conversation model that you define, you can create rich dialogs with a lot less code.

Although you can define conversation models in the developer console, ACDL provides a language specific to creating conversations that is much easier. It also allows for version control of the ACDL source code along with your skill's fulfillment and interaction model code.

Throughout this book, we've seen how to create voice-first applications for the Alexa platform. We've seen how to create interaction models that define how our skill will interact with its human users and how to develop fulfillment code to handle the requests that represent the user's spoken questions and commands. We've also seen how to customize Alexa's speech, target multiple languages, integrate with external APIs, create reminders and notifications, and make money by selling add-on capabilities in our skill.

The Alexa platform presents an exciting new form of human-computer interface in which both applications and their human users speak and listen to each other in a way that's as natural as human-to-human communication. I hope that this book has inspired you to create some amazing voice-first applications, and I can't wait to see (and talk to) what you create with what you've learned. Thank you for reading!

Running and Debugging Skill Code Locally

In chapter two, you saw several techniques for testing your skill, including semi-automated and automated testing tools. While automated testing gives the most consistent and reliable test results, they don't offer the same level of satisfaction you can get from actually talking to a real Alexa device (or through a virtual device such as the testing tool in the Alexa Developer Console) and hearing the results spoken back to you.

As you develop your Alexa skill, vocally testing along the way, you might find the repeated cycle of editing, deploying, and testing creates friction in your work. Specifically, the deployment step will bring you to a full stop while you wait for your skill's fulfillment code to be deployed to AWS Lambda.

If you are only making changes to the fulfillment code (not the interaction model), then you can tighten that development cycle by eliminating the deployment step and setting up your project to run locally. In this setup, Alexa will route requests for your skill's code to your local machine, enabling near-instantaneous turnaround on your changes and allowing you to debug your code while manually testing it.

This appendix walks you through setting up your skill for running fulfillment code locally, including tips on debugging your skill in Visual Studio Code. The first step is to deploy the skill's interaction model.

Deploy Your Skill

Even though you'll be running your skill's fulfillment code locally during development, the interaction model still needs to be deployed so that Alexa can understand user utterances, map them to intents, and process any custom types and utterances you may have defined.

For an Alexa-hosted skill, deploying a skill means committing and pushing the code to the Git repository:

```
$ git commit -am "...commit message..."
$ git push
```

On the other hand, if you have chosen explicit AWS Lambda hosting for your skill's fulfillment code, you'll need to use the ASK CLI to deploy the skill:

```
$ ask deploy
```

This will deploy the entire skill, including the fulfillment code. If you only want to deploy the skill metadata, which includes the interaction model, you can specify "skill-metadata" as the target:

```
$ ask deploy --target skill-metadata
```

Either way, this ensures that the interaction model is available in the Alexa platform. Once the skill's interaction model has been deployed, you are ready to start running the skill locally.

Running Skill Code Locally

Next, you'll need to install the ask-sdk-local-debug library. The following npm install command, executed at the root of the skill project will install the local debugging library as a dependency in your skill project.

```
$ npm install --prefix lambda --save-dev ask-sdk-local-debug
```

Notice the use of the --lambda and --save-dev parameters. The --lambda parameter specifies the location of the fulfillment code as being in the lambda directory. (This assumes that you run npm install from the project's root directory.) And because the local debugging library is a development-time dependency and is not needed by the skill itself, the --save-dev parameter ensures that the dependency will not be included when the skill's fulfillment code is deployed.

Finally, it's time to run the skill's fulfillment code. This is made easy with the ASK CLI's run command. From the skill's root directory, run it like this:

```
$ ask run
```

After a few seconds, you should be able to test your skill using the Alexa Developer Console or an actual device connected to your developer account.

What's the Local-Debugger.js Script in My Project?

When you first created your Alexa skill project, you may have noticed a script named local-debugger.js in the lambda directory. That is a now-deprecated script that offered a similar local run/debug experience as the local debugging library covered in this appendix.

You can ignore the local-debugger.js script or even delete it altogether. It's no longer recommended.

You'll know it's hitting your local code because the request and response will be logged in the same console where run started the local run.

Although ask run is about as easy as it can get to kick off a local run of your skill's fulfillment code, you'll more likely want to specify the --watch option:

```
$ ask run --watch
```

With the --watch option, the local runner will restart if it detects a change to the fulfillment code. This enables an efficient development process in which you can test and make changes in rapid succession, without having to stop to redeploy.

Debugging Skill Code

If you specify --wait-for-attach, then the local run will expose a debugging session that you can attach one of several Node.js debugging clients to, including popular JavaScript editors like Visual Studio Code and JetBrains' WebStorm. You can even attach Google Chrome's DevTools to the session and use the debugger in the browser to step through the code. How you do this will vary depending on which debugging client you are using, but the Node.js Debugging Guide[1] has instructions for several of them.

If you're using Visual Studio Code, it's very easy to attach a debugging session. All you need to do is open the "Run and Debug" view from the Activity Bar, then click the "JavaScript Debug Terminal" button to open a terminal window. From that terminal window, running ask run will run the skill locally and attach the Visual Studio Code debugger. The screenshot on page 346 highlights the relevant portions of Visual Studio Code for running the debugger.

---

1. https://nodejs.org/en/docs/guides/debugging-getting-started/#inspector-clients

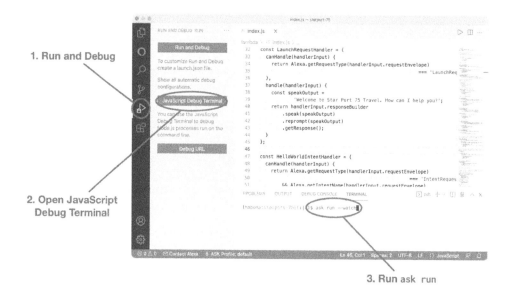

1. Run and Debug

2. Open JavaScript Debug Terminal

3. Run ask run

Now you can test your skill the same as if you had fired up ask run from the command line. But you can also set breakpoints in the code and step through the code.

Troubleshooting Your Skill

Sometimes, things don't go so well while developing a skill. When the unexpected occurs, how can you figure out what went wrong and correct it?

This appendix offers a few helpful troubleshooting tips for problems you might encounter while developing Alexa skills. This is by no means comprehensive, but it does cover many common situations with clues on how to get out of a jam.

"Hmmm. I don't know that one." or "Hmmm. I have a few skills that can help."

This is often the response when you are attempting to launch a skill, but the given invocation name doesn't match the skill's invocation name. While Alexa is very good at matching sample utterances to spoken utterances, even if they're not exactly the same, the invocation name must be given precisely as it is defined in the interaction model.

For example, if you were to say, "Alexa, open Star Port Seventy Five," but the skill's invocation name is "Star Port Seventy Five Travel", then Alexa won't know for sure what skill it is that you're trying to launch. If she can find a similarly named skill, she will offer that as a suggestion. Otherwise, she'll say that she doesn't "know that one."

A Skill Other Than the One You Expect Is Launched

There are no uniqueness constraints placed on a skill's invocation name. Therefore, it's very possible that there are other skills published that have the same invocation name as your skill. Unless you explicitly choose a particular skill and associate it with your account, Alexa will choose a random skill that matches the given invocation name.

When you deploy a skill for development purposes, it will automatically be associated with your account as long as you've not already associated a different skill with the same invocation name to your account.

This is a very common problem with "Hello World" skills. Let's say that you have just developed your very first skill with an invocation name of "Hello World" and then deploy it so that you can try it out. But suppose that there was an error deploying the skill and you didn't notice it before you said "Alexa, open Hello World." In that case, your skill has not been deployed and so Alexa chooses another skill with "Hello World" as the invocation name.

What's worse, though, is even after you realize your mistake and successfully deploy your skill, the other "Hello World" will still be the one that launches. It can be infuriating.

The way to fix this is to go into the companion application, find the wrong skill, and disable it. Then, the next time you launch your skill, Alexa should find your skill and not another one that happens to have the same invocation name.

An Utterance Is Handled by the Wrong Intent Handler

This could happen for a handful of reasons:

- Perhaps Alexa didn't hear the utterance well.

- Your interaction model has two or more intents with the same or similar sample utterances.

- You've not defined an AMAZON.FallbackIntent or a corresponding handler for the fallback intent.

- The canHandle() function on two or more handlers is written such that it matches the same request.

- You've not registered the handler with the skill builder.

The simplest explanation is that Alexa misheard the utterance. In that case, try again, speaking as clearly as possible. Or, try testing it with ask dialog or the developer console, typing in the exact utterance.

If that still doesn't work, then it's possible your interaction model has multiple intents defined with similar sample utterances. You can use the ask smapi profile-nlu command to see which intent the utterance matches to. For example:

```
$ ask smapi profile-nlu \
  --utterance "hello world" \
  --skill-id amzn1.ask.skill.5b59d242-8c3b-4ced-a285-1784707f3109 \
  --locale en-US
```

The response will tell you which intent was matched to the utterance as well as any other intents that were considered (if any).

If the utterance was not intended to be handled by any of your intent handlers, then perhaps you need to declare the AMAZON.FallbackIntent in your interaction model (and create a corresponding handler in the fulfillment code). Without declaring the fallback intent, all requests will be matched with the intent whose sample utterances are the closest to the given utterance, even if they're not very close at all.

If you have a fallback intent declared, but it's still not handling utterances you expect it to, then you may need to adjust the sensitivity in the interaction model. As a child of languageModel, add the following JSON:

```
"modelConfiguration": {
  "fallbackIntentSensitivity": {
    "level": "HIGH"
  }
}
```

The sensitivity level defaults to "LOW", but can be set to "MEDIUM" or "HIGH" to increase the sensitivity of the fallback intent.

If the utterance matched to the correct intent but is still being handled by the wrong intent handler, then you should examine the canHandle() function of the handler that is handling the request and compare it to the canHandle() function of the handler you expected to handle the request.

Finally, another common mistake is either not registering the handler with the skill builder in the call to addRequestHandlers() or registering a handler with a less restrictive canHandle() function higher in the list of handlers given to addRequestHandlers(). When determining which handler to handle a request, the first handler whose canHandle() returns true in the list of handlers given to addRequestHandlers() will be used to handle the request. If your intended handler isn't being registered or if it is registered after one whose canHandle() isn't restrictive, then another handler will be given the job of handling the request.

You See "<Audio Only>" in the Response

This error often means that what Alexa heard from the user didn't match an utterance for any of the skill's intents and there is no fallback intent to fall back on.

In many cases, a misunderstood utterance will be directed to another intent with a similar enough utterance. But if there's nothing even close to make a match and if there's no fallback intent, then you might get the "<Audio Only>" response.

To fix this problem, add a fallback intent and handler to your skill. Also consider expanding the collection of utterances in the skill's intents to capture more variations of what a user might say.

"There was a problem with the requested skill's response."

This message indicates that there was something wrong with the response sent back from the skill when handling a request. For example, if an error occurs during request handling, but there is no suitable error handler, the error itself will be returned instead of a valid response object.

To fix this problem, be sure that you have an error handler whose canHandle() function will return true in the event of the error. If you're unsure what the error was, then you might be able to find more information in the JSON Output when testing in the developer console. Or there might be some information in the skills logs in CloudWatch that will provide a clue to what went wrong.

"You just triggered {Some Intent}."

This message comes from IntentReflectorHandler, the intent handler included in index.js when the skill was first initialized. It indicates that although you have defined the intent in the interaction model and the utterance was mapped to that intent, there is no intent handler defined to handle the intent. Or, if you have defined an intent handler, it has either not registered with addRequestHandlers() or it has been registered after IntentReflectorHandler.

You can fix this by making sure you've defined an intent handler whose canHandle() method returns true for the given intent and including it before IntentReflectorHandler in the call to the skill builder's addRequestHandlers().

Skill ID Not Found when Deploying a Skill

This error happens when you try to deploy a skill that was previously deployed, but has since been deleted.

When you deploy a skill, it will be assigned a skill ID that is written along with some other deployment artifacts to the .ask directory in the skill's project directory. In order to get past this error, you'll need to delete the .ask directory. On a Unix-based operating system you can delete it like this:

```
$ rm -rf .ask
```

The next time you deploy the skill, it will be assigned a new, fresh skill ID.

Also, the URI of the AWS Lambda function which is the skill's fulfillment is also written to the /skill-package/skill.json file. For example, if you open the skill.json file, you might see the following endpoint property as a child of apis.custom:

```
"apis": {
  "custom": {
    "endpoint": {
      "uri": "arn:aws:lambda:us-east-1:494442948374:
              function:ask-starport-75-default-default-1625712152087"
    }
  }
},
```

You'll need to clear this URI, or else it will be deployed to try to use the old AWS Lambda function from the previous deployment. The skill.json file has other useful information in it, so you can't simply delete the file. But you can remove the endpoint property so that section of skill.json looks like this:

```
"apis": {
  "custom": {}
},
```

Now if you try to redeploy your skill, it should be able to deploy successfully and be assigned a new skill ID.

"Sorry, I had trouble doing what you asked. Please try again."

This message comes from the default error handler placed in the skill's fulfillment code (in index.js) when the project was initialized with ask new. If you see or hear this response, it means that Alexa found a matching intent for your utterance and it attempted to handle the request, but there was some exception thrown from the intent handler.

The exception thrown could be almost anything, depending on what your skill was doing when the exception was thrown. The best way to determine what the problem is (and then fix it) is to add a few logging messages in the intent handler and view the logs in CloudWatch.

It might be helpful to know that you are welcome to change the message in the default error handler to say anything you want it to say. This could be useful in making your skill unique among other skills, even in how it handles errors.

Index

Thank you!

We hope you enjoyed this book and that you're already thinking about what you want to learn next. To help make that decision easier, we're offering you this gift.

Head on over to https://pragprog.com right now, and use the coupon code BUYANOTHER2022 to save 30% on your next ebook. Offer is void where prohibited or restricted. This offer does not apply to any edition of the *The Pragmatic Programmer* ebook.

And if you'd like to share your own expertise with the world, why not propose a writing idea to us? After all, many of our best authors started off as our readers, just like you. With a 50% royalty, world-class editorial services, and a name you trust, there's nothing to lose. Visit https://pragprog.com/become-an-author/ today to learn more and to get started.

We thank you for your continued support, and we hope to hear from you again soon!

The Pragmatic Bookshelf

Build Chatbot Interactions

The next step in the evolution of user interfaces is here. Chatbots let your users interact with your service in their own natural language. Use free and open source tools along with Ruby to build creative, useful, and unexpected interactions for users. Take advantage of the Lita framework's step-by-step implementation strategy to simplify bot development and testing. From novices to experts, chatbots are an area in which everyone can participate. Exercise your creativity by creating chatbot skills for communicating, information, and fun.

Daniel Pritchett
(206 pages) ISBN: 9781680506327. $35.95
https://pragprog.com/book/dpchat

3D Game Programming for Kids, Second Edition

You know what's even better than playing games? Programming your own! Make your own online games, even if you're an absolute beginner. Let your imagination come to 3D life as you learn real-world programming skills with the JavaScript programming language—the language used everywhere on the web. This new edition is completely revised and takes advantage of new programming features to make game programming even easier to learn. Plus, new effects make your games even cooler. When you're done, you're going to be amazed at what you can create.

Chris Strom
(372 pages) ISBN: 9781680502701. $47.95
https://pragprog.com/book/csjava2

A Common-Sense Guide to Data Structures and Algorithms, Second Edition

If you thought that data structures and algorithms were all just theory, you're missing out on what they can do for your code. Learn to use Big O notation to make your code run faster by orders of magnitude. Choose from data structures such as hash tables, trees, and graphs to increase your code's efficiency exponentially. With simple language and clear diagrams, this book makes this complex topic accessible, no matter your background. This new edition features practice exercises in every chapter, and new chapters on topics such as dynamic programming and heaps and tries. Get the hands-on info you need to master data structures and algorithms for your day-to-day work.

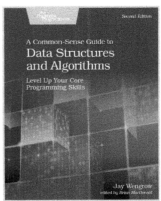

Jay Wengrow

(506 pages) ISBN: 9781680507225. $45.95

https://pragprog.com/book/jwdsal2

Practical Microservices

MVC and CRUD make software easier to write, but harder to change. Microservice-based architectures can help even the smallest of projects remain agile in the long term, but most tutorials meander in theory or completely miss the point of what it means to be microservice based. Roll up your sleeves with real projects and learn the most important concepts of evented architectures. You'll have your own deployable, testable project and a direction for where to go next.

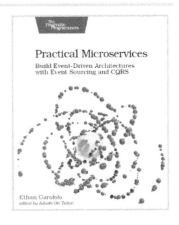

Ethan Garofolo

(290 pages) ISBN: 9781680506457. $45.95

https://pragprog.com/book/egmicro

Mazes for Programmers

A book on mazes? Seriously?

Yes!

Not because you spend your day creating mazes, or because you particularly like solving mazes.

But because it's fun. Remember when programming used to be fun? This book takes you back to those days when you were starting to program, and you wanted to make your code do things, draw things, and solve puzzles. It's fun because it lets you explore and grow your code, and reminds you how it feels to just think.

Sometimes it feels like you live your life in a maze of twisty little passages, all alike. Now you can code your way out.

Jamis Buck
(286 pages) ISBN: 9781680500554. $38
https://pragprog.com/book/jbmaze

Your Code as a Crime Scene

Jack the Ripper and legacy codebases have more in common than you'd think. Inspired by forensic psychology methods, this book teaches you strategies to predict the future of your codebase, assess refactoring direction, and understand how your team influences the design. With its unique blend of forensic psychology and code analysis, this book arms you with the strategies you need, no matter what programming language you use.

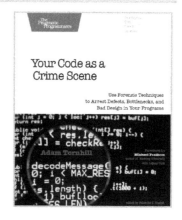

Adam Tornhill
(218 pages) ISBN: 9781680500387. $36
https://pragprog.com/book/atcrime

The Ray Tracer Challenge

Brace yourself for a fun challenge: build a photorealistic 3D renderer from scratch! It's easier than you think. In just a couple of weeks, build a ray tracer that renders beautiful scenes with shadows, reflections, brilliant refraction effects, and subjects composed of various graphics primitives: spheres, cubes, cylinders, triangles, and more. With each chapter, implement another piece of the puzzle and move the renderer that much further forward. Do all of this in whichever language and environment you prefer, and do it entirely test-first, so you know it's correct. Recharge yourself with this project's immense potential for personal exploration, experimentation, and discovery.

Jamis Buck
(290 pages) ISBN: 9781680502718. $45.95
https://pragprog.com/book/jbtracer

Seven More Languages in Seven Weeks

Great programmers aren't born—they're made. The industry is moving from object-oriented languages to functional languages, and you need to commit to radical improvement. New programming languages arm you with the tools and idioms you need to refine your craft. While other language primers take you through basic installation and "Hello, World," we aim higher. Each language in *Seven More Languages in Seven Weeks* will take you on a step-by-step journey through the most important paradigms of our time. You'll learn seven exciting languages: Lua, Factor, Elixir, Elm, Julia, MiniKanren, and Idris.

Bruce Tate, Fred Daoud, Jack Moffitt, Ian Dees
(318 pages) ISBN: 9781941222157. $38
https://pragprog.com/book/7lang

The Pragmatic Bookshelf

The Pragmatic Bookshelf features books written by professional developers for professional developers. The titles continue the well-known Pragmatic Programmer style and continue to garner awards and rave reviews. As development gets more and more difficult, the Pragmatic Programmers will be there with more titles and products to help you stay on top of your game.

Visit Us Online

This Book's Home Page
https://pragprog.com/book/cwalexa
Source code from this book, errata, and other resources. Come give us feedback, too!

Keep Up to Date
https://pragprog.com
Join our announcement mailing list (low volume) or follow us on twitter @pragprog for new titles, sales, coupons, hot tips, and more.

New and Noteworthy
https://pragprog.com/news
Check out the latest pragmatic developments, new titles and other offerings.

Save on the ebook

Save on the ebook versions of this title. Owning the paper version of this book entitles you to purchase the electronic versions at a terrific discount.

PDFs are great for carrying around on your laptop—they are hyperlinked, have color, and are fully searchable. Most titles are also available for the iPhone and iPod touch, Amazon Kindle, and other popular e-book readers.

Send a copy of your receipt to support@pragprog.com and we'll provide you with a discount coupon.

Contact Us

Online Orders:	*https://pragprog.com/catalog*
Customer Service:	*support@pragprog.com*
International Rights:	*translations@pragprog.com*
Academic Use:	*academic@pragprog.com*
Write for Us:	*http://write-for-us.pragprog.com*
Or Call:	+1 800-699-7764

Lightning Source UK Ltd.
Milton Keynes UK
UKHW031833260422
402095UK00003B/4